COGNITIVE THERAPY FOR DELUSIONS, VOICES AND PARANOIA

The Wiley Series in

CLINICAL PSYCHOLOGY

J. Mark G. Williams *School of Psychology, University*
(Series Editor) *of Wales, Bangor, UK*

Paul Chadwick, Cognitive Therapy for Delusions, Voices
Max Birchwood and Paranoia
and Peter Trower

Peter Sturmey Functional Analysis in Clinical Psychology

Frank Tallis Obsessive Compulsive Disorder: A
Cognitive and Neuropsychological
Perspective

David Fowler, Cognitive Behaviour Therapy for
Philippa Garety Psychosis: Theory and Practice
and Elizabeth Kuipers

Robert S.P. Jones, Stereotyped Movement Disorders
Peter G. Walsh and
Peter Sturmey

D. Colin Drummond, Addictive Behaviour: Cue Exposure
Stephen T. Tiffany, Theory and Practice
Steven Glautier and
Bob Remington (Editors)

Carlo Perris, Parenting and Psychopathology
Willem A. Arrindell and
Martin Eisemann (Editors)

Chris Barker, Research Methods in Clinical and
Nancy Pistrang Counselling Psychology
and Robert Elliott

Further titles in preparation: *A list of
earlier titles in the series follows the index*

COGNITIVE THERAPY FOR DELUSIONS, VOICES AND PARANOIA

Paul Chadwick
Max Birchwood
Peter Trower

Foreword by Aaron Beck

JOHN WILEY & SONS

Chichester · New York · Brisbane · Toronto · Singapore

Email (for orders and customer service enquiries): cs-books@wiley.co.uk
Visit our Home Page www.wileyeurope.com or www.wiley.com

Reprinted March 1997, June 1998, June 1999, March 2000, April 2001, June 2003, June 2004,
April 2005

Other Wiley Editorial Offices

John Wiley & Sons Inc., 111 River Street, Hoboken, NJ 07030, USA

Jossey-Bass, 989 Market Street, San Francisco, CA 94103-1741, USA

Wiley-VCH Verlag GmbH, Boschstr. 12, D-69469 Weinheim, Germany

John Wiley & Sons Australia Ltd, 33 Park Road, Milton, Queensland 4064, Australia

John Wiley & Sons (Asia) Pte Ltd, 2 Clementi Loop #02-01, Jin Xing Distripark, Singapore 129809

John Wiley & Sons (Canada) Ltd, 22 Worcester Road, Etobicoke, Ontario M9W 1L1

Wiley also publishes its books in a variety of electronic formats. Some content that appears in print
may not be available in electronic books.

Library of Congress Cataloging-in-Publication Data
Chadwick, Paul (Paul D.)
   Cognitive therapy for delusions, vocies and paranoia / Paul
Chadwick, Max Birchwood, Peter Trower; foreword by Aaron Beck.
      p.   cm. — (The Wiley series in clinical psychology)
      Includes bibliographical references and index.
      ISDN 0-471-93888-2 (cloth). — ISBN 0-471-96173-6 (pbk.)
      1. Delusions. 2. Hallucinations and illusions. 3. Paranoia.
   4. Cognitive therapy. I. Birchwood, M. J. II. Trower, Peter,
   1938–   . II. Title. IV. Series.
      [DNLM: 1. Delusions—therapy. 2. Hallucinations—therapy.
   3. Paranoid Disorders—therapy. 4. Cognitive Therapy—methods. WM
   204 C432c 1996]
   RC553.D35C46 1996
   616.89'70651—dc20
   DNLM/DLC
   for Library of Congress   96-1475
                                                                     CIP

British Library Cataloguing in Publication Data

A catalogue record for this book is available from the British Library

ISBN 0-471-93888-2 (cased)
ISBN-10: 0-471-96173-6 (paper)
ISBN-13: 978-0471-96173-4 (paper)

CONTENTS

About the Authors vii

Foreword *Aaron Beck* ix

Series Preface *J. Mark G. Williams* xii

Prologue xiii

Chapter 1   A cognitive view of delusions and voices 1

Chapter 2   The practice of therapy and the problem of
            engagement 25

Chapter 3   Delusions: assessment and formulation 45

Chapter 4   Challenging delusions 69

Chapter 5   Voices: engagement and assessment 91

Chapter 6   Disputing and testing beliefs about voices 115

Chapter 7   Cognitive therapy for paranoia 135

Chapter 8   Challenging cases and issues 163

Chapter 9   From a symptom model to a person model 175

References 187

Appendix 1 193

Appendix 2 195

Appendix 3 201

Appendix 4 203

Index 205

ABOUT THE AUTHORS

Paul Chadwick   *Royal South Hants Hospital, Southampton, UK*

Max Birchwood   *All Saints Hospital, Birmingham, UK*

Peter Trower   *University of Birmingham, UK*

Paul Chadwick completed his Ph.D. at University of Wales, Bangor, under Professor Fergus Lowe, developing a cognitive approach to assessing and modifying delusions. He did his clinical training at the University of Birmingham, followed by four years as a lecturer at the university and clinical psychologist at All Saints Hospital, Birmingham. He is now based in the Royal South Hants Hospital, Southampton, and is Honorary Senior Lecturer in the Department of Psychology, University of Southampton.

Max Birchwood is the Director of the Early Psychosis Service of the Northern Birmingham Mental Health Trust and a Professor of Psychology at the University of Birmingham. His clinical and research interests lie in the psychological understanding and management of psychosis and he has published widely in this area including: early intervention in psychotic relapse, family intervention, cognitive therapy for auditory hallucinations, acute psychosis and comorbid depression/suicidal ideation. His current work involves the development of early intervention approaches in the first episode of psychosis.

Peter Trower Ph.D. is a Senior Lecturer in the School of Psychology at Birmingham University and Consultant Clinical Psychologist for South Warwickshire Mental Health NHS Trust. He was a leading member with Michael Argyle of the Oxford University research team that originated the theory and practice of social skills training. More recently he has combined this interpersonal perspective with cognitive psychotherapy approaches to the psychoses.

FOREWORD

This work by Chadwick, Birchwood, and Trower is a significant break-through in the treatment of psychotic symptoms. It represents a sur-prisingly effective application of cognitive therapy to one of the most distressing and intractable set of clinical problems. From the very early years when cognitive therapy was found to be an effective approach to depression and anxiety disorders, modification of the original treatment protocols have been applied to a broad panoply of disorders. Skilled cognitive therapists, such as the present authors, tackled additional disor-ders and tailored their cognitive approach to the specific characteristics and demands of these disorders. Thus, practically all of the 'neurotic' disorders have been subjected to customised cognitive interventions whose efficacy has been demonstrated in outcome trials. The present authors have attacked the last remaining bastion of psychopathology and with their profound understanding have managed to scale its walls.

In this volume, Chadwick, Birchwood, and Trower describe their own work over the past decade developing and using cognitive therapy for delusions, hallucinations, and paranoia. In focusing in considerable detail on these three symptoms, the book nicely complements existing more general texts in this area. The authors' central proposition is that when working with these symptoms the therapist needs to address not merely the delusional ideas but also the associated issues of low self-worth, a point increasingly being recognised in the literature.

As the author of the first published study to show how a prototype cognitive therapy might be used to modify a *delusion*, I have long believed that some delusions respond to psychological therapy (Beck, 1952). It is pleasing to see how the authors have built on this report and recent breakthroughs to develop a comprehensive approach to cognitive assess-ment, formulation, and therapy for delusions—the topic of Chapters 3 and 4.

However, over the years I have been less certain that progress could be made using cognitive therapy to manage *auditory hallucinations*. The key insight of the authors is the view that an hallucination is an activating event and not an 'automatic thought'. This simple step suddenly clarifies the cognitive therapy approach to voices: an individual hears a voice (an A), which he or she interprets in a particular fashion (e.g. as friendly or hostile) and this meaning (the B) shapes the way he or she feels and behaves (the C). The immediate aim of cognitive therapy is therefore not to diminish the hallucinatory experience itself but to render it less distressing by altering its meaning.

In Chapters 5 and 6 the authors describe a well-developed approach to voices. To guide cognitive assessment, they use a semi-structured interview schedule and a self-report measure of the individual's voice-related beliefs, emotions, and behaviour. Chapter 6 describes the cognitive therapy for voices and presents a combination of standard cognitive therapy methods plus useful adaptations that the authors have originated specifically for working with voices.

In Chapter 7, on paranoia, the authors argue that there are in fact two psychologically distinct types of paranoia—persecution and punishment. In persecution paranoia, individuals believe that the malevolence they face is undeserved and they consequently feel angry. In punishment paranoia, individuals see themselves as bad and others as justified in punishing them, and the effect is predominantly anxiety and fear. The authors develop the implications for cognitive therapy of this original idea and illustrate how the process of assessment, formulation, and therapy is very different for each type.

In Chapter 8 the authors reflect on the central challenges to cognitive therapy for these symptoms, and it is interesting to note how many of these challenges apply to work with other problems. Indeed, one of the most exciting aspects of this book is that for most of the time the authors are approaching delusions, voices, and paranoia as a cognitive therapist would approach depression, anxiety, etc. In the final chapter the authors argue that working with symptoms is best achieved within the framework of an understanding of the individual's enduring psychological vulnerability. Again, this follows recent developments in cognitive therapy for depression and personality disorders. In fact, this makes good sense if one assumes, as the authors do, that all patients—indeed, all people—are perpetually struggling to construct a sense of self. This raises the possibility that a cognitive therapist trained in work with neurotic problems could, with minimal change, work with people troubled by delusions and voices. Training courses could be designed in the future to cover both. The major difference from working with depression and anxiety, which the authors highlight, is the problem of engaging clients in therapy. Engagement problems are similarly severe in clients with drug addictions and those with personality disorder, and this is clearly one of the major challenges currently facing cognitive therapy work with psychotic symptoms.

This volume is a treasure trove of understandings of psychotic symptoms and provides clear guidelines for the clinician for ameliorating them. All of us in the mental health field are grateful to the authors for sharing their wisdom with us.

A.T. Beck
Emeritus University Professor
University of Pennsylvania Medical Centre

SERIES PREFACE

The Wiley Series in Clinical Psychology aims to provide a comprehensive set of texts covering the application of psychological science to the problems of mental health and disability. The Series covers topics that are already central to the work of health professionals, but also includes areas that are at an earlier stage of development. Of all such areas, few have contained such exciting promise as the new developments in psychological treatments for people diagnosed as schizophrenic. For many years, symptoms of psychosis such as delusions, the hearing of voices or paranoia were felt to be beyond the reaches of 'talking therapies'. For example, part of the definition of a delusion was that it was a belief which could not be weakened by counter-argument or direct refutation. There is now a great deal of evidence that many 'classical' delusions held by people with a diagnosis of schizophrenia can, in fact, be changed during therapy. Furthermore, this is only part of an entire research endeavour that has shown increasing degree of continuity between 'normal' and 'abnormal' beliefs and experiences. What is also new is that such approaches are now co-existing with established psychiatric approaches to this difficult mental health problem. Mental health professionals are giving up the battle-lines of the past whereby one had to choose whether one was going to hold a biological or a psychological theory of psychosis. Biological, social and psychological factors are involved even in the severest mental health problems. Paul Chadwick, Max Birchwood and Peter Trower have been in the forefront of research and clinical work that has sought to understand how best to approach the psychological aspect of psychosis. This book promises to bring us up to date with their conclusions, and to give us invaluable insights for our own therapeutic practice. With a wealth of case examples throughout, all mental health students and practitioners will benefit from this book.

PROLOGUE: THE SYMPTOM MODEL

Few would doubt that the 'cognitive revolution' (Mahoney, 1974) within psychology has now happened. Although some have lamented the direction cognitive psychology and cognitive science have taken (Bruner, 1990), it seems that within clinical psychology the growth of cognitive models and therapies has been palpably in the best interest of those struggling with clinical problems. Indeed, a measure of this progress is that today it is almost inconceivable to think about psychological understanding and treatment of depression, anxiety and other emotional problems without at least considering the cognitive approach.

One major disorder which until recently has remained largely, and perhaps surprisingly, outside the cognitive approach is 'schizophrenia'. There have been a number of recent books and journal papers on the topic (e.g. Kingdon & Turkington, 1994; Perris, 1988; Chadwick & Lowe, 1990), but these are conspicuous by their scarcity. Also, there is a long history of attempts to identify deficits in cognitive functioning associated with schizophrenia, but these lines of enquiry have been disappointing and in any case have little in common with the clinical cognitive approach, which is concerned with issues of personal meaning and biased processing of threatening stimuli. Thus at a time when the clinical cognitive model was transforming how many people understood and treated clinical disorder, this new wave did not reach the psychoses—schizophrenia and manic depression.

In relation to schizophrenia, what makes this neglect even more surprising is that in the 1950s two of the leading figures in British and American psychology and psychiatry offered embryonic cognitive formulations and treatments of delusions (Beck, 1952; Shapiro & Ravenette, 1959). However, this early breakthrough heralded not a rush of research interest but a mere handful of studies over the subsequent three decades; those few studies to be published did at least offer crumbs of encouragement showing, for example, that with certain individuals it was possible to modify delusions using cognitive therapy (e.g. Watts, Powell & Austin, 1973).

In fact, before considering why the clinical cognitive approach to schizophrenia was so slow to take off, a wider point needs to be made. This tardiness may be a symptom of a more general malaise, namely, that *any* psychological therapy is typically applied less liberally to schizophrenia than to the so-called neuroses. Historically schizophrenia has been psychology's forgotten child (Bellack, 1986) and cognitive therapists are therefore not unique in being slow to address those problems associated with schizophrenia. Undoubtedly this oversight reflects the sheer number and severity of problems usually associated with schizophrenia: people so diagnosed are thought to suffer a daunting range of significant primary and secondary psychological disturbances (Birchwood, Hallet & Preston, 1988).

Notwithstanding this, there remains the question of why the clinical cognitive approach has been slow to make a mark on schizophrenia. It is our view that the major impediment to clinical cognitive approaches in this area has been the very concept of schizophrenia itself. In particular, the concept is laden with pessimistic and at times baffling presumptions which serve to banish psychological analysis. Moreover, there have been, and remain, very serious doubts about the concept's scientific validity and therefore about its capacity to spawn progress in research and clinical practice.

Let us begin with some of the presumptions. Schizophrenia, unlike most other clinical disorders, is characterised as being discontinuous from 'normal' experience; indeed, this presumption in part explains the psychiatric distinction between the neuroses (depression, anxiety . . .) and the psychoses (schizophrenia, manic depression). Delusions, for example, have traditionally been described as beliefs which are not weakened by counter argument or direct refutation. Well, what price cognitive therapy? If we accept this definition of delusion then psychotherapy is obviously out of the question, but so too is much of academic psychology. It is well known that core beliefs of all types are very resistant to change, and that this owes much to a variety of automatic (unconscious) and controlled (conscious) cognitive processes which govern attention, appraisal, action and affect. Psychology has well-established experimental paradigms for examining such cognitive bias. But if one accepts the view that an entire class of beliefs (delusions) is *utterly* resistant to change then it is difficult to understand this in terms of ordinary psychological processes, which account only for why change is resisted but not impossible.

In a similar vein, psychiatry traditionally ignores or dismisses as irrelevant much that from a psychological perspective is of central importance.

Berrios (1991) argues that delusions are not in fact beliefs, but 'empty speech acts, whose informational content refers neither to self or world' (p. 12). Again, in relation to voices, the question of why an individual's voice should have a particular content is insignificant from a psychiatric point of view and the emphasis is placed firmly on determining if the experience is a true hallucination and of what disorder it is symptomatic. And yet from a psychological perspective the content and theme of delusions and voices would be expected to contain significance and personal meaning and to connect to the individual's wider psychological vulnerability.

In this way a dichotomy emerges between, on the one hand those psychological principles which govern ordinary behaviour, and on the other hand schizophrenia, which obeys different laws. This dichotomy is, we believe, false and rests in part on conceptual confusion. For example, Berrios and others make a reasoned and reasonable statement if they assert that from a *psychiatric point of view* the content of delusions is insignificant, even irrelevant. But if they assert that the content of delusions and voices is of no *psychological significance either*, then they make either a conceptual or empirical claim. If the claim is empirical, then it is unsubstantiated and in fact flies in the face of an enormous literature, beginning with Freud, analysing how there are meaningful and important connections between content of delusions and personal vulnerability. If the claim is conceptual, then it rests on a logical error of the type highlighted by Ryle (1949). Ryle discusses how disciplines are equipped to consider certain questions but not others, and how when this is ignored it causes confusion and contention; Berrios may speak with clarity and authority on the question of the psychiatric significance of delusional content, but not about its psychological status.

Also, the empirical evidence points to a continuity between psychotic and other phenomena, not a discontinuity. For example, research shows that paranoid people show exaggerations of ordinary defences, such as the 'self-serving bias' whereby responsibility for failure is attributed externally and success internally (Bentall, 1994). Psychotic phenomena appear in other diagnostic groups, and research shows that the tendency to hallucination and bizarre (delusional) thinking appears to be spread across the population at large (Claridge, 1990). In spite of prodigious research endeavour, there is no convincing evidence for the idea that delusions result from qualitatively different reasoning; some studies indicate a bias towards conceptual thinking ('top-down') but others towards stimuli driven thinking ('bottom-up), but none offers convincing evidence of a deficit.

Thus we have argued that the insistence that schizophrenia is outside ordinary psychological functioning is unjustified and we think has retarded exploration of the applicability of cognitive theory and therapy. A second obstacle concerns the usefulness of the concept itself.

SHOULD WE ABANDON THE CONCEPT OF SCHIZOPHRENIA?

It is tempting, but conceptually muddled and hazardous, to ask the question: Does schizophrenia exist? Schizophrenia is not a 'thing' or object. Much has been written about this epistemological fallacy, as philosophers would call it, i.e. the fallacy of reifying—turning a metaphor into a real 'thing' (Sarbin, 1990). Most clinicians can usually agree that schizophrenia is a scientific concept invoked to describe certain symptoms (delusions, voices, thought disorder, etc.). We know that the individual symptoms exist, that they often appear together, and that individuals, their families and friends are frequently very distressed and disturbed—this is not in doubt. What is in doubt is if and how to group or categorise symptoms so as to best advance understanding and treatment.

Historically, clinicians have observed the range of patients' behaviour, affect and cognition, and have come up with different concepts, or diagnoses, with which to organise and categorise these experiences. Schizophrenia is one such diagnosis. The correct conceptual question to ask is therefore not 'Does schizophrenia exist?', but 'Is it helpful to place these identifiable experiences (delusions, voices, thought disorder etc.) into one category, which happens to be called schizophrenia?'. In other words, the way to assess the usefulness of a diagnosis is to enquire how it increases understanding and possible management (i.e. what is its 'cash value': Austin, 1976).

One thing may be gained by categorising symptoms together is that we are then better able to predict what will happen to them over time. Thus in relation to schizophrenia, the concept would have cash value if it were possible to predict the likely prognosis for those individuals who met the diagnostic criteria. A second type of cash value comes when putting things together in one category allows us to assert something about their aetiology. Thus the concept of schizophrenia would have cash value if all those people so classified shared a common aetiology or 'cause'. A third way in which the concept schizophrenia might have cash value is if it informed a clinician of the best treatment.

Scientifically, what we are discussing here is validity—a concept has validity if it brings one or more of the above advantages. If in spite of repeated investigation it fails to tell us something firm about aetiology, course or treatment, it should be abandoned in favour of new ways of categorising the clinical problems patients describe and these new systems should be tested. In two excellent and detailed books Bentall (1990) and Boyle (1990) have argued that the concept of schizophrenia is invalid and should be abandoned. Their points may be summarised as follows. There is no common symptom which everyone who has the diagnosis would show, and the symptoms that do define the diagnosis appear in other disorders—that is not a fatal flaw, but it means that the diagnosis is less informative to a clinician than it might be. The course and outcome of the disorder is extremely mixed and difficult to predict in advance. In spite of prodigious research endeavour, the cause(s) of schizophrenia remain elusive. Nor does it always respond to a particular class of treatment, and to that class alone (Bentall, Jackson & Pilgrim, 1988). What these authors are saying is that in effect there is no good reason to group the symptoms of schizophrenia into one category, or diagnosis, because the scientific requirements which warrant this are so far absent.

In no way do these arguments ignore or deny patients' distress and disturbance and their need for treatment, and it is wrong to level this accusation at Bentall, Boyle and others. The argument is a scientific one and concerns how best to organise and approach the clinical problems individuals present—indeed, the better the problem is defined, the more likely treatments are to be effective.

If one accepts that the concept of schizophrenia currently lacks validity, then how should clinicians approach psychotic phenomena like delusions and voices? Bentall et al. (1988) argue that the most parsimonious approach is to study individual symptoms. This recommendation has considerable appeal. On the one hand it satisfies those who reject the idea of syndromes, such as schizophrenia, and prefer to work with what is known. On the other hand it is still a sensible tactic for clinicians who do believe in syndromes and will continue to seek the most helpful way to categorise clinical problems, but who also recognise that the current concept of schizophrenia is flawed (e.g. Costello, 1993). Indeed, understanding individual symptoms is important even if one were to reject all the above criticism and embrace the current concept of schizophrenia.

We believe that Bentall et al.'s (1988) call to study psychotic symptoms, not syndromes, has been the catalyst for psychological exploration. Since the mid 1980s, when the criticism of Bentall, Boyle and others began to be widely known the psychological investigation and treatment of psychotic phenomena, and especially of delusions and voices, has flourished. In particular, the clinical cognitive approach has revealed much about how these symptoms are maintained, and has offered a new and exciting treatment approach through the use of cognitive therapy. In the process these experiences are increasingly being understood in terms of ordinary psychological principles and greater emphasis is given to the significance of individuals' attempts to understand their experiences.

This book describes our own cognitive therapy and research over the past decade with delusions and voices. In Chapter 1 we describe our view of the cognitive model and show why we think it is profitably applied to delusions and voices. In Chapter 2 we detail the central conceptual steps in cognitive therapy for these symptoms, and discuss the major threat to successful therapy—clients not engaging in collaborative empiricism. Chapter 3 details how the model applies to assessing delusions and Chapter 4 to their treatment. Similarly, Chapter 5 illustrates our unique cognitive assessment of voices and Chapter 6 covers intervention methods. In Chapter 7 we raise the idea that there are two psychologically distinct types of paranoia and we show how each requires a different style of assessment and intervention. The chapter ends with our theoretical speculation about how the two types reflect defences against two separate threats to the process of self-construction. Chapter 8 considers six major challenges to the use of cognitive therapy for delusions, voices and paranoia, and we conclude the book arguing for the need to continue working towards a person model, where understanding and treatment occurs within a wider understanding of the person's enduring psychological vulnerability, to replace the prevailing symptom model.

Notes

The names used to describe clients throughout the book are invented, and in many cases we have altered certain aspects of a person's history to further protect his or her true identity. We have tried to indicate in the text which clients were seen by which therapist; in general, unless stated otherwise, all clients discussed in Chapters 5 and 6 were seen by Max Birchwood, and all those discussed in Chapters 1, 3, 4, 7 and 8 by Paul Chadwick.

Not all dialogue is verbatim. In any instances where dialogue implies that a client has changed for the better, the dialogue is accurate. However, we use dialogue for this purpose very rarely. Rather we have used dialogue primarily to *illustrate* a point being made about a clinical process; whilst these dialogues often are verbatim, we have not felt restricted to using only such material at those points when we are making no claim about efficacy.

Chapter 1

A COGNITIVE VIEW OF DELUSIONS AND VOICES

THE COGNITIVE ABC MODEL

It is hard to define *the* cognitive model in clinical psychology because there is no one cognitive theory and therapy. Rather, over the last 20 or more years there has been a proliferation of theories and therapies, some specific to one disorder and others pertaining to all human behaviour, that have assumed the label 'cognitive'.

It is more straightforward to convey the *idea* of the cognitive model within clinical psychology. The well-used example is of a man lying in bed late at night who hears a noise downstairs. If he thinks he is being burgled he will likely feel frightened and may telephone for help. If he thinks it is his inconsiderate partner returning home late again, he will likely feel annoyed and may prepare for an argument. And so on. The central point is that responses to events are mediated by thoughts, images, and beliefs—a commitment to cognitive mediation may be the only attribute which is common to all cognitive theories and therapies (Brewin, 1988).

The cognitive model we use for working with delusions and voices draws mainly on Beck's cognitive therapy (e.g. Beck et al., 1979) but almost as heavily on rational-emotive behaviour therapy (e.g. Ellis, 1962; 1994) and represents an integration of the two (and see Trower, Casey & Dryden, 1988).

Possibly the clearest and heuristically most useful framework for cognitive psychotherapy is Ellis' (1962) ABC model. With one adaptation—that we include all cognitions under B—we use this framework in the present book (see Table 1). A stands for Activating event, B stands for Belief about the Activating event, and C stands for the emotional or behavioural Consequence that follows from the B, given A.

Table 1   The cognitive ABC model

A	B	C
Activating event	Beliefs (images, thoughts, beliefs)	Emotional and behavioural consequences

The ABC framework is deceptively simple—hence the line about cognitive therapy being as easy as abc—but it is a subtle and powerful model which, as we shall see, can guide assessment, formulation and therapy. For now, it is important to make two points about it. We are not arguing that beliefs *cause* feelings, not only because the concept of cause is a complex one but also the As, Bs and Cs usually occur as one unified experience; the merit of the ABC model is that it teases apart the components of experience in a very unique and useful way. Early cognitive formulations sometimes did mistakenly assert that beliefs caused emotional distress.

The second point which requires clarification at this early stage is the meaning of the notation B within the ABC model. In our cognitive therapy we include four cognitions: Images, Inferences, Evaluations and Dysfunctional assumptions.

Images are easily ignored when doing cognitive therapy but should always be explored. For example, an individual who is very anxious about public speaking and is contemplating a forthcoming event might have a sudden image of him or herself fainting on stage. Images are especially useful with individuals who struggle to come up with verbal Bs, but they are worth exploring with everyone.

Inferences are hypotheses which can be true or false—he does not like me, I am going to fail, this table was made from oak, or people are spying on me. Inferences tend to be sudden—what Beck has called automatic—thoughts which occur in abbreviated, often crude, language (e.g. he hates me, I'll fail, the bastards are at it again). Inferences are predictions or hypotheses about what is happening, will happen or has happened. All inferences go beyond the factual evidence.

One way of making an inference is by means of an attribution. People who fail an exam may attribute this to something internal about themselves (e.g. inability) or external about the situation or another person (e.g. an unfair test). They may predict it will only happen this once (unstable attribution) or will always happen (stable attribution). They may attribute the failure to just a deficiency in maths (specific attribution) or a general failing (global attribution). Abramson, Seligman and Teasdale (1978) theorised that depression was caused by a depressive attributional style, namely a tendency to attribute bad outcomes to personal, global and stable faults of character.

Beck (1976) has demonstrated how in clinical problems inferences in the form of anticipations and recollections tend to be distorted, or biased, because of the influence of mood. Beck identified six such errors:

- *Arbitrary inference* is where a specific conclusion is drawn quite arbitrarily.
- *Selective abstraction* is where the client focuses on a detail taken out of context, ignoring other salient features, and conceptualising the whole experience on the basis of this fragment.
- *Overgeneralisation* refers to the pattern of drawing a general rule or conclusion on the basis of one or more isolated incidents and applying the conclusion to virtually all situations.
- *Magnification and minimisation* are reflected in gross errors in evaluating the significance or magnitude or an event.
- *Personalisation* refers to the client's tendency to relate external events to himself. This is one form or arbitrary inference, in which the patient tends to blame himself for things that go wrong.
- *Absolutistic, dichotomous or black-and-white thinking* is the tendency to place everything into one of two opposite categories. Thus an error is a catastrophe, a failure is a complete failure.

An *evaluation* may be defined as a good–bad judgement, or a preference as opposed to an inference (Zajonc, 1980), for example, I prefer John to David, John did a bad thing, etc. It is Ellis who has most clearly and consistently separated inferences and evaluations and it is one of the fundamental principles of rational-emotive behaviour therapy that extreme and disabling emotion is functionally associated with different kinds of negative evaluation.

Of particular importance are what we call *person evaluations*. Person evaluations are defined as stable, global and total condemnations of an entire person, and they may be made about either oneself or someone else in one of three ways: 'other to self' where the other is making an evaluation of me, 'self to self' where I evaluate myself, and 'self to other' where I evaluate the other. The key point here is that it is not a piece of behaviour that is being judged as either good or bad (this would be a reasonable and useful exercise) but an entire person—for example, a person is saying I am a complete and utter failure in everything I do and I shall remain so, or you are totally and forever bad.

Assessing person evaluations is a key therapeutic task when working with delusions and we have developed our own self-report measure of person evaluations, the Evaluative Beliefs Scale or EBScale (Chadwick & Trower, 1993; Appendix 1). This measures the three directions of person evaluations (other-self, self-self, self-other) and covers the major areas of interpersonal concern—namely, unlovability, failure, inferiority, badness, weakness.

Dysfunctional assumptions (Beck et al., 1979) are fundamental rules or principles which guide behaviour. They are thought to have their origins in childhood and are therefore usually implicit but may be deduced from an individual's interpersonal behaviour. For example, a depressed woman appeared throughout her life to have tried to please everyone she met and in the process had utterly subjugated her own wishes and feelings. On those occasions when she *inferred* she had displeased someone she would feel despairing and empty and believe that she would be alone always and was utterly unlovable, a 'non-person'. Her dysfunctional assumption might be characterised as follows: In order to be a complete person I must have others around me. It followed from this that she must never risk upsetting others, for fear of being rejected. As part of cognitive therapy she was able to connect this rule to her early childhood, and in particular she recalled how she had felt despairing and empty and helpless when her parents had neglected her, and how she had slowly come more and more to care for them and others as a way of gaining contact and avoiding these painful feelings.

Clients are usually aware of their inferences (though as facts, not inferences!). This 'awareness' may take the form of words literally as we have described them above, but often, and probably indeed usually, they are aware of them as images, or fragments of images or sentences or imperatives. Clients are less often aware of their evaluations and only very rarely are they aware of their dysfunctional assumptions.

Five Fundamental Principles of the ABC Model

When introducing the cognitive ABC model we have found it helpful to define it in terms of five separate postulates. These postulates are like building blocks and we begin with the most primary and gradually unfold the complexities of the ABC model as the blocks are added.

Principle 1. All Clinical Psychological Problems are Cs

Cognitive therapy is committed to easing severe emotional distress (depression, anxiety . . .) and disturbed behaviour (self-harm, avoidance), and in this sense these are the ubiquitous psychological problems to which cognitive therapy is addressed. This is a very specific definition of a clinical psychological problem—extreme emotional and behavioural disturbance; it does not imply that milder upset and disturbance is not a problem to the individual, merely that it is not a pathological one requiring therapy. If, for example, an individual expresses considerable sadness following a loss this would be seen as an ordinary response; if the feeling was severe depression this would be deemed a problem. Rational-emotive behaviour therapy has most clearly distinguished between extreme and mild emotional upset. The major examples are anger or rage compared with irritation, depression compared with sadness, and anxiety compared with concern.

Locating clinical problems at point C may at first appear odd; in everyday jargon it is events that are usually called problems, such as losing a job or partner. But the cognitive model would say that an event is a problem only if it is associated with significant emotional distress; if an individual is not excessively upset by losing a job, then it is not in this sense a psychological problem. A behavioural problem may be either doing something that the individual strongly wants not to do (smoking, self-harm, heavy drinking, etc.) or not doing something that the person strongly wants to do (avoidance). Similarly, an emotional problem might be experiencing extreme anger, anxiety or depression, or a lack of feeling (dissociation, minimisation). We caution against the easy mistake of locating the problem at point B—a dysfunctional belief. The importance of identifying and changing the B is not as an end in itself, but as a means to an end, namely to resolve the problem at point C. We will define and describe Cs in detail in the practitioner guidelines section below.

Principle 2. Problems arise from Bs, not As

When patients begin therapy and are asked to say what is troubling them, they almost always offer an event (an A), such as divorce or redundancy, or an emotion or behaviour (a C), such as anxiety or violence, or both an A and a C. Thus people might say 'I've lost my job and that's made me feel depressed', or 'going to work makes me feel lousy', or 'my friend treated me badly and that made me hate him'—indeed, this is true in everyday speech too. For most people the A and C is as much as they are aware of and they begin therapy as A-C theorists, saying that such and such an event happened and it made them feel such and such an emotion. (In fact when a client describes an event (A) the description often contains one or more Bs—for example, someone might say 'I was ignored by a friend at a party', taking this to be factual, but on examination it is clear that the person is inferring that the friend saw him and chose not to acknowledge him. More on this in Chapter 2.)

However, the cognitive model asserts that Cs are not products of events (As), but reflect the personal meaning (Bs) the event has for the individual. In other words people's actions and feelings (C) arise from their interpretations of events, and are not inevitable consequences of those events. Events such as going to the shops, losing a relationship, failing at a task, or being snubbed, all provoke significant emotional distress only in certain people and at certain points in their lives; this reaction is not an inevitable consequence and occurs only when these events have a particular personal meaning. This is probably the *cardinal* principle of the cognitive approach. This is the point of the much-quoted saying from the ancient Greek Stoic philosopher Epictetus: 'Men are disturbed not by things but by the views which they take of them . . . when, therefore, we are hindered, or disturbed, or grieved, let us never blame anyone but ourselves: that is, our own judgments' (Montgomery, 1993). Indeed, this commitment to a mediational view has been put forward as the only attribute that is common to all the cognitive behaviour therapies (Brewin, 1988).

As was mentioned earlier, we do not favour the view that Bs cause Cs, for a mixture of philosophical and phenomenological reasons. Philosophers have long argued that it is false to assert that a cognition (belief, intention, image, etc.) can cause a behaviour, because a cognition is not an entity (see Searle, 1983). Also, there is uncertainty about what criteria should be used to decide if any event X may be said to have caused another event Y. From the point of view of phenomenology, the Bs and Cs within the ABC model are not discrete sequential entities but part of the same phenomenon—a person does not think 'I might fail' and only having thought this start to feel anxiety and look for an escape route—rather, having such thoughts and feelings and behavioural impulses is what it is to experience anxiety.

The purpose of separating experience into As, Bs and Cs is that it has considerable utility; it draws the therapist's and client's attention to all aspects of the client's experience (events, cognitions, behaviour and feelings), and facilitates cognitive therapy in numerous ways.

Philosophical Origins

As has been noted elsewhere (e.g. Blackburn & Davison, 1990) the philosophical origins of the cognitive perspective are best introduced through the thinking of Kant (see Magee, 1987). Kant was troubled in general by the conflict between physical sciences and fundamental ethical and religious convictions, and in particular by the presupposition within physical sciences that whatever happens is determined by antecedent events and could not have been otherwise. A world where events were completely determined appeared to Kant to leave no room for ethical and religious ideas. Kant's solution to this problem was to draw a distinction between 'things in themselves' (noumena) and 'things as they appear' (phenomena), and to argue that people could never claim knowledge or understanding of the noumenal world. No one was justified in claiming to experience or understand the world as it really is, the noumenal world (Kant, 1787).

The basis for this argument was that in order for an individual to experience anything at all, to be a subject of experience, he or she must possess sensory, intellectual and conceptual capacities of one kind or another. In order for an object to be experienced, it must fit in with these predispositions—individuals can experience no other kinds of objects. It was therefore inevitable that people must always experience a world of appearances, comprising 'things as they appeared' to subjects, but could never experience the world in itself.

Kant went on to specify those capacities which people could not help but impose upon objects if they were to perceive them and understand them. These were that events be perceived as located in space (space) and occurring in temporal sequence (time), and that they be perceived as orderly and predictable (causality). In other words, Kant argued that all perception and knowledge was sense-dependent and mind-dependent; because people could never experience objects other than in terms of time, space, and causality, Kant argued that whilst these concepts specified the fundamental forms of any possible world of appearances, they could not be assumed to exist in the world as it really is. In short, it is impossible for people to perceive, understand, or discuss objects as they really are because the processes of perception and understanding inevitably impose structures or forms. And if this is true for physical reality, how much more true for evaluations of that reality.

Kant's position is perhaps of more benefit to cognitive therapists than to religious leaders, as the strength of the argument condemns God either to the world of appearances or to something which cannot be meaningfully discussed. What it does for cognitive therapy is set out the importance, and limit, of the cognitive model. In short, the cognitive approach emphasises the crucial role of the B in the ABC. This may seem obvious, but stands in clear contrast to other models, both professional and lay, which are AC approaches—Cs are directly caused by As.

Principle 3. There Are Predictable Connections between Bs and Cs

In this section we shall first illustrate how inferences and evaluations are connected and then spell out how they connect to affect. To recapitulate, there are different types of Bs—images, inferences, evaluations and dysfunctional assumptions. There are a number of different types of evaluations, but probably the most important are person evaluations—that is evaluations of the whole person, be it self or other.

It is central to our understanding of the cognitive model that when people are emotionally distressed there is always both inferential and evaluative thinking involved. This is because inferences are recruited by evaluations: for example, if people have an enduring vulnerability to seeing themselves as total failures (negative self-evaluations) they will habitually infer that a task is going to go badly, they will fail, their shortcomings are obvious and others will label them as failures, and so on. So, even though person evaluations are enduring and are not tied to a specific situation or context, and inferences are always bound by a context, the two are inseparable. REBT theorists describe this elegantly by saying that if you listen closely to an inference you can always hear the implicit evaluation (Wessler & Wessler, 1980).

There are specific relationships between the content of Bs and the type of emotion felt (and behaviour enacted) at C. The three primary cognition-emotion links are anxiety, depression and anger, though there are many other emotions which are related to these (e.g. jealousy, guilt and shame).

Beliefs about threat—psychological or physical danger—are related to anxiety and often to avoidance and escape behaviour. The intensity of the anxiety is related to beliefs about the intensity, probability and assessment of coping responses. Anxiety beliefs and emotions are usually future-oriented.

Beliefs about loss—of status, self-worth, freedom, or important others—are related to depression and withdrawal behaviour. The intensity of the Cs related to beliefs about helplessness and/or hopelessness. Depressive beliefs and emotions are usually past-oriented.

Beliefs about infringement of rights and negative self-other evaluations are related to anger and aggression. The intensity of anger and the expression of aggression are related to beliefs about relative status, threat to status, and revenge-seeking. Angry beliefs and feelings can be future, present or past oriented.

Principle 4. Core Bs Arise from Early Experience

To summarise so far, we have argued that it is the personal meaning events have for people which determines if they are distressed and disturbed, and we have examined some of the different cognitions involved (inferences, evaluations . . .) and spelt out some specific connections to affect and behaviour (e.g. beliefs about threat go with anxiety and avoidance). Thus, following a failed driving test, if I condemn myself as an utter failure then I will experience depression, if I regret the outcome and resolve to get better I will experience merely disappointment, and I will feel angry if I condemn the instructor as a worthless fool who wouldn't know a good driver if he fell over one.

But why is it that certain people have a generalised tendency towards, for example, negative self-evaluation? This is a very big question and a full answer is unavailable. It is likely that babies are genetically endowed with vulnerabilities towards anxiety, paranoia, depression, etc., and that their experience serves to maintain, enhance or diminish these individual propensities (Gilbert, 1992). For the present purpose, one important conclusion may be offered—*early relationships have a profound impact and for the majority of patients it is here that the origin of their problems lies.*

This conclusion has been an essential feature of Beck's theorising for many years (Beck, 1984) although it has featured less strongly in REBT, also for theoretical reasons. Adapting the work of Blatt and his colleagues (e.g. Blatt & Zuroff, 1992) we believe the most fundamental Bs (dysfunctional assumptions and person-evaluations) are laid down in early life and reflect the amount of attachment (closeness) and autonomy (self-definition) the child has. Blatt has developed a cognitive developmental theory in which he argues that personality development involves two dynamically related motivations:

1. Relatedness—the capacity to establish increasingly mature and mutually satisfying interpersonal relationships.
2. Self-definition—the development of a consolidated, realistic, essentially positive, differentiated and integrated self-identity.

These two motivations are contingent on each another, and evolve together; that is, in order to attach closely to another person, I risk temporarily sacrificing autonomy, whereas to develop and explore my autonomy and self-definition, I must separate from an attachment figure. The two themes of attachment and autonomy run through a number of psychological theories, including Bowlby's distinction between attachment and separation, and Beck's concepts of sociotropy and autonomy.

While normal development might be described as a combination of the two, individuals place relatively greater emphasis on one or other. Thus, there are two broad personality configurations, each with preferred modes of cognition, behaviour, defence, adaptation. Briefly, Blatt and Zuroff (1992) offer good evidence that three types of early experience threaten healthy psychological development, defined as a reasonable balance between attachment and autonomy. First, children of caregivers who tended to be inconsistent, neglectful, rejecting, abandoning seem to be very vulnerable to feelings of dependence: they risk feeling empty and despairing if isolated. Second, children of caregivers who tended to be intrusive, controlling, judgemental and punitive seem to avoid others, to be critical of others and themselves, and are prone to feelings of worthlessness. Third, a significant disruption or loss of attachment figure (death, abandonment), or a significant trauma, may push an individual into either of the above, depending on the individual's age and how the individual interprets the loss (e.g. punishment, 'I killed the parent', etc.).

Reformulating this from a cognitive perspective, this means individuals are made sensitive to certain events (As) which will trigger existing negative self-evaluative beliefs and associated affect and behaviour. Individuals develop an interpersonal style which protects this vulnerability, and guards against future re-experience of the shame, loneliness, despair etc. This interpersonal style, or self-presentation behaviour draws particular behaviour from others and individuals quickly become locked in, interpersonally. For instance, if a person who fears criticism behaves in a confrontational manner, this is likely to draw either competition or submission, but not co-operation, from others (see Gilbert, 1992).

Principle 5. Weakening Beliefs Weakens Associated Distress And Disturbance

From a therapist's perspective, the most important asset of the cognitive model is that it creates a new point for the intervention—namely, the Bs. Weakening inferences and evaluations associated with emotional problems is one means by which to ease those problems. Beck et al. (1979) for example, shifted understanding of depression from being primarily an affective problem to a cognitive one, by focusing attention on the associated beliefs, thoughts and images and offered a new treatment approach through the systematic weakening of these beliefs, and thereby the depression also, using cognitive therapy.

DELUSIONS

At the age of 18 Alan's parents began noticing that he was behaving oddly towards them, and at times they felt threatened. He began to make strange references to 'knowing what was going on', and things finally came to a head when he assaulted them. Alan had become convinced over the course of a few months that his parents had been replaced by aliens, and that the surrogates were plotting to kill him. His delusion elaborated until he believed that he was the master of the universe and that his battle with aliens would decide the future for planet Earth.

Defining delusions is notoriously difficult. The traditional approach has been based on establishing qualitative differences between delusions and other beliefs. In this vein, the American Psychiatric Association offered the following definition in the revised *Diagnostic and Statistical Manual III* (American Psychiatric Association, 1987):

> A false personal belief based on incorrect inference about external reality and firmly sustained in spite of what everyone else believes and in spite of what constitutes incontrovertible and obvious proof or evidence to the contrary. The belief is not one ordinarily accepted by other members of the person's culture.

In keeping with others (Garety, 1985; Harper, 1992) we shall consider these DSM IIIR criteria in turn, reviewing the major problems with each. This will alert the reader to the central problems with the traditional approach to definition of delusion, and will render the looser and latest definition—in DSM IV—understandable.

Defining a delusion as a 'false belief' has been criticised on two grounds. First, delusions need not be false. If an individual believes his partner to be unfaithful without evidence for this, he might be said to have a delusion of jealousy even if the partner were actually being unfaithful (Brockington, 1991). Second, defining truth and falsity is so troublesome that one thinker has concluded that 'it is nearly hopeless for a lone clinician to try to judge whether a belief is a delusion by determining its truth value' (Heise, 1988, p. 266).

The firmest evidence for the criterion of being based on 'incorrect inference' came with the discovery that people with delusions follow biased reasoning (see Bentall, Kinderman & Kaney, 1994). It has emerged that under certain experimental conditions people with delusions appear to show bias in their attributional style, in their judgement of covariance, and in their probabilistic reasoning (Garety, 1991). However, these data are inconclusive. First, in some instances research on probabilistic reasoning has found that deluded people are more, not less, rational than others. Second, there is evidence for competing theories. For example, the reasoning of deluded people has been found to be excessively influenced by stimuli ('bottom-up') in one study and in a second study to be excessively influenced by prior beliefs, expectations, etc. ('top-down'). Also, it is not always clear how specific findings in analogue studies might apply to delusional thinking. For example, analogue studies are easily able to measure how many items of information are used to form hypotheses in experimental situations, but how might it be established if delusions are formed on the basis of less information than, say, religious beliefs or depressive beliefs? There is no convincing evidence for either a general bias (i.e. one applicable to all material) or a specific bias or a cognitive deficit in the process of delusion formation.

The criterion of being 'firmly sustained' shifts the focus from formation to maintenance. The implication is that all delusions are held with total (or near total) and unwavering conviction. Although this may be true of many delusions it is not true of all delusions; Brett-Jones, Garety & Hemsley (1987) showed that conviction can be less than total and can fluctuate quite dramatically. Again, Harrow, Rattenbury & Stoll (1988) found in a sample of 34 people diagnosed as schizophrenic, that even at the height of the disorder six individuals (18%) showed only partial conviction. Despite this the evidence is nonetheless clear that many delusions are held with strong or total certainty, but this seems to be the *sine qua non* of core beliefs of any kind and does not imply anything pathological or abnormal about deluded people.

The next and related criterion, that delusions are unmodifiable or utterly insensitive to reason, is distinct from the preceding criterion in that it introduces the idea that delusions resist active attempts at belief modification. However, there are strong empirical grounds for rejecting this association. There have been a modest number of studies, including our own, reporting attempts to weaken delusions, with generally favourable results (Alford, 1986; Alford & Beck, 1994; Beck, 1952; Chadwick & Lowe, 1990; Chadwick, et al., 1994; Fowler & Morley, 1989; Hartman & Cashman, 1983; Hole, Rush & Beck, 1979; Johnson, Ross & Mastria, 1977; Kingdon & Turkington, 1994; Lowe & Chadwick, 1990; Milton, Patwa & Hafner, 1978). It might be more reasonable to assert that delusions are difficult to modify, sometimes fiendishly so. This position would acknowledge that the class of beliefs called delusions varies considerably along a number of dimensions, and it would encourage examination of the multitude of factors which might be thought to influence therapeutic outcome. It would also encourage an exploration of whether delusions are more difficult to modify than political or religious beliefs, or the core beliefs associated with sexual abuse, and anorexia, for instance.

The final criterion, 'in spite of what almost everyone else believes' relates to the unusual content, or bizarreness, of delusions. Delusions are beliefs which the vast majority of the individual's group do not hold. However, using this as a point of definition may be questioned on empirical grounds, for research has demonstrated how difficult it is to rate the 'bizarreness' of delusions (Kendler, Glazer & Morgenstern, 1983), and on conceptual grounds because of the shifting sands of what people in different cultures, groups, and periods of history will believe (Harper, 1992).

One further approach to defining delusions, which retains the character of the traditional view, is to propose a disjunctive definition. Thus, Oltmanns (1988) lists eight defining characteristics of delusions, and suggests that none be viewed as either necessary or sufficient. Research could then begin to resolve which characteristics are most important. An advantage of this strategy is that it acknowledges individual differences, and recognises the need for empirical investigation. Nonetheless, if the individual criteria do not distinguish delusions from other beliefs, then even a disjunctive definition would seem flawed.

Traditional criteria have also been challenged by a radical and exciting call to define delusions (and hallucinations) as points on a continuum with normality, position on this continuum being influenced by dimensions of thought and behaviour, such as degree of belief conviction and the extent of preoccupation with the belief (Strauss, 1969). Rather than playing down individual differences and commonality with other beliefs, Strauss' perspective embraces them and elevates them to the position of defining characteristics. This view has shaped our view of delusions and hallucinations enormously.

Therefore the last 20 years has seen a shift in emphasis away from discontinuity to continuity, and from qualitative to quantitative differences. Individuals with paranoid delusions, for example, are acknowledged to be thinking and behaving in ways which can be detected in ordinary people. It is implicit to this view that delusions need to be studied on an individual basis, and that specific and varied dimensions of thinking and behaviour need to be covered. It is encouraging to note that this shift has been reflected in the less absolute DSM IV definition of delusions (American Psychiatric Association, 1994). In particular, it is noted that delusions 'usually involve a misinterpretation', the 'distinction between a delusion and a strongly held idea is sometimes difficult to make and depends on the degree of conviction', and determining bizarreness 'may be difficult to judge'. There is no direct assertion of unmodifiability.

An ABC Perspective

In this section we argue that the cognitive ABC perspective offers a helpful framework within which to understand the experience of delusions. In particular it provides a much needed conceptual framework for under-standing delusions, clarifying current confusion and offering a new ap-proach to treatment.

Delusions within an ABC analysis are obviously Bs—that is, they are delusional interpretations of an event (A) and may or may not be associ-ated with distress and disturbance at point C. Thus the concept of delu-sion implies an inference has been made, as in the DSM IIIR definition considered earlier. In Table 2 we illustrate the ABC approach to delusions by listing an ABC analysis of the major types of delusions—the examples listed are those offered by clients.

At an immediate level, depicting delusional experience in this way en-sures that attention is paid to the environmental and bodily events (As), clarifies that the delusion is but one possible interpretation placed on events, and shows if the delusion is a problem (i.e. distressing or disturb-ing) to the client.

In addition to those benefits mentioned above, the ABC perspective on delusions also brings much needed conceptual clarity. It clarifies that a delusion always contains an explicit *inference*, but that *evaluations* are usually implicit and will need teasing out through thought chaining. This means that in most cases cognitive therapists need to use thought chain-ing to go beyond the delusional interpretation in order to uncover the critical evaluative beliefs. Only when both the (delusional) inferential and evaluative thinking is exposed will the emotional and behavioural con-sequences be fully understood (see Principle 4 of the cognitive model above).

Thus, the cognitive model clarifies how delusions relate to other import-ant beliefs and to distress and disturbance. For example, with the delu-sion of reference (Table 2), the client infers that the doctor is passing a message to him through his walk that he, the doctor, sees the client as totally inferior, a nothing—that is, he was evaluating the client's entire person. But this inferred other-self evaluation will not fully account for the client's emotional experience of shame, because the client might think to himself that the doctor is an ass who's opinion is worth nothing. Further thought chaining revealed that the client accepted the doctor's evaluation of him; in other words, he made a negative self-evaluation that he as a person was inferior and a nothing. This accounts for the emotional upset, and clarifies the two main therapeutic goals for cogni-tive therapy for delusions—to weaken the delusion, and to weaken associated negative evaluative thinking. In subsequent chapters we go into the intricacy of cognitive assessment and therapy for delusions in considerable detail.

Table 2 A cognitive ABC analysis of delusions

Delusion	Antecedent	Belief	Consequences
Mind reading	Client cannot find a word, therapist supplies it	She read my mind, I've found her out, I knew it	Elated Pressure to tell people
Paranoid	Car horn sounds outside house	They have come for me, to kill me	Fear Runs from flat
Thought broadcast	Client shopping Hears man say what he was thinking	My thoughts are being transmitted to others	Panic Escape
Thought insertion	Client has sudden intrusive and shocking thought	It's not mine, someone put it in my head with a special machine	Fearful, exposed Urge to hide
Reference	Doctor walks past window, head held high	He thinks he's better than me, he's letting me know	Shame Moves away from window
Grandiose	The Queen says on TV she loves all her children	She means me, she loves me, I *am* her daughter	Elation
Infestation	Scalp itching	They are biting me again, I can't stand it	Anxiety Helplessness
Somatic	Wakes feeling tired, aching	I've got AIDS, I'm going to die	Terror Immobilised
Capgras	Father supports client's admission to hospital	He's not my dad, dad wouldn't do it, he's an alien	Frightened Withdraws, clenches fists
Cotard	Fails to respond to once enjoyed activity	I feel nothing, I am dead	Emptiness Suicidal
Control	Moves to push daughter out of open window	I didn't do that, they made me do it, they did it, it's not my fault	Reassured Passive

The ABC perspective also brings much needed conceptual clarity to the debate, which was touched upon earlier in this chapter, surrounding the role of reasoning in the formation and maintenance of delusions. On the one hand, Maher (1974) has long argued that delusions result from ordinary reasoning processes in the face of abnormal, or unusual, perceptual experience. On the other hand, researchers have argued that delusions result from reasoning deficit or bias. Claims for a *deficit* in reasoning are unsubstantiated. The case for a reasoning *bias* appears stronger, with numerous studies demonstrating that people with delusions display bias in different features of automatic and controlled processing (see Garety, 1991).

However, there are three significant obstacles to progress in this field. First, if a robust bias were to emerge, it might well be a consequence of delusional thinking rather than the delusion being a consequence of the bias—thus, this research may not reveal anything direct about formation. Second, the extensive data from research looking at non delusional thinking in people with delusions offer conflicting indications as to the type of bias expected to produce or maintain a delusion. Certain studies find evidence for exaggerated 'top-down' processing, where individuals are excessively guided by beliefs at the expense of stimuli (e.g. Huq, Garety & Hemsley, 1988); other studies find evidence to show that people with delusions are unusually quick to reject their hypotheses and are therefore excessively 'bottom-up' in their thinking (e.g. Garety, Wessley & Hemsley, 1991).

The third problem concerns research investigating bias in delusional thinking. This research consistently shows that deluded people process salient (usually threatening) stimuli differently from ordinary material. But so do people who are depressed, who have an eating disorder, who are anxious, etc.—this is not evidence of anything new or unusual. Also, such research does not yield evidence of a *general* bias in reasoning; only of a specific bias for material of personal significance.

We believe that the cognitive ABC clarifies the role of reasoning in the maintenance of delusions. First, it is implicit to the model that cognitive bias is specific—that is, it is to be expected only when the individual is distressed, angry, anxious, etc. A general bias would not be expected. Thus, in relation to delusions, the standard cognitive distortions (selective attention, overgeneralisation, arbitrary inference, personalisation) would be expected only when the delusion was 'on-line'. This fits our clinical experience. Second, the cognitive model states clearly that inferential thoughts, such as delusional interpretations of events, are necessarily influenced by antecedents (external or internal stimuli) and enduring beliefs (evaluations and dysfunctional assumptions). Therefore, delusional interpretations would not be hypothesised to result solely from either top-down or bottom-up influences.

What is clear is that certain delusions are much more strongly influenced by activating events (especially perceptual abnormalities), others more so by evaluative beliefs. Examples of the former include experiences of passivity, reference, thought insertion or broadcast. It is at this point that the contribution of Maher (1988) is perhaps most significant, with his formulation of delusions as reasonable explanations of abnormal perceptual experiences. In contrast, other delusions—especially grandiosity and paranoia—seem much more to reflect a psychological motivation, perhaps to protect the individual's sense of self (Zigler & Glick, 1988). The popular debate about whether delusions are all either reasonable explanations of abnormal experiences, or unreasonable explanations driven by motivational force, is an example of absolutistic thinking once again being unhelpful, and recognition is growing that some delusions are the result predominatly of perceptual abnormality, others predominantly of psychological motivation (Garety, 1991).

VOICES

In this section we describe the experience of voices and introduce our ABC approach. We believe the cognitive ABC model is an exciting, new approach to understanding the experience of hearing voices. First, it draws attention to neglected features of phenomenology. Second, it attaches great importance to the individual's effort after meaning and generally places the individual at the heart of the theory and therapy. Third, it better accounts for differences in coping behaviour and distress and finally it creates a new treatment.

Hearing Voices

Vinny has lived in Birmingham for most of his life. At the age of 18 while at work he began hearing voices. He recalls this experience vividly:

> They say things about me all the time, I never get a moment's peace. They swear at me and criticise everything I do, like saying 'What's he doing that for', 'Look at the bastard, they're all taking the piss'. There's one main voice, I don't know who it is, I hear it really clear through my ears. I once thought it came from the birds. When I was in jail it told me to drink my piss from the slopping out bucket, so I did. It once told me to go and stand on a street corner and like an idiot I did, and nothing happened! I lost my girlfriend through it; I used to get really angry, I couldn't cope with it.

Leonard is a European immigrant to the UK who began hearing voices soon after an occasion in church when he saw a figure appear out of the ground amidst 'a crescendo of light and sound'. Five years later he continues to hear several voices, whom he identifies as his ancestors. He has an intimate relationship with them and views them as akin to guardian angels who provide companionship; they offer advice on simple matters (e.g. where to buy the cheapest loaf of bread or encouraging attendance at clinic) and prophesy the future—once, for example, telling him that if he went to a ballroom dance then he would meet a woman who would want to marry him (he believes he has met his intended but she has yet to propose marriage).

Leonard is able to initiate contact with the voices by saying 'Uncle B'. The voices can be tetchy if he refuses to heed advice. He has few close friends and acknowledges that without them his life 'would be a void'. His voices are demanding and he has to pay them back by praying to them. Latterly he has become disillusioned with them; their promises to protect his car from vandals, and arrange for a beautiful woman to come and see him remain unfulfilled.

Auditory hallucinations are traditionally associated with a diagnosis of schizophrenia. In the World Health Organization's International Pilot Study of Schizophrenia (WHO, 1973) auditory hallucinations were reported by 73% of people diagnosed as having an acute episode of schizophrenia. Yet they can be reported by individuals who have been sexually abused, or suffered a bereavement, as well as by individauls diagnosed as having a manic depressive illness or an affective psychosis. Indeed, because they feature in many different disorders, the importance of auditory hallucinations in differential diagnosis has been doubted (Asaad & Shapiro, 1986).

In addition, it appears that auditory hallucinations are not restricted to clinical groups. Auditory hallucinations can be reported by individuals who, while showing signs of a specific clinical disorder, display insufficient for a firm diagnosis to be made (Cochrane, 1983). Again, it appears that under laboratory conditions many ordinary people display a propensity to report hearing sounds which are not there, prompting researchers to speculate that proneness to hallucinate may be a predisposition spread across the general population (Slade & Bentall, 1988). Current opinion in psychology veers towards accepting the possibility that hallucinations lie on a continuum with normality (Strauss, 1969).

The auditory hallucination itself can be a noise, music, single words, a brief phrase, or a whole conversation. Voices are defined as auditory hallucinations which are perceived as someone talking. The experience of hearing voices is a powerful one that demands a reaction. However, the experience is also very personal, as the case examples show.

An ABC Analysis of Voices

The case for viewing voices from a cognitive ABC perspective may appear less obvious than that for delusions—after all, delusions are beliefs, the cornerstone of the ABC framework. Our progress in developing a cognitive model of voices began with the insight that voices are not thoughts (Bs), they are activating events (As). This simple observation was the clue to our cognitive formulation of voices (Chadwick & Birchwood, 1994): a voice is seen as an activating event (A) to which the individual gives a meaning (B) and experiences associated emotional and behavioural reactions (C). This manoeuvre has a profound impact upon the psychological understanding and treatment of voices because it makes clear that distress and coping behaviour are consequences not of the hallucination itself, but of the individual's beliefs about that hallucination. In Table 3 we offer two examples of an ABC analysis of voices, one for a voice believed to be benevolent and one malevolent.

Table 3   ABC analysis of voices

Activating event	Beliefs	Consequences
Richard hears a voice say 'Hit him'	It is God testing my strength and faith	Does not comply Feels pleased
Jenny hears a voice say 'Be careful'	It is the Devil, he is watching waiting to get me	Terror Avoids going to shops

There is an immediate and striking connection between this view of voices and our earlier discussion of delusions. Indeed, beliefs about a voice (e.g. it is the Devil punishing me) formally speaking are secondary delusions. Thus our approach to voices is once again actually a cognitive approach to delusions, but to a specific class of delusions—those which are secondary to the same type of activating event, namely voices. In this respect this entire book is really about cognitive approaches to delusions, and we hope this will be reflected in conceptual unity across chapters on voices and delusions.

The reconstruction of voices in terms of As, Bs and Cs has intuitive appeal because serious disturbance associated with voices, like so many other symptoms, is located in the way an individual feels and behaves—a central principle of the cognitive model. People who hear voices are typically referred for therapy because they are desperate, depressed, angry, suicidal, helpless, harming themselves, isolated, violent, etc. This point is implicit in traditional treatment approaches, which have usually been directed at easing distress and altering behaviour (methods of anxiety reduction, punishment procedures) as well as at eliminating the hallucinatory experience (medication, ear plugs, headphones). Such treatments were based on the premise that a particular individual's coping behaviour and affect followed necessarily from the nature of his or her hallucination (e.g. Benjamin, 1989, p. 293).

However, this explanation may be too simple. Research has shown how voices with similar contents may evoke differing coping behaviour (Tarrier, 1992). Also, an inventive study by Romme and Escher (1989) has revealed how voices frequently do not evoke a sufficiently strong reaction to bring the individual to the attention of services, even when the content is extremely serious. It would appear that the nature and strength of an individual's response to voices is mediated by psychological processes.

Empirical Support for the Model

We have gathered strong empirical support for the cognitive model of voices, which rests on two pivotal predictions. First, that emotion and coping behaviour is indeed connected to beliefs about voices; this is the major premise of the model. The second prediction is that beliefs are not direct interpretations of voice content—if this were so, then differences in coping behaviour and distress might be accounted for just as well by inspecting voices content (an A) as beliefs (Bs). Our research has produced strong evidence for both hypotheses (Chadwick & Birchwood, 1994; 1995; 1996).

We have developed a comprehensive therapeutic approach for working with voices from a cognitive perspective, which includes a semi-structured interview schedule and 30 item self-report measure (see Chapter 5), and an adapted version of cognitive therapy (see Chapter 6). Research using this approach has shown that beliefs about voices do predict coping behaviour and distress, and do this better than voice content. Four types of belief are of particular importance; those about the voices identity, purpose (is it trying to harm or help me), power or omnipotence, and beliefs about the consequences of obedience and disobedience.

Around 80% of all voices are believed to be extraordinarily powerful, or omnipotent, and this belief seems to rest on four types of evidence. First, collateral symptoms often contribute to a sense of a voice's omnipotence. One man, for example, was commanded by his voice to kill his daughter; he recalled an occasion when she was standing by an open window and he experienced his body being moved towards her. A second man heard a voice telling him that he was the son of Noah, and occasionally when he heard his voice he experienced concurrent visual hallucinations in which he was dressed in a white robe and walked on water. Second, people frequently attribute events to their voices, and then cite the events as proof of the voices great power. Thus, although two individuals cut their wrists under their own volition, both subsequently deduced that the voices had somehow made them do it. Similarly, one man attributed responsibility for his having sworn out loud in church to his satanic voices. Third, about three-quarters of voice hearers we have seen are unable to influence either the onset and offset of their voices or what was said, once again suggestive of the voices' power.

Finally, almost all voices give an impression of knowing all about people's past histories, their present thoughts, feelings and actions, and what the future holds. Frequently voices refer to behaviour and thoughts of a highly personal and emotive nature, such as a criminal act or personal weakness, which the individual feared others knowing. Perhaps because of this lack of privacy, individuals would often attribute more knowledge to the voice than the content actually displayed. So general statements like 'We know all about you' are interpreted as referring to specific actions. Understandably, this appearance of omniscience leaves many individuals feeling exposed and vulnerable.

A belief that a voice is extremely powerful, or omnipotent, is associated with higher depressive symptomatology (Chadwick & Birchwood, 1996). Bauer (1979) coined the phrase to be 'caught in the voice's power' to portray this facet and it is to be expected that under these circumstances individuals should experience depressive symptomatology because they are in the presence of a controlling other from whom they cannot escape. This is known to produce a sense of helplessness and powerlessness in all individuals (Gilbert, 1992) and an important part of cognitive therapy for voices is helping individuals break free of this control.

An orthogonal but equally important belief concerns a voice's identity and purpose—that is, why is this voice talking to me. On the basis of beliefs about identity and purpose, people usually believe voices to be either malevolent or benevolent. Beliefs about malevolence take one of two forms; either that the voice is a deserved punishment or an undeserved persecution. For example, one man believed he was being punished by the Devil for having committed a murder, and another man believed he was being persecuted without good reason by a spiteful ex-employer. The punishment-persecution distinction (Trower & Chadwick,

1995) is of fundamental psychological importance and it is a theme which runs throughout this book.

Beliefs about a voice's benevolence are more varied. For example, one woman believed that she heard the voice of a prophet who was helping her become a better mother and wife, and one man believed that the voices were from God and were there to help develop a special power. Many people hear a mixture of benevolent and malevolent voices, but in our experience each individual voice is either one or the other.

Connection between Beliefs, Coping Behaviour and Affect

We organise behavioural and emotional response to voices into three categories. Engagement comprises co-operative behaviour (e.g. elective listening, willing compliance, seeking contact with voices, trying to call them up) and positive affect (e.g. joy, reassurance, amusement). Resistance comprises resistant and combative behaviour (e.g. arguing, covert and overt shouting back and swearing, non-compliance or reluctant compliance when pressure is extreme, avoidance of cues that trigger voices, and distraction) and negative affect (e.g. fear, anxiety, anger, depression). Indifference is defined as not engaging with the voice, and is very unusual in clinical groups.

In our first study (Chadwick & Birchwood, 1994) using a semi-structured interview schedule (Appendix 2) we found that voices believed to be malevolent were resisted, and benevolent voices were engaged with. However, in order to establish the reliability and validity of these concepts, we have developed a 30 item Beliefs About Voices Questionnaire (Chadwick & Birchwood, 1995: Appendix 3) to measure malevolence (6 items), benevolence (6 items), resistance (9 items) and engagement (8 items) and power (1 item). A statistical analysis conducted on a preliminary sample of 60 completed questionnaires has shown the BAVQ to be both reliable and valid and again strongly reinforced the connections between resistance and malevolence, engagement and benevolence (for details see Chadwick & Birchwood, 1995).

In particular we have been interested in the connection between depressive symptomatology and beliefs about voices. The 26 individuals in our sample of 60 who believed their voices to be malevolent were almost twice as *commonly* depressed as those without paranoid beliefs, and also more *severely* so. These data suggest that in hallucinated individuals paranoid secondary delusions are unlikely to be defending against depression (Zigler & Glick, 1988). Believing a voice to be very powerful was also associated with higher levels of depressive symptomatology, and this dimension was orthogonal to that between malevolence and benevolence. Powerlessness in the face of an inescapable and powerful other is known to be associated with depression (Gilbert, 1992).

Connection between Beliefs and Content

Having found that differences in coping behaviour and distress were rendered understandable by reference to beliefs about malevolence and benevolence, it remained to be shown that voice content could not account for these differences with equal clarity. In other words, the distinction between malevolence and benevolence needed to say something about the maintenance of voices which could not be said by inspecting voice content alone.

It is clear that there is a link between voice content and the person's associated feelings and behaviour, and therefore that in many cases resistance and engagement might have been predicted on the basis of content. However, the class of belief was not always understandable in the light of voice content alone. Between one third and one half of all individuals who have taken part in our research held beliefs which were either not explicable by reference to voice content, or directly at odds with it. Two voices of benign content were believed to be malevolent; for instance, one of these voices simply urged the individaul to 'take care', 'mind his step', and 'watch how he went', yet he believed these words to have been spoken by evil witches intent on driving him mad. The reverse was also true; two voices commanded the hearers to commit suicide, yet both were believed to be benevolent. Three voices commanded the hearers to commit murder (in two instances, of immediate family members), and yet again were believed to be benevolent. Perhaps most strikingly, one woman's voice identified itself as God and yet she disregarded this and believed it to be an evil force.

We have found the meaning individuals attach to their voices renders their coping behaviour and affect understandable; when beliefs are not taken into account, many responses seem perplexing or incongruous (see also Strauss, 1991).

SUMMARY

Out of the events and facts of everyday life each one of us builds over time a unique picture of the world, our selves and our interpersonal relationships. We make judgements about these interpretations and depending upon those judgements, we react with positive or negative emotions and in ways to defend or enhance ourselves interpersonally. However, our understanding can be distorted and our evaluations extreme and negative, and we experience extreme emotional and behavioural problems. One way of analysing this highly complex process is within the framework of the ABC cognitive model. In this framework the As are the objective facts of life, the Bs are on the one hand the inferences out of which we build our picture of our worlds and our selves, and on the other hand the evaluations with which we judge that world and our selves. Finally the Cs are our emotional and behavioural reactions to the world as we understand and judge it. In this chapter we have introduced this general framework for thinking about ordinary behaviour and shown how it applies very well to delusions and voices, experiences thought to be outside the realm of such analysis. In what follows we explore this application in detail.

Chapter 2

THE PRACTICE OF THERAPY AND THE PROBLEM OF ENGAGEMENT

THE PRACTICE OF COGNITIVE THERAPY

In this chapter we intend to lay out the framework of cognitive therapy, and show how we can go about producing therapeutic change by modifying the inferences and the evaluations with which people construct their world, their selves and their future. We begin by explaining some of the prerequisites for this type of therapy, then describe what we see as the eight major conceptual steps in this form of therapy. These steps represent those many aspects of the work of Beck (1976; Beck et al., 1979) and Ellis (1994) that we have found to be most helpful and most easily integrated with one another. By necessity our coverage in this chapter of the practice of cognitive therapy is incomplete—otherwise we should need two books, one on cognitive therapy, one on its use with psychosis—but we hope to give a framework which will usefully ease the reader through the subsequent chapters.

This general eight-step approach draws on ideas and procedures developed largely for work with emotional disorders. We find it works well with psychotic problems with, generally speaking, few and slight adjustments, which are addressed in the appropriate chapters. There is one exception, which we find to be a difficulty in cognitive therapy with people who have delusions and voices to a far greater degree than is usual in many other groups, that is, the problem of engaging clients in therapy. We discuss the engagement problem in detail in the final part of this chapter, listing the major blocks and offering some strategic moves to overcome them.

Prerequisites

There are at least two important prerequisites to the practice of effective cognitive psychotherapy. The first is the use of good basic counselling skills in order to

- establish a good working alliance,
- engage the client fully in collaborative empiricism (see Beck et al. 1979),
- understand the client's unique perspective and feelings,
- help the client carry out the difficult and often painful work of therapeutic change.

This material is extensively available elsewhere (e.g. Egan, 1990) and will not be repeated here.

The second prerequisite is a sound knowledge of the principles of cognitive formulation and intervention and the use of a cognitive framework, such as the ABC framework, described in Chapter 1. In other words the therapist should be fully informed of the theory and use the theory to guide the practice. In the next section we look in detail at the process of gaining a clear ABC assessment, and of proceeding to intervention. This process takes place within a general psychological assessment and formulation of a client's history and present difficulty.

Eight Basic Steps from Assessment to Intervention

The first two or three sessions with the client should be conducted in a non-directive manner using basic counselling skills to encourage the client to tell his story, including current problem, precipitating events, and earlier learning and traumatic experiences which may have contributed to characteristic vulnerabilities. The therapist can use the ABC model as a background heuristic to develop hunches, give ideas for further elaboration and so on. When a point is reached where the therapist has a general picture and feels that rapport is reasonably established, she then seeks to become more specific, and the work that is specific to cognitive therapy begins. We have devised an eight-step sequence to take the reader through the basics in a structured way. These eight conceptual aims are all defined in terms of the ABC model offered in Chapter 1. We give the steps briefly below, then we describe each of the steps in detail.

1. Ask the client for a problem he wants to start with.
2. Assess either the activating event (A) or emotional problem (C).
3. Assess whichever remains.
4. Connect A to C and check that is what the client is most worried about.
5. Assess Beliefs (images, inferences, evaluations) using thought chaining.
6. Formulation: (a) show the B–C connection, and (b) offer a developmental formulation.

7. Establish the client's goals and consider his options.
8. Challenge beliefs.

These steps may appear deceptively easy—converting them into practice is a complex art. What we are proposing is a sequence of conceptual steps, not a sequence of technical ones—knowing which techniques to use when a theoretically driven, flexible and innovative collaboration is required with the client. The whole process is lengthy and dynamic, with stages being recycled, depending on progress with a problem, tackling a new problem and so on. Let us go through this process in detail.

1. Focus on a Problem

The therapist 'changes gear' from the early explorative, client-centred counselling phase and tells the client that she now has an overall picture, and the time has come to start dealing specifically and practically with the main problems. She may then ask: 'what problem would you like to work on first?' It is not always easy to engage this change from the general to the specific. A client may have talked extensively and given a complex and confusing picture, or have been taciturn and given short and vague answers. In either case it will be useful to use those counselling skills that help to make the client more concrete, especially open questions such as 'What's bothering you most at the moment?' 'Can you give me an example?' 'What actually happened?' 'Can you tell me in more detail about the problem at that time?' The 'problem' that the client eventually describes should contain elements of at least the A—a situation or event or subjective experience—and a C—how they felt about it or reacted behaviourally. Sometimes there will also be a B—an interpretation of some kind. The therapist's task is to unpack 'the problem' into the ABC components, as outlined in the steps that follow. When collecting this type of information, it is useful to write it down in three columns under the headings: Activating event (real or anticipated), Beliefs (images, inferences . . .), and Consquences (emotional and behavioural disturbances).

As the therapist and client analyse a number of problems in this way, the therapist may soon see a theme emerging from apparently quite disparate problems, and start to intuitively formulate ideas about the underlying dysfunctional beliefs.

2. Assess the C

We pointed out in the last chapter that the nub of the 'problem' was the C—the client's emotional turmoil and distress and his destructive or disturbing or self-defeating behaviour. While of course it is true that the beliefs at B and triggering life events at A are instrumental in creating problems at C, we would not want to offer cognitive therapy to someone who seriously upset no-one (including himself), no matter how bizarre his beliefs or bad the events. It is essential therefore to establish that the client has a moderately serious problem at C, and then to obtain a factually accurate account of the Cs. We divide the Cs into related emotional and behavioural reactions; in practice either may be used to help deduce the other.

Emotional Cs. It is useful to separate the emotional Cs into two elements— the intensity of emotion and the type of emotion. People respond emotionally to negative life events all their lives, but do not need psychiatric or psychological help for their emotional reactions—though they may seek a variety of solutions to the negative life events. People generally seek psychotherapy when their feelings reach distressing proportions. This then is the first dimension of emotion the therapist will want to establish—where, on a dimension of intensity, does the client's experience lie: terrified or just worried, depressed or just sad, enraged or just cross? It is often useful for a client to rate intensity on a ten-point scale where 0 is neutral or no emotion, and 10 is the strongest and most intense they can imagine. The therapist needs this information to know first, whether the client really needs psychotherapy or simply moral support and practical advice, and second, to make progress later in establishing the belief. This second point is essential for the successful conduct of therapy, since the therapist must have identified a strong emotion at C in order to be able to get to the important B. The client who is merely worried at C will hardly be responding to 'catastrophic' inferences and person evaluations but probably thinking quite realistically about some event A.

We are not suggesting that the therapist simply accepts the word of a client who reports being merely worried or a bit sad. Many clients are inhibited about admitting to strong feelings, or are even unaware of them through years of inhibition. The therapist should therefore probe for the depth of feeling. This requires a good counselling 'attitude' in which the therapist makes the client feel safe enough to explore his negative feelings. If you cannot get a strong emotion descriptively, you may certainly get the physiology ('I'm not anxious, my heart's just pounding'). Furthermore the emotion will *express* itself not only in the internal physiology but in verbal and nonverbal behaviour. This is known as emotional leakage. This helps a therapist to interpret the likely feeling. For a client who is really unused to identifying feelings, basic *gestalt* awareness exercises can be useful (e.g. Clarkson, 1989).

Some clients have the reverse problem—rather than repressing their feelings, they are over-sensitised to them. People vary in the threshold or tolerance level at which point the emotion is triggered, so that the client with a very low threshold will react very quickly to minor levels of aversiveness—for example the person who reacts angrily to the slightest inconvenience, or panics at the slightest twinge or pain. Rational-emotive behaviour therapy (REBT) theorists refer to this as low frustration tolerance.

The second task for the therapist is to establish the *type* of emotion the client is experiencing. Clients often do not or cannot express clearly the type of emotion they experience about an event. For example the client may report feeling upset, but does this mean he feels anxious or depressed, hurt, guilty or ashamed, or something else? As a rule of thumb, there are three primary negative emotions, namely anxiety, anger and depression, with numerous secondary emotions which are permutations of these, such as guilty depression or shameful depression. The therapist can usually get the client to nominate one of the primary emotions as closest to how he feels.

Behavioural Cs. Behavioural Cs may be either an action, or an unrealised impulse to act. The *type* of behaviour is usually related to the type of emotion, and this is because people do not just respond emotionally to their interpretations of events but actually do something about them. Anxiety emotions are usually accompanied by avoidance or defensive behaviour, ranging from an extreme of avoiding or leaving situations, to less overt forms such as gaze aversion and other subtle non-verbal responses. Depression is accompanied by inactivity and withdrawal, and anger by overt or muted aggressive behaviour. Although these behavioural ways of coping with an event often achieve a short-term benefit, such as reducing stress by avoidance, in the longer term they nearly always maintain or worsen the problem.

It is rare that clients give neatly distinguished emotional and behavioural Cs. Indeed, the ABC separation is, to begin with, in the therapist's mind only. From a client's point of view all three components are experienced as one, and the therapist's task is to distinguish between them.

Three words of caution concerning likely pitfalls assessing Cs are required. First, ensure the C is severe. Second, in certain situations clients veer between two differing emotional reactions, such as depression and anger. When we come across this, conducting an ABC assessment, we find it helpful to reflect it to the client and agree to look at each separately. Third, clients often merge primary and secondary reactions. With a secondary ABC the C from the primary ABC has become the A for a second ABC. For example a client may feel angry and aggressive (C) about some event (A), but then feel anxious (new C) about having been angry and aggressive (the new Activating event). Such cycles are common in practice, and can be quite confusing. Clients react to an event, and then react to their reaction.

3. Assess the A

The task in clarifying As is to get the client to give an objective and factual account of a *specific* event that triggered the Cs, and preferably a recent one. By far the most common error is to attempt an ABC assessment beginning with a general A (e.g. doing badly at work).

The therapist gently directs the client's attention to the event that directly triggered the particular C described earlier. There is virtually no limit to what can be an A event. An A event is anything that a person attends to and appraises at B, and consequently reacts to at C. The most obvious A events are actual situations or incidents that arise in the here-and-now daily life of the client, or are memories of events from the recent or distant past, or are predictions of events the client thinks may or will happen, or are pure imaginings. However, As can equally be a person's own feelings and behaviour (Cs can be As), or a person's own thoughts and beliefs (Bs can be As). It is important that the therapist helps the client build a detailed and *factual* description of all aspects of the situation in order later to be in a position to challenge the client's distorted picture.

Clients will not usually give their therapists neatly clarified A events. Very commonly they will give factual descriptions that combine A with elements of B. For example a client offers as a factual description of events the following: his boss passed him by in the street (an A), saw him (an inferred B) and ignored him (a second inference). Having made the distinction, the therapist needs to communicate this to the client and help him discriminate between subjective judgements and objective facts.

4. Confirm A–C is the Problem

The therapist communicates to the client her understanding of the A-C connection in a paraphrase. For example 'You say you felt depressed (C) and withdrew (C) because you argued with your partner (A)'. The therapist then checks that this A-C is what the client is most worried about ('Is this the problem that is bothering you most at the moment?'). The therapist must be careful not to underestimate the power of the A-C connection. Clients really do feel at the mercy of As—in very powerful emotions it seems overwhelmingly the case. They feel overwhelmed by events or experiences and no longer in control. Researchers are finding more and more that clients are responding to what are called *biologically* prepared stimuli—apparent social and physical dangers that are triggering evolved and powerful survival mechanisms such as fight, flight, freeze and faint, and subordination and defeat states (Gilbert, 1989).

5. Assess B

The therapist's task now is to assess the related images, inferences, evaluations and dysfunctional assumptions (see Chapter 1). Before doing this the therapist wishes the client to understand that the meaning events have for him (the Bs) is central to understanding his problem; gaining a common perspective on this point is essential to the process of change. First, she needs to clarify with the client that the A-C analysis is lacking in that the event alone (A) does not account for the client's reactions (C). This is because he might in principle have responded differently—the therapist argues that what is lacking is an understanding of the personal meaning the event had for the client.

Thus, the therapist assumes the client has an AC theory about his problem, and the therapist seeks to inculcate an ABC theory—that we are disturbed not by things in themselves but by our interpretations of them. There are a number of quick ways of helping the client to gain this insight. One of the most straightforward is to give a simple A—suppose they hear a tap at the window at home at night—and vary the emotional response at C—get them to imagine they felt anxious, then angry, then pleased, and to report their thoughts at B in each case that led to the change in C.

The therapist then turns to the client's A-C problem and says that the next task will be to explore the client's own beliefs at B. The major way to uncover the client's specific Bs is to use theoretical knowledge about the main B-C connections (see Chapter 1) to guide a process of thought chaining. Chaining almost always begins with an inference. To get started the therapist focuses the client on the specific A-C episode, and asks him something like 'What was going through your mind when you were feeling . . .'. Several inferences may be connected in a chain. Let us imagine a client who feels depressed (C) when his girlfriend does not phone as promised (A), and infers it means she has gone out with another man (first inferred B), which means she doesn't like the client (second inferred B) which means no woman will ever like him (third inferred B). It is rare for the client to be aware that his thinking takes the form of an inference—even less an inference chain—but the inference is there, unverbalised, and the therapist can draw it out and make it explicit in the way described.

We have argued that how people respond emotionally at C reflects a combination of inference and evaluation, and nestling at the bottom of a chain of inferences is one or more evaluations. Usually it is possible to scent the evaluations that are implicit in an inference statement. Evaluations are attributed *by* individuals *about* individuals or circumstances. An individual may evaluate a part or a whole—for example, a single behaviour ('that was a bad action'), a person's trait or role ('he is a bad teacher') or the whole of a person ('he's a totally bad character').

Only certain kinds of evaluations are associated with extreme distress. Of paramount importance, we believe, are negative person evaluations—interpersonal global and stable judgements of a person's total worth. Since global negative person evaluations are such a key component of the assessment process we have developed the Evaluative Beliefs Scale specifically for this purpose (Appendix 1).

A client who is very emotionally disturbed at C is probably harbouring a global negative evaluation, either for self or other, or life circumstances. When the emotion is anger the therapist is looking for a negative self-other person evaluation. So, if our imaginary client who fears he has been jilted feels strong anger with his partner, he will be making some form of negative judgement about her as a person. When the emotion is either anxiety or depression a thought chain often uncovers first an inferred other self-negative person evaluation, and leads ultimately to a self-self one. To return to our example, if the man feels depression he may believe his girlfriend, who is now with someone else, views him as totally inadequate and he may agree with this judgement, thereby making it self-self. In point of fact, other-self evaluations may be deduced and hence inferences (e.g. you ignore me and from this I *infer* you see me as totally worthless or require no inference (e.g. you tell me this explicitly).

Virtually all negative person evaluations arise because an individual has judged that he or another has fallen short of some interpersonal rule, or dysfunctional assumption, which determines his sense of self-worth (see Chapter 1). For example, a client might behave according to an implicit rule, 'It would be terrible if I made another mistake—it would make me completely worthless. It *must* never happen.' Such demands are often expressed spontaneously in automatic thoughts ('I mustn't get it wrong . . .') or emerge during or at the end of an inference chain assessment.

6. Formulation: (a) Connect Bs to Cs (b) Connect the Current ABC to Early Psychological Development

We see a full cognitive formulation as an integration of a current ABC analysis and a historical or developmental assessment.

In the process of assessing the As, Bs and Cs, the therapist has also produced a cognitive formulation of the current problem. This formulation shows specifically what cognitions at B are generating emotional and behavioural disturbance at C, given A. Or in ordinary language, it connects a person's feelings and behaviour in a situation to the personal meaning the event has for him. The therapist conveys this insight by showing how the event alone does not necessarily lead to the feelings and behaviour the client experienced; he at another time in his life, or another person, may have responded differently. However, a global, stable negative self-evaluation always implies depressed feelings.

The therapist and client will also want to be thinking about a longitudinal or developmental formulation, in order to consider why the latter should have his particular vulnerability. Vulnerability is defined as negative personal evaluation, and associated distress. This formulation concerns the origins of the client's psychological vulnerability (usually in early childhood), how the client evolved an interpersonal style which protected him against re-experiencing negative self-evaluation and distress, and times when episodes of distress have occurred (often triggered by life events). In particular, she will have in mind the two central threats to self discussed in Chapter 1, namely a lack of attachment or a lack of autonomy. It bears stating that a therapist may constantly update her hunches about the developmental formulation as more information emerges.

7. Set the Goal and Establish the Options

The therapist asks the client to re-state the problem in terms of an ABC formulation, and to compare this with his original A-C statement of the problem. Next, the therapist asks the client to state the first goal of therapy ('What would you like to be different/to change?'). Despite the work on Bs, the client may still see the goal as changing the A—the situation or event. Here we draw on the advice of Dr Al Raitt, REBT therapist and trainer, who has a useful method for running through a client's therapeutic options. In essence you advise your client that there are only four ways in which anyone can respond to problematic situations:

1. They can try to avoid or escape from them.
2. They can do nothing, i.e., resolve to 'put up with them'.
3. They can try to change them in some way, e.g. persuade their employer not to dismiss them.

The fact that the client is in therapy suggests that all these responses have failed. The therapist is now in a stronger position to offer the fourth option:

4. They can reduce their incapacitating emotional and behavioural disturbance by working to change their core beliefs.

It can also be pointed out that success at changing B will optimise success at changing A—this is, if the situation is changeable anyway—since they will be able to more effectively think out practical steps to solve the problem.

8. Challenge Beliefs

If the client agrees with this option then he and the therapist may begin the process of cognitive intervention, challenging beliefs through a mixture of disputing and empirical testing. This requires some particular skills of interviewing style which seek to give as little direct advice to the client as possible but instead seek to elicit suggestions and solutions from the client, and in this way build on the client's own capacity to problemsolve. This procedure, known as the Socratic method, is based around the use of open and closed questions, and is an invaluable addition to basic counselling skills. A useful account is given in Beck et al. (1979).

Through the developmental formulation the therapist and client discover an alternative to the client's core belief—for example, replacing 'I am totally unlovable' with 'I have never felt loved by significant people'. These two possibilities are then compared through discussion of the evidence and direct testing. It is important to use some methods which stir the client's emotions.

Disputing and testing inferences   Disputing inferences is based on the 'scientific' method, in which hypotheses are made and then supported or disconfirmed by looking at the evidence. In particular the therapist helps the client to become more aware of the specific cognitive distortions (see Chapter 1) which colour his automatic inferential thinking, and to systematically seek to reduce their influence. The classic challenge to an inference is: 'where's the evidence?'

Testing inferences involves what rational emotive behaviour therapy calls risk taking—that is, clients gradually work towards attempting the feared task in order to test their inferences that they will certainly fail, be rejected, etc. Of course, this might happen. Inferences may or may not be true and this needs to be reflected in the choice of what test to use and when. A powerful example of this procedure is Clarke's cognitive therapy for panic disorder (Clarke, 1986). Here the client's inference is that symptoms such as racing pulse and pains across the chest are certain indicators of an imminent heart attack. The alternative belief is that the symptoms are harmless side effects of overbreathing. After rating his conviction in each belief, the client agrees to an empirical test. In this test it is easy to show that the symptoms only occur when the client over-breathes, and stop immediately he stops overbreathing. The client then re-rates his conviction level, and commits himself to giving up his un-founded belief.

This method of disputing and testing can be used on a host of different kinds of inferences—for example all those listed in step 7 above. Of spe-cial importance are inferred other-self evaluations. Sometimes clients in-fer global negative evaluations from others (e.g. 'people see me as totally and forever bad') and they then use these assertions as evidence that they are indeed worthless, bad, etc. The challenge centres on the nature of a second, concealed inference that if the other believes something to be the case, this must be right. So for example, in answer to the question 'how is their opinion you're no good evidence that you're *actually* no good?' the client might say 'if that's what they believe, then it must be true'. Now the therapist switches to challenging this underlying inference. One way is to suggest an absurd other to self inference, e.g. 'suppose I said you were a unicorn—would you be one?'. At this stage the client takes the point intellectually. The therapist might then proceed to say 'suppose I said you were a totally bad person, how would you feel?'. This usually makes the point emotionally. Only when other's behaviour gives a hint (or stronger) that they reject us in ways we fear to be accurate are we persuaded they are right. In other words, we agree with them because we already believe it to be true. Indeed, the therapist hopes to show more than this, namely that because we believe we are bad, we attribute this evaluation to other people even where it does not belong.

Disputing and testing evaluations. Within rational emotive therapy there are many types of evaluations, only some of which produce severe dis-tress and require challenging. We shall illustrate the process in relation to negative personal evaluations, the type we find to be most useful, though the methods are applicable to others as well. There are three major steps when challenging person evaluations and each uses a range of disputing and testing and experiential work.

First, the therapist clarifies that the person rating is indeed global and stable and works to question and break this. The purpose is to encourage the client to rate behaviour only and to avoid global judgements about people, as if they were either all this or all that. The principle for this type of challenge is: rate the behaviour, not the self, i.e. behaving badly (if you did) doesn't mean *I'm* bad. Part of this process involves looking at evi-dence, and part looking at insight methods to convey first, the impossibility of anyone being totally and forever anything, and second, the origins of the painful person evaluations.

One important piece of evidence for a self-self evaluation is often that the client believes other people evaluate him in an identical way. We have discussed how to challenge this above. Another type of invalid evidence the client might offer is the way he feels. For example he may say the evidence he is 'no good' is that he feels depressed about himself—that surely proves he's no good, because if he was any good, he wouldn't feel depressed. This is an example of what Burns (1992) calls 'emotional reasoning'. Emotions can't be used as evidence for anything other than the self-evident truth that the person is *having* the emotional experience. The client can also be reminded that the emotion is the consequence, not the cause of his belief.

The second important aspect of challenging evaluations is for the therapist to draw out the implicit rule, or dysfunctional assumption, which drives the self-evaluative process (see Chapter 1); for example, beliefs of the type 'My worth is contingent upon my having success, or respect, or love . . .'. The therapist and client work collaboratively to expose such assumptions, to explore their effect on his interpersonal relationships, to trace their origins, and to assess if it fits what the client has learned about himself, others and the world.

Finally, the client and therapist plan a specific kind of test, developed in Ellis' REBT, called shame-attacking. Shame is one of the prime emotional consequences of global self-evaluations of stupidity, inadequacy, uselessness, worthlessness and so on. This exercise is different from risk taking in that the client is surprisingly *not* asked to do something to show he is capable of it, such as succeed at something, or win someone's approval. The idea is that the client wilfully plans to fail, or not gain respect, or make a fool of himself in order to recognise emotionally and intellectually that he can survive these ego threats and need not live in fear of them. The point of the exercise is to challenge the general dysfunctional assumptions that underlie global person evaluations—that people have worth only if they are successful, or loved, or respected, etc. Instead it affirms the opposite belief that a person is worthwhile despite doing things wrong simply because humans are fallible. Shame-attacking needs very careful planning and timing, but offers the client a greater potential emotional security than risk taking because it confronts the fear most directly.

Planning 'homework' can be a useful addition to therapy time. Any of the processes so far described may be set as a collaboratively agreed task for the client to attempt. The steps for homework are first to have clearly in mind the client's original (dysfunctional) belief and a competing alternative (functional) belief, second to decide on a homework assignment which will truly test the beliefs but is a manageable step for the client to take, and thirdly to set the homework for the following week or specified time.

We use homework with many clients, but some prefer not to work in this way, which is fine. However, beliefs rarely change as a result of intellectual challenging, but only through engaging emotions and behaving in new ways that produce evidence that confirms new beliefs. Indeed, clients are resistant to carrying out homework not least because it creates anxiety. The therapist wishes the client to experience this essential work in sessions, or outside, or ideally both.

THE PROBLEM OF ENGAGEMENT

The reader may raise an important question about using cognitive psychotherapy in the way we have described above. Surely it is not appropriate to use 'ordinary' cognitive psychotherapy—developed for and practised with a wide range of 'ordinary' problems, such as anxiety disorders, depression or anger problems—with clients who are so different, who have such extreme experiences as hallucinations, delusions and paranoia? This assumption undoubtedly has contributed to the delay we have lamented in introducing this form of therapy to psychosis sufferers. But as we argue in Chapter 1, there is no evidence for such an assumption, psychosis sufferers are not discontinuous from sufferers of any other mental health problems. They experience the same emotional and behavioural problems as other people and we suggest for this very reason ordinary cognitive therapy is indeed relevant and effective for this client group.

As we stated earlier however, there is one significant obstacle to overcome, namely, the problem that certain client groups are far more difficult to engage in therapy than others. This, too, is not peculiar to people with psychotic symptoms, but it certainly pertains to them. In the remainder of this chapter we consider this obstacle. In what follows we do not cover the basic counselling strategies for engaging clients and working with transference issues, but look at what are several additional threats to engagement common in our client group. Readers interested in the more fundamental issues are referred to Storr (1979) or Egan (1982).

In our clinical practice we find engaging to be perhaps the biggest challenge facing a therapist. It is noticeable that many individuals either never attend or do so for a few sessions and then stop. Once individuals get past the opening stages of cognitive therapy they usually see therapy through. This pattern of high and early drop out is found in those few research trials so far carried out on cognitive approaches to psychotic problems (e.g. Tarrier et al., 1993).

In Table 4 we list the seven major threats to engagement we have encountered in our therapeutic work. We see these threats as general in that they cut across work with delusions, voices and paranoia: threats or problems specific to a symptom (e.g. voices) appear in the appropriate chapter. In the next section we look at each of these threats in turn, first describing how engagement is threatened and subsequently offering some thoughts about ways to minimise the likelihood of drop out.

Table 4   Major threats to engagement

Threat	Common example
Failure in empathy	Therapist unable to empathise with unusual experience
Therapist beliefs	Delusions always resist therapy
Client beliefs	Therapist will be punitive and controlling
Relationship too threatening	Client has poor experience of mature interpersonal relationships
Client sees no potential benefit	Client expects therapist to want merely to stop the voices
Framing delusions as beliefs, not facts	Client suspects he is disbelieved
Developing a rationale for questioning delusions	Client anxious

A Failure of Therapist Empathy

Most of us have felt depressed, anxious and angry and our experience of emotional disturbance of this kind helps us to understand these feelings in our clients. But we cannot always make this assumption with psychotic symptoms. Far fewer therapists will have heard voices or held bizarre delusional ideas, and this may threaten comprehension of and empathy with the client.

Indeed, Karl Jaspers the 'father of phenomenology', went so far as to suggest that a failure of empathy and intuitive understanding of the person with a psychosis is diagnostic—he used the term 'abyss' to characterise this discontinuity of understanding between experience that was normal (and neurotic) on the one hand and psychotic on the other (Jaspers, 1962). In the mind of many professionals and perhaps clients too will be firmly entrenched the notion of discontinuity—that is, one may accept and try to empathise with a client's distress yet one may not feel one understands it.

It seems reasonable to expect this difficulty to be more pronounced with certain experiences above others. Delusional experiences which centre on an unusual perceptual experience are a likely case in point. An experience of passivity, for example, is something that may be more difficult to intuitively understand than believing that one is being persecuted, the latter being an exaggeration of ordinary behaviour.

One of the central tasks in the opening phase of therapy is bridging as far as possible the 'discontinuity gap' that Jaspers refers to. We find the cognitive ABC approach very useful in this respect because it clarifies which parts of an individual's experience the therapist is and is not able to understand intuitively. It may be that many therapists are unable to understand what it is actually like to have an experience of passivity (an Activating event) in the same way that they may understand what it is like to fail at something important. Certainly we find ourselves acknowledging to some of our clients that certain of their experiences are beyond our experience. But empathy does not require that we have exprienced all that our clients have experienced, but only that we recognise and understand how they feel and think and behave within this context. What seems to us very understandable are the ways our clients who experience unusual perceptions made sense of them (the Beliefs and personal meanings) and the associated feelings and behaviour (the Consequences).

This then is the bridge in cognitive therapy for psychotic symptoms; to acknowledge, if it applies, that an aspect of the client's experience may be beyond a therapist's empathy, but the client's human response to it is not and it is this response which is a foundation for empathy.

Therapist's Beliefs about Clients

In one sense a failure to empathise may relate to a second threat to engagement, namely a therapist's beliefs about psychosis and the likely impact of psychological therapy on it. If a therapist has the view that psychotic behaviour is discontinuous and beyond her comprehension and empathy then this is likely to be reflected in her feelings and behaviour towards the client and, in sessions, her expectation of change.

There are many other beliefs therapists may hold about clients which jeopardise therapy—we have given merely one to illustrate the point. We believe this danger is best offset in supervision, an important function of which is to draw out these beliefs, to analyse them, and to limit their impact within sessions.

Client's Blocking Beliefs

Clients too will enter therapy with beliefs which make them less likely to engage in therapy. Most clients have general fears about therapists using power in a punitive or controlling way; for example, clients often fear that if they discuss the extent of their involvement with delusions or voices, this will lead to either an increase in medication or a hospital bed, or both. These concerns are not simply 'bizarre' or 'paranoid'. Nor are they all examples of transference—that is, meanings and feelings which are trans-ferred from formative interpersonal relationships—in the majority of cases they are expectations learned from bitter experience of health care. For example, it is well documented that clients often experience treatment as disempowering (e.g. McGorry et al. 1990). The client may come with expectations that he will engage in a therapy that is further disempower-ing in which he is to play the role of a passive patient.

Again, in the client's mind first and foremost will be the expectation that the therapist is likely to disregard his beliefs, perspective and experience and (although mental health professionals rarely say this outright) view the client's beliefs exclusively within the framework of 'madness'. An-other common belief is that therapists will be too ignorant of the client's experience to be able to be of benefit. The fear of a therapist as adversary is common but should not be a problem if a therapist adheres to a gentle collaborative therapeutic style.

So, a therapist has in mind that a client will almost certainly hold a number of beliefs which jeopardise therapy, and she targets much of her early behaviour in therapy at reassuring the client, but she does this gradually and implicitly. The process by which these 'blocking' beliefs are weakened is critical. Although we have in mind the ABC model, we do not set out to examine and dispute and test blocking beliefs explicitly. Rather we have found it more helpful to slowly and often implicitly offer a particular view of how we as cognitive therapists work, how we view people, and how we view the process of therapy. It is worth providing the client an opportunity to vent frustration and anger with services.

It is important for therapists to discuss with clients their position on possible increases or decreases in medication and hospitalisation, and the kinds of circumstances where these options might need to be raised and discussed. This makes clear that these measures might be used—indeed, there are circumstances where neither therapist nor client is able to prevent this—but only as ways of protecting clients.

Above all, the relationship should be safe and collaborative so that the client is able to take part in an ABC assessment of voices without fear of 'losing face'. As ever, the therapist pushes the idea that she is committed to reducing the client's distress and disturbance, thereby improving his quality of life.

Engaging in a Therapeutic Relationship

Many of our clients have a history of impoverished interpersonal relationships and they can experience one-to-one interaction as stressful and be hyper-vigilant to what they perceive as threatening or rejecting behaviour by a therapist. This is not to imply that individuals with delusions and voices are exclusively impoverished in this way, or that the impoverishment reflects an inborn difficulty on their part to relate to others. We are simply acknowledging that this is a common problem among our clients, and highlighting that it makes interpersonal contact especially difficult for them.

Where this problem is particularly acute, it can be useful to sacrifice some of the basic boundaries and principles of psychotherapy. To begin with informal almost casual initial contact may be tolerated better by vulnerable clients. Sessions may usefully be shorter and more frequent. In addition, it is often most productive to structure the sessions and to avoid lengthy silence. Also, as we discuss later, we do not press the client to disclose delusional ideas.

Viewing Delusions as Beliefs, not Facts

This and the next engagement problem occur early in the actual process of cognitive therapy. The first problem to be encountered is the necessary move of conceptualising a delusion as a belief (B) and not a fact (an Activating event). This move is an essential part of cognitive therapy for all emotional problems, and in our experience is tricky at the best of times. With depression, for example, clients often struggle to appreciate that their sense of worthlessness, which is so concrete to them, is actually a belief they hold and is different from knowledge of events and facts. With delusions there is the added complication that the therapist might be perceived as being just another person who disbelieves the client.

There are two central points to bear in mind when seeking to reconceptualise delusions as beliefs, not facts—why it is being done and how it is done.

The purpose of clarifying that delusions are beliefs, not facts, is to empower the client and offer him a way of easing his distress. If the client really is being persecuted by a powerful organisation, or has a radio transmitter and receiver in his head, or has AIDS, neither the therapist nor he can actually change this. Yet this is what he wants, and he is therefore frustrated and helpless as well as other distress. However, if the client believes these are true, but does not know it, then he gains the freedom to examine his beliefs and perhaps change his distressing feelings and behaviour and experience himself. In this sense it is in his best interest for the delusion to be false.

How this process takes place is critical. The process of Socratic questioning is not one of persuading a client that he is wrong and that you, the therapist, are right. This mistake is made all too often. Rather in Socratic dialogue the therapist helps the client to draw on his own doubt and experience in order to realise that there are other ways in which he is able to make sense of his experience. So, when the therapist pursues the conceptual step of clarifying that a delusion is only a belief, she has in mind drawing on the client's own doubt, past or present, the client's own contradictory experience and behaviour, and on the client's own concerns about the possibility that the delusion is wrong. It is our experience that very many clients have double awareness of delusions—on the one hand, they believe them firmly and are distressed and disturbed by them, yet on the other hand they behave in ways which appear to fly in the face of the delusion, and they believe that working with a therapist might ease the problem.

Finally, the therapist really must accept that it is okay if the client does not alter his belief. The process is collaborative empiricism, not indoctrination.

Developing a Rationale for Questioning the Delusion

The second engagement problem in the process of cognitive therapy which most easily trips up therapists, and loses clients, is ensuring that both have a common rationale for questioning the delusion. Clients are usually well used to being told by family and carers that their beliefs are wrong, that they are deluded. It is easy for a therapist to prepare an intervention well and embark on it before the client really is clear of the purpose and possible benefit of this. It is revealing to turn the engagement question on its head and to consider why a client should ever wish to engage in cognitive therapy. With emotional problems clients identify their problems as depression, anger, anxiety, guilt, etc., and it is from this they wish to be free. In this sense at least they have a motivation to engage in therapy and to work at changing how they feel. However, with delusions and voices this is not so; clients predominantly present problems which they believe are actual events (persecution, voices, passivity). This means that they have no clear objective and therefore have no particular motivation to engage.

Although we separate this threat to engagement and the previous one, the challenge in cognitive therapy is to guide the client smoothly through both. The key reason for a client to reconsider delusional beliefs is that it will help him feel less distress and it will free him to behave differently and to pursue the things he wants more directly.

What the therapist does gradually through the unfolding cognitive ABC assessment is clarify with the client that he is experiencing emotional and behavioural problems, and that these are tied to his beliefs (delusional and evaluative). The therapist needs then to explore with the client how the delusion affects his life now, both the advantages and disadvantages, and how his life would be different (i.e. better and worse) if the delusion were false. In this way, the therapist slowly encourages the client to view the delusion not as an important discovery which serves to help him (e.g. the belief that people are watching him and trying to harm him) but as a belief which leads him to experience distress (e.g. fear, anxiety) and behave in ways he would rather not (e.g. avoid things he would otherwise like to do).

Again, the process here is critical. Whereas with anxiety or depression the therapist may proceed relatively quickly through this type of provisional ABC assessment, we tend not to do this with people who are deluded. Rather, the therapist has in mind a process of slowly moving a client through the conceptual steps in cognitive therapy thereby creating safety as well as insight and motivation. This process should seem seamless from a client's perspective, even if a therapist prefers, as we do, to divide the process into steps.

SUMMARY

In this chapter we have described in eight conceptual steps the way we practise cognitive therapy. This theoretical framework for progress in therapy enables a therapist to use techniques flexibly, creatively and collaboratively with clients. This eight-step framework is one we use with all of our clients. On the whole this framework has required little adaptation when clients are deluded, hearing voices or paranoid. Those specific innovations appear in the relevant chapters in this book. The one major adaptation from work with clients with emotional disorders has been the need to ease individuals very gradually into therapy. It is because this issue is so important that we have considered it here.

Chapter 3

DELUSIONS: ASSESSMENT AND FORMULATION

ABC ASSESSMENT OF DELUSIONS

There is general disagreement over the purpose of assessment—some see the function as solely paving the way for intervention, without a need for any surplus exploration of childhood and development, whereas others view a full historical exploration as essential (Segal & Blatt, 1993). Even within the two major schools of cognitive therapy there is disagreement over the centrality of assessing childhood, with Beck giving this a far higher importance than Ellis. When assessing delusions we spend usually at least six sessions on assessment and this covers current functioning and taking a developmental history, because we find that both are useful to subsequent cognitive therapy. Sometimes this process takes much longer; some individuals take many sessions of this before revealing any delusional thoughts. Thus we rarely begin intervention (i.e. disputing and testing of beliefs) before session seven at the earliest.

We see a number of advantages to delaying intervention. First, when working with delusions, many of which are very complex phenomena, if a challenge is begun too early at a point when the therapist does not appreciate the complexity and range of delusional and evaluative thinking, it is unlikely to appear compelling to the client. Second, it allows the relationship and trust to grow—while we do not believe a sound therapeutic relationship is sufficient to produce change, we think it necessary. Third, it compels the therapist to confront any wishes to rush in and help, or 'rescue', the client. The most commonly advanced disadvantage is that it is unethical to hold back an intervention when a client is in distress; however, we believe the three points listed adequately meet this criticism.

Cognitive assessment and cognitive therapy is a form of psychotherapy and it must always adhere to good therapeutic practice and principles. In the following chapters we hope we have stressed this and given sufficient space to those aspects of therapy which may be common to other therapies or other presenting problems.

How to Begin

Very often we find that for the first one or two sessions we hardly steer the client at all. Rather we listen to his story and begin to get a feel for areas of discomfort; we reflect back what seem important feelings and experiences, and we point out when we are lost and ask for clarification.

In our experience it is as well *not* to begin by discussing the delusional experience, unless of course this is what the client wishes. Rather, the therapist might explore two areas; first, how the person felt about coming to the session (and discussing any previous absenteeism) and related thoughts and impulses; and, second, how the client came to be referred.

Exploring how the individual felt leading up to the session follows the standard ABC structure: in our experience the most common reaction is anxiety and a wish not to attend and the associated meaning may give an early clue to the client's areas of vulnerability—perhaps being exposed as bad, or being rejected by the therapist. In the process the therapist is also conveying the general cognitive ABC approach, and showing concern about the client's distress. Many clients will not have encountered before this simple interest in their concerns about therapy and it may help the client to settle by removing any blocking fears and easing anxiety.

If the individual does not spontaneously raise concerns about the therapist it may also be helpful to ask about this directly. In our experience most clients have some anxiety about meeting health professionals. Raising this issue gives the therapist an opportunity early on to clarify what she is not (e.g. prescriber of medication, someone to help with housing and money problems) as well as what she is. In particular, we emphasise again and again that our interest is in listening to what is distressing and disturbing the client and in helping him to be less distressed and disturbed. This places us firmly on the side of the client and also sets an agenda for therapy.

A second theme which needs to be examined at the outset is how the client came to be referred. This issue is usefully considered in all therapy, but especially with so-called 'psychotic' symptoms, where the individuals themselves may not see a problem. Indeed it is quite common for individuals to be referred by a family member or another professional without their knowledge, or consent.

If the client concurred with the decision to refer, then the therapist may begin to explore what it is that troubles the client. If not, and the client says he does not have a problem and does not need therapy, this needs to be taken seriously. Within the cognitive perspective this may be taken as meaning that at this point in time he is free of significant emotional distress or behavioural disturbance. However, this may not be what the client intended to communicate. For example, clients who say they do not have a problem are often implying that they do not wish to be told yet again that they are deluded and their beliefs are wrong, or schizophrenic and in need of medication. That is, they are rejecting an approach that had hitherto been offered.

The cognitive therapist has to convey that her interest is in the client's emotional and behavioural problems. In particular she wishes to explore if in these terms the client has problems he would like to change. The therapist and client then search for such problems over an agreed number of assessment sessions. This process imparts one of the major tenets of the cognitive model, namely that problems are located at point C in the ABC heuristic.

This definition of problems in terms of distress and disturbance is, we believe, one of the greatest strengths of the cognitive model, one that encourages a therapeutic alliance and avoids much conflict. What most clients will have been told by other professionals is that they do have a problem— it is their symptoms. Those who experience primary experiences, such as voices, are usually told that this experience is their problem, or at least a sign of the problem. In other words, within the ABC framework most clients are told that their problem is an A (e.g. voice) or B (e.g. delusion); we think this approach encounters resistance which might be avoided by attempting to establish a shared view of the problem in terms of Cs.

And what if even after prolonged assessment and exploration a client does not present significant distress or disturbance? Our opinion may be summed up as 'no Cs, no cognitive therapy'. Cognitive therapy is a collaborative process and presumes a common focus for change— emotion and behaviour—and if this is not present then progress within this model is impossible. The therapist of course has other therapeutic options, perhaps a behavioural intervention.

Problem Clarification: the ABC Approach

The formal aim of a cognitive assessment of current delusional experience is to carry out an ABC assessment—that is, to identify the antecedents, the affective and behavioural consequences, and the delusional and evaluative beliefs. When possible we follow the standard strategy of first getting either an A or C, then getting the other. It is important that the therapist move backwards and forwards between the As and Cs refining each many times. Exploration of the Bs comes last, although it may sometimes be easier or tactical to begin with the B, perhaps because this is where the client starts.

Almost invariably we seek to gain a firm grasp of the delusional (usually inferential) thinking before attempting to identify the evaluative beliefs, or themes, implicit in the delusion. Also, because of our dissatisfaction with current definitions of the words schizophrenia and delusion, in speaking to the individuals we do not use these labels to describe their experience. Nor do we tell clients that their beliefs are a sign of illness. Although our position is taken on theoretical grounds, it is possible that it may also have the effect of reducing psychological reactance (Brehm, 1962), and therefore may be justifiable on therapeutic grounds too.

The following interchange illustrates the process of getting started, and looks at an initial ABC exploration of a delusion (later in this chapter we shall look at how to search for an evaluative theme). The man in question, Peter, believed that he was HIV positive; the belief persisted in spite of considerable counter-evidence, including two clear HIV tests. During the assessment Peter referred to people treating him badly as a consequence of his having HIV and although it does not come out in the extract below, there was in fact a strong paranoid delusion. (Note that in all exchanges in this book T stands for therapist and C for clients.)

T: Peter, I have received a referral letter from your GP telling me a little about you and your problem. I think it would be helpful if you were to tell me in your words what it is that is troubling you.

C: I'm HIV positive.

[At this point the therapist did not know if this was true (and therefore an A) or an inference (B) which may or may not be true.]

T: You are HIV positive. That's very upsetting to discover. How long ago did you find out?

C: Well I've known for about 3 years and its ruining my life. People don't want to know me, even my family. I feel lonely, I'm fed up. I can't believe the way I've been treated.

[Peter has listed a number of Cs (lonely, fed up) and As or Bs (people don't want to know me, it's ruining my life) and has hinted at possible anger on his part (I can't believe the way I've been treated). The therapist decides to clarify if the statement 'I am HIV' is an inference or fact.]

T: It's clear that you are very upset and lonely, and that others close to you have disappointed you. Perhaps we could talk about how the problem has affected you and others in a little while, but first it would help me to find out when it was that you were told that you were HIV.

C: No-one told me, I found out. I started noticing physical things which were different. I get a tingling, burning in my arms. I feel weak, pale.

[It sounds as if the client has inferred that he is HIV. The therapist thinks it might be difficult to pursue this without challenging Peter, so decides to get the Cs and maybe come back to As.]

T: So you have spotted physical changes, you feel weak, pale and you have a burning in your arms. How did you feel when you spotted these changes?

C: To begin with I hardly noticed what was happening. I didn't know what was happening. But then I thought I must have HIV and things seemed to make sense, it seemed to make sense of a lot of things. The way I felt, the way people didn't want nothing to do with me.

T: Sounds as if once you thought you had HIV you had a sense of someone having switched on a light, you could suddenly see things clearly. I wonder how you felt, though.

C: I was frightened. Very lonely. I was going to die.

T: You thought you were going to die and felt very frightened and lonely. Did you want to do anything?

C: I wanted to be with my family.

T: So, Peter, you spotted bodily changes which at first were puzzling but not distressing. Some while later the idea occurred to you that these bodily changes might be the result of HIV and this thought seemed to make a lot of sense, but was also very frightening and you felt acutely lonely. And it sounds as if you feel angry with others for treating you badly. Is that correct? (Peter agrees.)

In this dialogue the therapist first frames Peter's experience in terms of As, Bs, and Cs, and locates the problem in the Cs. The therapist's concluding statement summarises the ABC assessment and enquires about the client's reaction to it. From this point there are many possible leads to pursue. For example, although it is clear that Peter's own initial 'diagnosis' was an inference, the therapist has yet to establish if a medical diagnosis of HIV has since been made. Also, Peter describes how others have treated him badly and he attributes this to his having HIV—either of these points might be explored, or Peter's reaction to this mistreatment.

Indeed, delusions are frequently very far reaching in their implications and meaning, and we commonly find that many different ABC analyses are required in order to sample the range of emotions and meanings incorporated in a delusional belief system. In Peter's case further assessment revealed clear paranoid and depressed beliefs.

It is often helpful to complete an ABC assessment form with a client, and perhaps to subsequently ask a client to keep an ABC diary of emotionally distressing events occurring in between sessions. One of the merits of this process is that it explicitly separates the antecedent experience and the delusional interpretation, thus paving the way for cognitive challenge. What the diary format makes apparent is that while the antecedent happened and is a statement of fact, the delusion is an interpretation of it, an inference which is either true or false. Hitherto the client has seen both the A and B as indubitable. This separation frees the therapist and client during cognitive therapy to explore other, hopefully more compelling interpretations (see Chapter 4).

Having constructed an initial ABC analysis the therapist may then proceed to develop the cognitive assessment of delusions by further exploration and measurement of the As, Bs and Cs.

Assessing Activating Events

Assessing activating events is an important and perhaps underrated aspect of the cognitive assessment, and one which has significant implications for treatment. It may be achieved simply through careful discussion, or using ABC diaries, or by more formal measurement methods.

In general, when assessing As it can be beneficial for the therapist to have in mind the distinction made in Chapter 1 between problems associated with attachment issues and those associated with issues of personal control and worth. Often the type of event which triggers delusional thinking, and associated distress and disturbance, provides a clue to the client's enduring psychological vulnerability. For example, one client's first episode of illness began soon after the death of his father and the end of his marriage—two instances of traumatic interpersonal loss. This theme was played out in his delusion, which related to his having the power to change history and prevent loss through accidental death and war; the delusion hinted at the client's sense of responsibility and guilt over his own losses, and reversed his sense of powerlessness. However, there is no one-to-one relationship between trigger events and enduring vulnerability (see Blatt & Zuroff, 1992), nor would one be expected given that in the cognitive approach it is how events are *interpreted* that is vital.

The first important rule with assessing As, and one commonly broken, is to get the client to focus on a *specific* event associated with emotional distress. When so doing, the therapist needs additionally to bear in mind that triggers may be internal as well as external. In panic disorder, for example, extreme panic and a wish to flee may be triggered by slight changes in bodily state (Clarke, 1986).

Second, it is important to identify settings in which the client does not experience delusional thinking, as well as those in which he does. This knowledge exposes opportunities for intervention. The therapist might, for instance, wish to reduce delusional thinking early on in therapy in order to engender a sense of optimism. Alternatively she may wish to get clients to practise first increasing and then decreasing the frequency of delusional ideas and associated affect, in order to demonstrate that the client has control over them: this method has been used successfully in the treatment of obsessive ruminations (Salkovskis, 1989) as well as in our own work with voices (see Chapter 6).

There is yet another reason to focus on As. Delusions are widely held to be more or less reasonable attempts to make sense of compelling and often distressing events (Maher, 1988). Often these are so-called primary experiences, for example voices, experiences of reference and control. Clients often see these experiences as *evidence* for their delusions. For example, they may say 'I know I am being watched because red cars keep going by my window'; or 'I know when people are reading my mind because they scratch their noses in a certain revealing way'; or 'I know people are trying to kill me because I hear them threaten me'. Part of cognitive therapy for delusions involves working systematically through items of evidence and seeking non-delusional but plausible interpretations of them.

Assessing Affect and Behaviour

The intention in this section is not to recommend one measure ahead of a second, nor to review the numerous general and specific measures of affect and behaviour, but rather to stress that a measure of each is required if the clinician wants to know about process and outcome in cognitive therapy.

Emotion. Cognitive therapy is often misrepresented as being primarily designed to change the way people think, and as having little to say about emotion. In fact this is nonsense; the individual's problem is defined in terms of emotional distress and disturbed behaviour, and the object of cognitive therapy is to change this—the method is to weaken associated beliefs. This means that the measurement of affect and behaviour is vital.

In more than one respect it is fortunate that there is only a discrete number of extreme and negative emotions. As well as limiting our opportunity for distress, it also makes the task of measuring emotional distress more straightforward, such that there are a number of well-established standardised measures of each. The choice of which emotion(s) to assess will be guided by the ABC assessment, which will have indicated which distressing feelings are associated with the delusional thoughts—the choice of which measure(s) to use will be influenced by the usual factors (client's capacity for form-filling, if a self-rating or interviewer rating is preferred, etc.). In addition, it can be worth using an individualised measure of emotional distress; the one commonly used to measure different aspects of delusional experience is a personal questionnaire format (Garety, 1985). In relation to measuring affect the client chooses the exact word he wants in order to capture how he feels, and then uses this label to monitor affective state. However, a word of caution is in order; sometimes clients may offer a label such as 'concern' and 'disappointment', which within the cognitive model is not an extreme and 'target' emotion; in such circumstances it may be worth drawing out what the client probably experiences is something more severe.

Behaviour. Measuring behaviour associated with delusions is much more difficult than measuring affect. This is because it can be hard to identify one or more reliable and frequent behavioural correlates, and also even where one exists, it is often unclear how to interpret an observed increase or decrease.

There may be times when a behavioural measure is impossible. One man, Larry, believed that in a previous incarnation he had been Leonardo da Vinci; however, he neither painted or designed rockets, nor talked about his presumed identity. The belief interfered with his life only to the extent that he thought about it a lot, and frequently misinterpreted what others said.

Very often the problem is that the behaviour is only loosely associated with the delusions—that is, the therapist is prone to record false positives and negatives. For example, it is common for staff on wards to observe an in-patient to discern which aggressive and violent behaviour is motivated by delusions or voices. The usual error in such exercises is for all such subsequent behaviour to then be attributed willy nilly to 'psychosis'.

However, a more careful assessment may have revealed that aggressive or violent behaviour is a result of frustration, anger and angry thoughts, not delusional ones. Research studies have consistently struggled with only limited success to show robust connections between delusions and behaviour (e.g. Buchanan et al., 1993).

At times the important behaviour may be obvious (attacking a believed persecutor) but of very low frequency. In these circumstances, the therapist might want to ask the client to rate his urge to do the thing, or to monitor behaviour which lies earlier in the chain of actions leading up to the attack.

Yet another problem arises with interpretation of an increase or decrease in target behaviour. Many individuals who are coming to doubt their delusions actually may increase their delusional behaviour in a process of reality testing (see Garety, 1991). In other words, an increase in behaviour during therapy can be a positive or negative sign, depending on its meaning.

Finally, for some clients what they are not doing is as significant as what they are doing. Avoidance is often a big problem for individuals who are deluded. The way to access this is to enquire how the individual's life would be different if he did not believe whatever it is that he believes. For example, a client who were able momentarily to suspend his conviction that he was being persecuted, might recognise that he would travel freely were it not for this belief. This process may take some time, but is a powerful inducement to engaging in cognitive therapy because the client comes to recognise that it is the belief, not events, that precludes him from doing things that he would like to do and misses. Thus the delusion may be seen less as an important discovery, one which saves the client from being attacked when outside, and more as an obstacle to getting what he wants in life.

Assessing Beliefs (Bs): Delusions

Delusions are complex beliefs and current approaches to assessment and measurement reflect the need to consider many different features, or dimensions, of delusional thinking. These include; conviction; preoccupation; formation; evidence for and against; susceptibility to change (accommodation and reaction to hypothetical contradiction). We shall discuss each in turn.

Conviction. By convention, conviction (how certain a client is of a belief) and preoccupation (the amount of time spent thinking about the belief) are the main measures of delusional thinking, and of how it changes in therapy. How conviction is measured probably reflects the clinicians interest in measurement and research as much as the client's ability and wishes! A simple percentage rating (0=zero conviction to 100=absolute) is certainly adequate for most settings. As an alternative personal questionnaire methods, though more complex, do have internal reliability checks.

Blocks To Assessing Conviction

Often when the therapist is assessing delusional conviction the client will ask if the therapist believes the delusion (and hence him) and perhaps may even say she must believe it, otherwise it is pointless their discussing anything further. What does the therapist do? Two possibilities which should be ruled out are to collude, and agree with the client's delusion, or challenge the delusion in what would have to be a confrontational and ill-prepared fashion. Rather the therapist needs to convey her uncertainty and to encourage an atmosphere of collaborative empiricism. Let us return to Peter, the man who believes he is HIV positive—the therapist may say something like the following:

T: The belief that you are HIV could of course be right, unfortunately many people are HIV. Equally it may be that you are wrong, which would be great news for you. At this point I have no way of knowing which is true, but perhaps we can look into this more together.

This then is the therapist's first response to the client who asks if he is believed. In our experience this usually satisfies the client because what he is really hoping for at this early stage is for someone to try hard to understand his perspective, not necessarily to agree with it. Perhaps he is also expressing his frustration that so few people will have taken time to do this in the past. This indicates a second response the therapist might wish to make when the client asks if he is believed, namely, to comment on the process rather than the content. If there is time for the therapist to reflect and listen she may be able to detect behind the tone of the client's request a powerful emotion. Frustration is certainly a common one, but sometimes it can be despair at the sense of forever being cut off from others, or perhaps the client is looking for an outlet for anger. On the whole we find that when a client asks us a direct question we more often than not find ourselves commenting on the process rather than the content.

There is yet a third response, and one which is of central importance in cognitive therapy. That is, the therapist conveys what really concerns her about the client is his distress and disturbed behaviour (the Cs); given that these are consequences of the beliefs, not events, it seems important for client and therapist to assess the accuracy of those beliefs.

Preoccupation. There are two central issues surrounding the measurement of preoccupation, those of reliability and interpretation of change. By necessity preoccupation is a retrospective measure and hence of uncertain reliability; for this reason a diary approach to measurement is sometimes preferred (see Slade & Bentall, 1988). We have tended to use a simple ordinal scale to capture how much the person is preoccupied and detect any gross changes over the course of therapy. We prefer to operationalise the different scale points rather than use subjective ratings, although we have no data to say that this is a better method. A typical example would be to rate the statement: 'In the last week I have thought about my belief' as 0 (not at all), 1 (3 or 4 times in the week), 2 (every day) and 3 (many times every day).

Perhaps of more importance is the question of interpretation. Although it is usually thought to be true, we doubt that a fall in preoccupation is to be expected or is necessarily desirable during or even soon after therapy. As part of the process of change in cognitive therapy for delusions, many individuals will spend time thinking about their beliefs, perhaps even testing them out, and may therefore show as more preoccupied. Indeed, cognitive therapy encourages greater attention to and consideration of distressing thoughts and beliefs (Beck et al., 1979). The concept of preoccupation therefore may need to be broken down into its constituent parts such that it is possible to predict an increase in one type (e.g. critical analysis of delusion) and a decrease in another (e.g. unquestioning acceptance). A similar concern was mentioned earlier in relation to the use of behaviour change as an outcome measure: some individuals show an increase in delusion related behaviour during and following intervention because they are actively seeking to reality test the belief.

Formation. How might you, the reader, assess how you formed a religious or political belief? Undoubtedly there would be some important influences of which you were aware, but surely many influences of which you were partially aware or unaware; and if you offered an account of how you came to form your belief, would this be accepted as accurate or merely as your construction today based on the relatively few influences of which you were aware? And how might you begin to establish criteria for weighing your belief against that of another person—whose is the more rational or reasonable?

When examining a client's recollections of how this delusion was formed, we do not assume that this recall is factual, or even that the client would have access to all the influences. We are looking for stages and interpersonal themes contained in the process of formation.

Clients are asked how they came to form their beliefs, and whether the realisation was an immediate or gradual one. The intention is to look for different stages in the client's delusional thinking, and to see if the delusion might be connected to certain important experiences or events, and is in this sense understandable. So, one client, Derek, who stated that he had the power to change the course of history, was asked how he first came to this realisation. Although Derek did not list a series of clear stages that preceded the formation of the delusion, these were certainly apparent in his words.

Soon after the unexpected death of his father, to whom he was very close, and the breakup of his marriage some seven months later, Derek began to experience delusions of reference and thought broadcasting. For example, people on the television, radio and in public places appeared to be both talking about him, and to hear and speak his thoughts. Derek recalled believing at first that someone was playing a trick on him; however, this was quickly succeeded by intense fear and anxiety. He recalled inferring some time later that one implication of his experiences was that he was able to communicate with people on the radio and television because he need only think something and they would hear it. A second implication was that he must be in some way a significant person for them to go to all this trouble. The client reported subsequently hitting on the fact that he was often 'communicating' with people on recordings and films made a long time ago, and that the actors in question were often dead. This further suggested that he was able to communicate with people from the past, and this in turn suggested that he might be able to prevent certain events such as wars and accidents and to create others. Hence, he had the power to change history. This sense of comprehension brought order where there had been chaos and carried a powerful sense of relief.

It does not always prove possible to uncover in such detail different stages in clients' understanding of the genesis of their delusions. However, more often than not there is a traumatic emotional experience and a related interpersonal theme running through. In Derek's case, the evaluative themes of guilty self-blame and responsibility for emotional trauma, and a sense of loss and helplessness were close to the surface.

Evidence. Collecting evidence for and against a delusion is an essential part of cognitive assessment. We assess historical evidence and counter-evidence by asking the client about events which have occurred in the past which either supported the delusion or ran counter to it. We include events which predate the formation of the delusion because once formed delusions often guide the reinterpretation of past experience.

Garety and her colleagues have developed a measure called 'accommodation' in order to assess the client's awareness of confirmation and disconfirmation once therapy is under way. Accommodation is usually measured at the start of every session by asking if anything has happened since the last session to alter the delusion in any way. In relation to disconfirmation, accommodation assessed the extent to which it was observed and the extent to which it impacted on the delusion. For example, in the Brett-Jones, Garety & Hemsley (1987) study responses were categorized as shown in Table 5.

Table 5 Summary of scales and scoring for RTHC and accommodation (adapted from Brett-Jones, Garety & Hemsley (1987))

RTHC	Accommodation
Categorical (0 to 4)	Categorical (0 to 5)
Situation ignored, dismissed or persistently denied as being possible	No instance given or one given but no effect on belief
Situation accommodated by alteration in content	Content change or belief replaced by new belief
Belief changes in conviction but not content	Conviction changes but not content
Belief dropped in face of contradictory evidence	Belief dropped and not replaced due to some objective event
	Change in preoccupation or interference but not content

Assessing for accommodation complements well the use of ABC diaries, because in respect of confirmation they are two nets to catch the one fish. It is quite common for an individual to have made no recordings in the ABC diary and yet to report a powerful instance of confirmation at the start of the session, and vice versa. Indeed, although accommodation was conceived as a measure of susceptibility to change, this may be a misleading description because individuals who report no instances of disconfirmation appear to respond well in cognitive therapy—in fact it is rare for individuals to report any such instances.

In our research, for example, (see Chadwick & Lowe, 1994) in a total of nearly 100 assessment sessions, only two disconfirming events were reported, both by the same woman. And yet disconfirmation was occurring, and in quite direct ways. Derek, for example, who believed that he could communicate with people in the past and thereby change the course of history, tried and failed to do this numerous times each day and yet never felt compelled to abandon the delusion. All 12 individuals frequently reported events which they perceived to support their delusions, though many of these were not obviously supportive. For example, Larry reported how a young dishevelled woman had once asked him for money at a bus stop. Although at the time he did not recognise the woman, he later deduced that she was an old acquaintance in disguise and that she had planned the meeting to remind him of her presence. Much of the evidence was of this type, that is, reconstruction of past events in line with a delusion. For instance, Dick went through Polytechnic enjoying satisfactory contact with his lecturers and only years later came to 'realise' that they had been reading his mind and persecuting him.

Research data such as ours are often used to support the argument that delusions, perhaps all strongly held beliefs, are maintained through a strong confirmation bias (Maher, 1988). It is important, however, not to infer from this specific bias in delusional thinking a general cognitive bias or deficit. Data such as ours offer no support for the existence of a general confirmation bias in deluded individuals—indeed, evidence exists that under certain experimental conditions, people with delusions may be *less* attached to their interpretations than pscyhiatric and ordinary controls (see Garety, 1991).

Reaction to Hypothetical Contradiction

A measure which appears a far more promising way of tapping susceptibility to change is RTHC, (Brett-Jones, Garety & Hemsley, 1987) a measure of people's potential for accepting disconfirmation. A plausible hypothetical event that is inconsistent with the delusion is described and the individual is asked how if at all such an occurrence would alter the delusion. Following Garety's recent work, prior to posing a hypothetical contradiction, the therapist first asks the client if he is able to think of an event which would lead him to modify or doubt his belief.

A rule of thumb for RTHC is to keep the hypothetical event as simple and plausible as possible. For example, a man who believed that Elvis Presley on his death had taken over his mind and body was asked if this belief would be altered in any way if Elvis appeared on television and said that he had stage-managed his death to avoid the glare of the public eye. A second man believed that a woman whom he had not seen since childhood has been reading his mind and determining things which happened to him was asked if this belief would be altered in any way if he were to meet the woman and she should deny it.

In practice we explore past experience of disconfirmation and reaction to hypothetical contradiction together, and we do it in a comparatively casual manner, as illustrated in the following dialogue which begins with an enquiry about accommodation and flows through past experience of disconfirmation to current reaction to hypothetical contradiction.

T: Belinda, has anything happened in the past week to alter in any way your belief that you are the daughter of Princess Anne?

C: Well, I was watching TV on Wednesday and I saw the Queen and she looked very concerned about me; she looked very old.

T: What effect did this have on your belief?

C: Well, it proved it is all true, I really am her granddaughter.

T: Aha. So seeing the Queen on TV reinforced your belief. And nothing has happened in the past week to make you modify the belief or doubt it?

C: No.

T: Has anything ever happened over the years to make you doubt your belief?

C: Going back ten years I was told twice the royals were coming to get me back. I got all my jewels out of the safe at the solicitors and waited at the door. My dad and husband pleaded with me to unpack. I was told they were coming for me. I just sat there and waited and waited and waited, but no one came. My dad and husband told me to go to bed and sleep it off. Now you can see why I tried to commit suicide.

T: That is a very distressing memory. (Pause). And that experience led you to doubt that you were Anne's daughter. These days you seem very sure of the belief again—indeed, you couldn't be more sure—I wonder what has raised your confidence?

C: Well I've been convinced again. I couldn't have dreamed this up, I don't have the imagination. And seeing them on TV and hearing things has convinced me.

T: Right, so in the past your experience sometimes went against the belief and at those times you doubted the belief—that seems very sensible. Recently events have seemed consistent with the belief and your conviction has risen. Is there anything you can think of which if it happened in the coming week would make you once again doubt the belief?

C: (Pause) No, I can't think of anything.

T: Put another way, what would have to happen for you to decide that your beliefs are wrong?

C: I don't know, I can't think of anything.

T: Belinda, I wonder if I can think of an event which, if it happened in the next week, might lead you to doubt your belief that you are the daughter of Princess Anne. Let's imagine that you were to actually meet Anne, but she was to say to you that she was not your mother and had not been doing the things to you over the years that you think. If this were to happen would it alter your belief in anyway?

C: No, I'd think she had been hypnotised to say it.

In our own research (see Chadwick & Lowe, 1994) RTHC did indeed appear to be connected to response to cognitive therapy. Eight of the 12 individuals responded on at least one occasion that the instance of hypothetical contradiction would lead them either to reject their delusions or to lower their degree of belief conviction and all eight did lower their degree of conviction in the face of the interventions. Conversely, two of the four people who stated that the instance of hypothetical contradiction would not affect their delusions did not lower their belief conviction during the subsequent interventions. However, the relationship was not one-to-one; two individuals gave negative responses to RTHC that were at odds with their positive response to treatment

It is our impression that some individuals are far more prepared than others to question their delusions and that results on the RTHC measure reflect this. While a change in belief conviction is undoubtedly related to weight of counter-evidence, cognitive therapy for any problem is rarely so persuasive that people have no option but to relinquish their core beliefs and it is not surprising that people will vary in their openness to change—indeed individuals frequently are not. In part, openness seemed to be linked to the degree of affect that the delusions still commanded. For example, two people with delusions related to long-standing auditory hallucinations gave the impression at the outset of our study of no longer being 'caught in their voices' power' (Bauer, 1979) to the degree that they had once been; they had perhaps come to expect that their voices' promises and threats were unlikely to be realised. This suggests the possibility that delusions might not necessarily become harder to modify with time.

Assessing Core Evaluative Beliefs (Bs)

When assessing the Bs the therapist is looking at clarifying not only the delusion, but also any evaluative beliefs, or themes, associated with it. Of special importance are the evaluations of self and other—that is, the person evaluations (see Chapter 1). This is one of the most challenging of all aspects of cognitive therapy for delusions, but also one of the most critical because it often throws light on the possible defensive function of the delusion and this material may be used in therapy to help to render the delusion more understandable. In our experience, this defensive function usually may be understood as an attempt to defend the self from threat, and especially to prevent negative self-evaluative thinking from becoming dominant, with its associated despair and guilt or shame.

Having completed an initial ABC assessment of current functioning, how then is the therapist to move from the delusional inferences (or automatic thoughts) to the evaluation? The traditional move would be to use thought chaining to progress from the surface inference to the deeper evaluation by *supposing that the inferences is true*. This technique of repeatedly assuming that an inference is true is used routinely with emotional problems concerned with anxiety, depression and anger, and lays bare the client's negative evaluations of self or other. The following dialogue illustrates the process being used to connect three delusional automatic thoughts to two deeper evaluations.

T: John, let us imagine just for a moment that your neighbour is spying on you. What would be so bad about that as to make you feel such extreme terror?

C: He's checking to see if I am alone in the house.

T: So you think he would check if you are on your own. Let us assume for a minute that that is true also, what would he want to check that for?

C: They may be planning to come and get me, to punish me.

T: You believe they want to come and get you, punish you?

C: Yeah, they hate me, they think I'm evil, they want to get rid of me.

T: They hate you and see you as evil. Do you believe that they hate one or two things about you, think that bits of you are evil, or that you as a person, the whole of you is evil?

C: The whole of me.

T: And how would you feel if they did think this about you, that you are evil through and through?

C: I'd feel terrible, I'd hate myself.

T: So if they evaluated you in this global way then you would hate yourself. And how would you be evaluating yourself?

C: I'd hate myself. They'd be right, I am evil.

In this dialogue the therapist uses thought chaining to move through a sequence of inferential automatic thoughts to arrive at two evaluations, first a negative other-self person evaluation (You are totally evil) and finally a self-self one (I am totally evil). This specific tactic of first clarifying the other-self evaluation and then proceeding to the self-self evaluation is commonly used in cognitive therapy and is a useful way to overcome a common defensive tendency to avoid attending to negative self-evaluative thinking. This tactic works particularly well with paranoid delusions (see Chapter 7) which are characterised not merely by fear but either anger or anxiety and guilt. It also works well for other delusions in which these emotions feature large—for example, delusions of guilt. The therapist each time has in mind the same conceptual 'prompts':

• complete a current ABC assessment,
• explore current delusional automatic thoughts,
• look for other-self, self-other or self-self negative person evaluations.

However, if handled in a clumsy manner it can be risky for the therapist to ask a client to assume temporarily that a delusion is true and proceed to exploration of what might follow from this premise. To begin with such a statement is easily misunderstood as being an agreement that the delusion really is true, or at the very least may provoke a debate about the therapist's own conviction that the delusion is true—thus missing the point of the exercise, which is to move beyond the delusional thinking.

Also, delusions can be unlike inferences associated with anxiety, depression and anger in the respect that their content is sometimes fantastic. It is stretching logic to class as inferences—defined as statements which may or may not be true (see Chapter 1)—delusional statements like 'I am dead', or 'My parents have been replaced by aliens from outer space'. In such cases the therapist needs to choose her words very carefully when seeking to connect an inference to an associated evaluation. It might be asking too much of a client's tolerance to say something like 'What is *so* bad about having your parents replaced by aliens as to make you depressed', or 'What is so bad about having the secret service plotting to kill you', or 'What is so bad about having a radio transmitter implanted in your brain and a camera in your vagina?'

In other words, because the content of delusions often goes beyond the realms of possibility, many are obviously terrible and it would often be perceived as insensitive to imply that on their own, such inferences are insufficient to produce extreme distress. It is as if certain delusions lie somewhere between inferences and evaluations—they cannot really be said to be possibly true, but neither are they explicitly evaluative. Other connecting prompts are probably safer, such as 'What is the worst thing about . . .' (e.g. believing your parents have been replaced by aliens), 'What sort of person do people see you as in order to treat you in this way?' (e.g. to implant a transmitter and camera).

When working with delusions where the content is grandiose, we find that an unconventional approach is often required to move from inferences to evaluations. In these cases what the therapist needs to do is ask the client to *imagine that the delusional inference is false*, not true, and to explore how this would affect the client. Once again, the therapist would be looking for the client's self-self, self-other and perceived other-self evaluations, and these would relate to the self without the fantastic or grandiose attribute. The reason for this is that the negative self-evaluative belief does not follow directly from the delusional inference. Grandiose delusions are thought to be defensive mechanisms for preventing negative self-evaluation (Neale, 1988) but the mechanism is such that the client's threatened negative self-evaluation (e.g. I am utterly bad) is actually reversed in the delusion and the client becomes utterly good and worthy. The clue to the defended negative self-evaluation lies in the nature of the grandiose belief, but accessing it directly requires that the client temporarily imagine the delusion to be false. In this way the individual's vulnerability is revealed and may be addressed in therapy.

So for example, one client, Michelle, believed that she had been transformed into a god. The therapist clarified that this meant, among other things, that she was an utterly good and worthy person. However, were the delusion false she and others would judge her to be bad and dirty because of her strong, culturally forbidden sexual urges and behaviour. The therapist was able to use this insight to explore the possibility that the grandiose delusion was a way of defending against this underlying negative self-evaluation, and to work on the evaluation with Michelle.

This unconventional approach may also be useful for working with clients with somatic delusions. If we return to Peter, the client who believes he is HIV positive, the therapist asks Peter to imagine that the delusion is false in order to reveal that the delusion is not the sole cause of his distress, that there are also evaluative beliefs.

T: Okay. I want you to imagine that the bodily changes you mentioned are not signs of HIV, but of a milder and treatable medical condition; if this were true, would you feel the way you do now?

C: No, obviously not. I'd be so relieved.

T: So if the bodily changes were due to a mild condition you wouldn't feel frightened and you wouldn't feel isolated and lonely. Is that it?

C: Well, I wouldn't feel frightened because I wouldn't be dying. But I might still feel alone (pause) and I still wouldn't like the way I'd been treated.

T: So if you were not HIV positive, one of your problems, that of fear, would go. But you might still have two problems, loneliness and anger. And we could then work together to help you feel less lonely and angry. And if you were HIV positive, which is what you believe to be true, then you have all three problems—loneliness, fear and anger. Well, some people who are HIV positive are able to overcome just these sort of problem feelings, and it might be that you could do the same. Either way, we can work together to help you reduce what it is that bothers you so much, the fear and isolation and anger that you feel currently.

In general, when searching for evaluations we have two general pieces of advice. First, the process is deductive; the ABC analysis will have revealed the affect and behaviour tied to the delusional automatic thoughts, or inferences, and from this the therapist is able to deduce the type of evaluations present (e.g. anger implies self-other, depression and anxiety imply other-self and self-self) Second, as Deck has emphasised, the process of cognitive therapy is collaborative—if the thought chaining process is stuck but the therapist has a hunch about the evaluative belief, then it is quite permissable for her to tentatively enquire if her intuition is correct. All too often therapists think they have to wait—and wait—until the client provides the next link in the chain.

FORMULATION

In this chapter we have concentrated on those features of psychological assessment which are unique to cognitive therapy, and this has been described within an ABC cognitive framework. However, to arrive at a formulation for an individual the therapist must clearly do much else besides. Within the cognitive model formulation connects early experience, interpersonal style, significant life events, onset, and current ABC analysis of problems. Formulations are tentative and speculative, and are likely to develop as therapy progresses.

Bette

Bette was in her forties and was divorced with children. She was a pleasant and likeable woman and a caring, considerate and loving mother. She was referred by a clinical psychologist because of a long standing and fixed delusion that was associated with considerable distress and disturbance. She believed that she was an evil witch who contaminated others, and this delusion had resisted different medical treatments. Bette was happy with the referral and held no particular anxiety about therapy. She experienced moderate to severe depressive symptomatology and in the recent past had experienced visual hallucinations and imperative voices commanding her to shave off her hair and mutilate her scalp, which she did. The psychiatrist involved had given Bette a diagnosis of borderline psychosis with delusional system.

Bette described her life as having been difficult and said she had 'never really enjoyed living much'. Throughout her childhood—indeed her life—she had felt unwanted and had a sense of being a nuisance, 'in the way'. She recalled sometimes wishing that her mum 'was not there' and said once that she did not like her mum. She described feeling angry with her mum for having brought her into the world, but her anger was usually blocked or turned inwards, and was directed at others only during admissions to hospital. She felt very close to her dad and 'valued his opinion above all'. There were hints that she felt inferior to her sibling; Bette certainly had always had an uncomfortable sense that she was unable to do things as well as others, and she tended to be a little subordinate.

She and her husband first met when she was 20 and they courted for many years before marrying and buying their own home. During their 12 years together he subjected her to quite appalling torment. Within two weeks of marriage he sent her home for a week, to be by himself; thereafter he continued this pattern of sending her away when he had enough of her. To have him reject her and condemn her as bad was a desperate blow, and was exactly what she most feared. For example, he would fluctuate moment by moment between kindness and cruelty; an everyday occurrence might be for him in an intimate manner to buy her a cake and then once she began to eat it to say 'people as fat as you shouldn't eat cakes'. He repeatedly told her and their children that she was a witch and satan. He taunted her about her admissions to hospital and commonly threatened to have her 'put away again'. Over and over again he would deny certain facts and then mock her confusion between what was and was not true. When finally Bette insisted on a separation, he told her he intended to win custody of the children and then give them to her as a present.

Bette's first admission to hospital came after the birth of their second child, and from her recollection sounded like post-natal depression. She recalled not wanting the child and thinking that she was unable to do anything right for it or anyone else. There were seven subsequent admissions over the duration of the marriage, and a number of genuine suicide attempts.

Bette reported having believed for about eight years that she was evil and contaminated others, with very high conviction. This belief was referred to in the psychiatric case notes as an 'unshakable belief'. In fact during the assessment period Bette's conviction was not total, but was always very high (in the range 80–100%). Preoccupation was also high, with Bette typically experiencing delusional ideation four or five times each day; these thoughts were often triggered by contact with her ex-husband, or times when her children behaved nastily. When preoccupied with her delusion she would feel very guilty and low and would view herself as 'no good' and 'unwantable'—the associated negative self-evaluation—and as therefore being responsible for other people treating her badly. She had a strong urge to commit suicide, genuinely believing that others would be better off without her, and had planned when she would do this. In the past she had written suicide notes, walked down to a local river intent on suicide, and had actually attempted suicide.

The cognitive formulation attached importance to Bette's childhood. It was hypothesised that Bette's early childhood was characterised by limited emotional support and attachment, especially with her mother. This left a very strong and largely unfulfilled need for attachment and affection from others, and a strong fear of future experiences of feeling unwanted, isolated and lonely. In this sense Bette's interpersonal style revealed a strong need to establish and maintain attachment. Her father she felt closer to, but contact had been limited. She identified very strongly with him and rejected her mother's ways; she did not like much of her mother's character and often wanted her out of the way.

The sense of anger which Bette attributed to her mum having brought her into the world may have been more about her mother's failure to love her properly once she had brought her into the world. The sense of being no good was thought to originate from two main sources; first, she may have assumed the blame for her parents limited interest in her (and their possible preference for her sibling) and put this down to there being something wrong with her. Second, her rejection of her mum and anger towards her may well have felt shocking and bad—this anger at mum was usually expressed most clearly when in hospital, perhaps because the setting provided a degree of safety.

Her hypothesised psychological vulnerability from childhood meant that her husband's behaviour was doubly important because for her it represented a first experience of someone, she thought, preferring, wanting and loving her. His cruelty could hardly have been more disturbing because it fulfilled her two main fears; he rejected her and told her she was bad. The birth of the second child came at a time when the marriage was clearly poor and painful. It is understandable that Bette did not want to have another child and should feel so ambivalent towards it. However, to her these feelings and thoughts must have seemed like further telling evidence that she was no good, now as a mother—she had rejected her mother and now her child.

It was hypothesised that the delusion and associated self-evaluation represented a crystallisation and magnification of concerns which had been very long standing. On the one hand there was her badness and on the other her accepting responsibility for others disappointing and bad behaviour towards her.

SUMMARY

When assessing delusions the therapist tries to identify the delusional and evaluative thinking, as both are believed to be tied to the emotional distress and the client's psychological vulnerability. Accessing evaluations is complex, and in certain circumstances requires an unconventional tactic—that of assuming that the delusional inference is false, and exploring what distress remains. This information is used in conjunction with that covered in a standard psychological assessment (childhood, developmental history, life events) to construct a provisional formulation which drives the process of disputing and testing the evaluative and delusional beliefs.

Chapter 4

CHALLENGING DELUSIONS

INTRODUCTION

To many readers the idea of trying to modify a delusion will seem at best futile and at worst harmful. Medical and nursing professions in the UK have long advised students and staff that delusions cannot be modified and that the best practice is to avoid discussing them with clients. In this section we apply a cognitive therapy style challenge to these beliefs, and suggest that the intransigent thinking may lie more with some professionals than their clients.

If the claim that delusions are not open to modification is intended as factual and based on observation (*a posteriori*), then two philosophical principles should be operative. First, we should seek to falsify the claim and not abide by it (Popper, 1977)—that is, we should seek those conditions where the statement falls down because in this way we advance knowledge. In other words, therapists should actively and imaginatively seek conditions under which delusions *are* modifiable. The second principle is this; if we do find even a few such instances of falsification then we have proved the statement to be false as it stands and there is a need for the theory to be adjusted or abandoned. An example commonly used to illustrate this process is the claim all swans are white (cf. all delusions are unmodifiable). Once a single black swan is discovered, the statement all swans are white is falsified. (In fact a single refutation is considered insufficient grounds for a theory to be rejected.)

Since 1952 there have been a number of published studies reporting attempts to weaken delusions with generally favourable results (see Chapter 1). It therefore seems plain to us that the statement 'all delusions are unmodifiable' is similarly false, having been disproved many times over, and should be abandoned. (We are not asserting that all delusions are modifiable, or even that a specific proportion is, merely that some palpably are: future research will clarify the factors which shape outcome.) If, however, psychiatry wishes to assert the statement delusions cannot be modified as an *a priori* statement—that is, as one which is necessarily true by virtue of the meaning of the terms (e.g. a square has four sides)—then the statement has to be true (see Magee, 1987) but this position is untenable in relation to delusions. It would mean, for example, that delusions were not being described and defined on the basis of clinical observation and practice. Also, it would mean that a belief could be called a delusion just up to the point at which it responded to psychotherapy, whereafter it could no longer be so named. Again, it would mark an end to the exciting and persuasive move towards investigating dimensions of delusional experience.

It might be more reasonable to assert that delusions are difficult to modify, sometimes fiendishly so. This position would acknowledge that the class of beliefs called delusions varies considerably along a number of dimensions, and it would encourage examination of the multitude of factors which might be thought to influence therapeutic outcome. It would also encourage an exploration of whether delusions are more difficult to modify than political or religious beliefs, or the core beliefs associated with conditions such as anorexia.

The second persistent idea which has deterred therapists from applying psychological therapy to delusions (and one which is incompatible with the first) is that weakening or removing a delusion is harmful to the individual concerned. Where the previous discussion might be captured in the question 'can a delusion be modified', this second issue asks the question, 'should a delusion be modified'. The idea is that if a delusion is formed to protect the individual from unacceptable threat, then removing it is to re-expose the person to the threat.

Yet for many people being deluded is associated with severe emotional and behavioural disturbance and it therefore seems, to us at least, questionable for a therapist to decide in advance to withhold therapy on the grounds of an unproven belief that deluded people are best left deluded. And should this argument not apply equally well to medication? However, the claim that having a delusion weakened is harmful is an empirical one and therefore cannot be settled dogmatically, and it is on empirical grounds that we reject it. Evidence from research into cognitive therapy for delusions suggests the weakening of a delusion is associated with a decrease in emotional and behavioural distress (see Chadwick & Lowe, 1994).

Indeed, the idea that weakening a delusion is harmful may rest on a failure to distinguish aetiology and maintenance. Historically it has been argued that inividuals form delusions because they are faced with what seems an insufferable threat, and that the delusion is a form of psychological defence without which the person would 'inwardly collapse' (Jaspers, 1962). While this may be an adequate account for the emergence of delusions (it is unproven) it says nothing whatsoever about an individual's likely response to losing a delusion some years later.

This is not to remove a therapist's prerogative, based on a sound formulation of an individual case, to withhold cognitive therapy, or for that matter any other therapy. Nor is it to suggest that the weakening of a delusion will *never* be associated with increase in distress and disturbance. Regrettably this does seem to be the case for a minority of individuals; but even in these few cases there is no clear causal connection between the increased distress and the loss of the delusion, only a temporal one. Individuals can get worse during or following all forms of therapy and it is the therapist's job to be alert to this possibility and take remedial action when necessary.

We suspect that the position therapists adopt on this general issue may reflect their implicit beliefs about the power of therapy. We do not believe that cognitive therapy is so powerful that individuals are swept along by it and somehow compelled to change, even if their will is not to. Our clients demonstrate numerous ways of not changing and we respect and accept this. Rather, cognitive therapy works well when the therapist and client share a common purpose and work together in pursuit of it, and our view is that a legitimate common purpose is to reduce distress and disturbance by weakening delusions.

THE PROCESS OF CHALLENGING DELUSIONS

Although certain delusions are beyond the realms of possibility, as a rule of thumb it is nonetheless useful to conceptualise them as inferences, statements which may or may not be true. It highlights that the challenge is one of reviewing evidence, generating an alternative framework, and empirical testing predominantly through risk taking (see Chapter 2). Also, labelling delusions as inferences highlights that the therapist needs to try and identify and weaken not only the delusions but also the associated evaluative beliefs, especially evaluations of self (e.g. I am totally bad) and others (e.g. you are totally inferior).

In this section we consider the process of working with the delusional (inferential) beliefs and the associated evaluations. To ease comprehension we have divided the description of cognitive therapy for delusions into discrete chunks. In particular, we have separated attempts to weaken a delusion through verbal discussion (verbal challenge) from planned empirical testing (reality testing). We have further subdivided the verbal challenge section into procedures related to delusional (inferential) thinking and evaluative thinking. These separations are useful in that they clarify in the therapist's mind the central conceptual tasks in therapy, but should not be taken as rigid divisions in the way therapy is practised. By now it should be plain that the cognitive approach is first and foremost a conceptual position from which to view a person's current problem and psychological development. Once the conceptual perspective is clear the therapist is well placed to draw on therapeutic techniques from the cognitive literature and elsewhere in order to best pursue specific goals.

The therapist hopes that through cognitive therapy the client will gain four insights regarding the delusion. First is the recognition that the delusion is a belief, and not a fact of life. Second is that it represents a reaction to, and attempt to make sense of, certain aspects of his life: in many cases there is a discernable psychological motivation for this (e.g. anxiety reduction, warding off negative self-evaluation). Third, is the recognition that the delusion carries an emotional and behavioural cost. Fourth, as the client considers, discusses and tests the delusion, he comes to recognise it is false and rejects it in favour of a more plausible and personally significant explanation (a new B) with which to make sense of his experience (A).

In terms of the ABC model, this means:

1. The client recognises the delusion is a Belief and not an Activating event.
2. The client understands more about how the delusion (Belief) was a reaction to and way of explaining his experience (Activating events).
3. The client recognises that much of his distress and disturbance (emotional and behavioural Consequences) is tied to the delusion (Belief) and is therefore not an inevitable consequence of experience (Activating events).
4. Through a process of collaborative discussion and direct testing the client rejects the delusion in favour of an alternative explanatory framework (new B) which is less distressing and disturbing (new Cs).

Process of Challenging Associated Evaluations

What part does identifying and challenging evaluations play in this process? We showed in Chapter 3 how to connect delusions—inferences, or what Beck calls automatic thoughts—to evaluations by using thought chaining. The role of evaluative beliefs in the process of challenging delusions is twofold. First, the therapist seeks to help the client connect the delusion to the associated evaluations, such that the delusion becomes more understandable in terms of its possible psychological function. In other words, *it is the associated evaluative beliefs which provide a clue to the interpretation of the possible psychological meaning and function of the delusion.* Second, the therapist wants to weaken the negative evaluations, in particular of self, in order to reduce the client's distress and vulnerability.

So for example, in Chapter 7 on paranoia, we show how delusions relating to punishment are associated with and driven by a strong negative self-evaluative belief about badness. In such instances the therapist seeks to convey this understanding to the client and to use it as a rationale for questioning both the delusion and the self-evaluation in therapy. Again, in Chapter 3 we described a woman who believed she had been transformed into a god and was therefore an utterly good and worthy person. This belief was hypothesised to be a defence against her vulnerability to seeing herself as totally bad and evil—the justification for this hypothesis being current theory on grandiosity, and the findings that the negative person evaluation could be accessed by thought chaining and had been conscious and dominant prior to the delusion being formed.

PROCEDURES FOR WEAKENING DELUSIONS

Disputing (or verbal challenge) comprises four elements. First, the evidence for the beliefs is challenged, and in inverse order of its importance to the delusion. Second, the internal consistency and plausibility of the delusional system is questioned. Third, following Maher, the delusion is reformulated as being an understandable response to, and way of making sense of, specific experience, and a personally meaningful alternative is constructed. Lastly, the individual's delusion and the alternative are assessed in the light of the available information.

Challenging the Evidence for the Belief

Watts, Powell & Austin (1973) argued that a danger when trying to modify delusions, indeed, all strongly held beliefs, was psychological reactance (Brehm, 1962) whereby too direct an approach served only to reinforce the belief. Two principles which Watts et al. offered to minimise this possibility were to begin with the least important belief, and also to work with the evidence for the belief rather than the belief itself.

Accordingly we usually begin the verbal challenge of delusions by questioning the evidence for the belief, and this process begins with the least significant item and works up to the most significant item. Our preferred approach is that with each item of evidence the therapist questions the client's delusional interpretation and puts forward a more reasonable and probable one. The customary approach in cognitive therapy is for the client to be asked to generate the alternative interpretation(s), rather than the therapist supply one, but we have found that for certain clients this conventional tactic is a weak intervention.

When the therapist questions the evidence for a delusion she has in mind two distinct but related objectives. One is to encourage the client to question and perhaps even to reject the evidence for his belief, and in this way perhaps to undermine the client's conviction in the delusion itself. For some individuals challenging the evidence is a very powerful intervention and one that produces a substantial reduction in delusional conviction. However, more commonly this does not happen, but challenging evidence is still valuable in that it does impart insight into the connection between events, beliefs, affect and behaviour. This is the second objective of challenging evidence, to convey the essentials of the ABC approach— that is, that strongly held beliefs influence behaviour, affect and interpretation for all people (see Vygotsky, 1962). Our core beliefs *recruit* or bias our everyday inferences and automatic thoughts. However, this means that we often impose an interpretation onto events which is unwarranted, and because we are prone towards selectively processing information that confirms our beliefs, this goes undetected. Therefore we are all very prone to self-deception.

In other words, it is understandable that a client should interpret a particular event in line with his delusion because this is merely one occurrence of a general tendency, a confirmation bias, common to us all. In therapy, we often convey the ordinariness of this process with everyday examples, such as the habit rival politicians have of interpreting the same report or finding in different ways that reflect their different political position. An awareness that beliefs may govern behaviour is a vital first step in all cognitive therapies.

As well as governing the way a person approaches and interprets a new event, delusions may also lead clients to reinterpret past events in line with current beliefs. It was St. Augustine who said that there is only ever the present—the past present (recollection), the present, and the future present (anticipation). In our own research much of the evidence put forward for delusions was of this type—that is, the reconstruction of past events in line with a more recently formed delusion (Chadwick & Lowe, 1994). For example, one man, Dick, went through polytechnic enjoying a good working relationship with his lecturers, and only came to 'realise' some years later that throughout the lecturers had been reading his mind and persecuting him.

The therapist seeks to stress how the client's delusional interpretation owes more to the guiding influence of belief than to any salient features of the situation. Having considered the alternatives the client is then asked to rate his conviction in each; regardless of how convinced he remains that the delusional interpretation is correct, we usually move on to the next piece of evidence. The therapist does not have to change what the client thinks, but only to offer a fresh insight into the way he is thinking.

One client, Larry, believed that he had been Leonardo da Vinci in a prior life. As part of this delusion he believed that all the experiences and knowledge people gained in their prior lives were retained in what he called the subconscious mind. The piece of evidence he rated as most important to the Leonardo belief was that he had a picture in his mind of a design for a helicopter and submarine, which he believed were drawn by Leonardo. His interpretation was that Leonardo's designs had seeped through from his, Larry's, subconscious into consciousness, and therefore proved that he had been Leonardo. Without being requested to do so, Larry drew the designs. The counter argument put forward was based on the drawings; where Larry's helicopter showed a contemporary rotory propellor, Leonardo's design showed an entirely different screw shaped one. The pictures Larry drew were therefore not Leonardo's, and most probably came from a book. It was stressed that Larry's interpretation was reasonable, given his belief, but was mistaken, and therefore offered him a valuable insight into the way beliefs become self-fulfilling.

A less clear-cut challenge is more usual. Charlie, for example, held that noxious and poisonous gases were sent through the walls and fireplace into her end-of-terrace house. She believed that the gases were pumped through with a heavy iron machine of some sort. This claim was based on the fact that she occasionally heard what sounded like a heavy metal object being dragged around next door. However, the sound was heard only occasionally, even though the source of the gas switched often: indeed, although Charlie claimed that the gas was often pumped through from the ground floor of her neighbour's house, she only ever heard the 'machine' in her neighbour's upstairs bedroom. Also, not only did the gases frequently come through when she did not hear the machine being moved, but she also heard the machine on occasions when the gases did not come through. Therefore, it was suggested that it was Charlie's belief about the gas that led her to interpret the occasional dragging noise as the movement of a heavy pump.

Affect plays a vital role in people's delusional thinking, and it is common for a client to take his associated affect as evidence for his delusion—what is referred to in the literature as emotional reasoning. This phenomenon is well recognised in the literature on depression (Williams, 1992) where depressed people often say things like 'I must be a bad mum, I feel so guilty when I see my children'. With delusions a similar thing occurs frequently. For example, people who believe they are being persecuted often take their fear and anxiety as evidence of an actual threat, rather than as being part of what it is to perceive a threat.

Terry, for example, believed that his appearance was sinister and suspicious, and that he was suspected of various criminal offences for which some form of retaliation was going to be taken. All his evidence for the delusion related to occasions when he had thought people were suspicious of him and he had experienced strong anxiety and guilt. He took these emotions as proof of his badness, reasoning that if he had nothing to hide he would not feel this way. Consequently although he was never accused of anything by anyone, he always said to himself 'Today I was lucky, I got away without being challenged', rather than questioning the delusion.

The event Terry put forward as most integral to the belief took place when he was on a training course. While walking through the town one evening a passing police car pulled over and a policeman briefly questioned him. Over the subsequent week he saw a number of different police cars. He believed that the police had questioned him and subsequently placed him under surveillance because of his sinister and suspicious appearance. This view was challenged as follows. First, Terry stated that he had felt so nervous walking through town that he had 'jumped' on seeing the police car; this may have accounted for the policeman stopping to 'have a word'. Second, the policeman did not ask Terry where he lived or worked and having spoken to him drove off; Terry was certain he was not followed home. Terry's conclusion (that he was placed under surveillance) therefore did not fit with his own perception of the episode, but made sense only when his delusional belief and affect were 'on line'.

A further strength of challenging evidence is that it begins to clarify a picture of the client's psychological vulnerability. Bette (see Chapter 3), who believed that she was an evil person who contaminated others considered her husband's unkind and cruel behaviour over a number of years to be the single most potent piece of evidence for this belief. He could only have behaved in this way, she reasoned, both because he had recognised what an evil person she was, and because he had also been contaminated by her. What made the delusional interpretation so compelling to Bette was her affect and the sense of her own badness, which was stirred so adeptly by her husband on occasions such as these. What the therapist and Bette did when considering this evidence was reveal her propensity for internalising badness and responsibility—and this anticipated the subsequent discussion of the historical origins of this propensity.

There is a risk that challenging evidence lasts too long. If a client produces a list of evidence as long as his arm, then the therapist will have to try and classify it. For example, Derek, who believed that he could communicate with people in the past and thereby change history, offered numerous instances when he had heard dead singers and film stars refer to him— rather than discuss each in turn, these were all classified as resting on a primary experience and discussed *en masse*.

Challenging the Delusion Directly

Procedurally the therapist attempts to weaken the delusion in three overlapping stages. These stages are first described, and then examples involving all three are given. First, any inconsistency and irrationality within the client's belief system is pointed out; this is tantamount to posing the question 'Would it make sense for things to be as you say they are?' Second, the delusion is recast as a reaction to and attempt to make sense of certain experience, and third it is shown how from within the client's own perspective the delusion lacks internal and external validity and carries significant personal cost.

Inconsistency and Irrationality

Although delusions contain differing degrees of inconsistency and irrationality, they all seem to contain some. However, we should not feel too smug because it appears that few complex belief systems are watertight; for example, it has been observed that all the major religious belief systems include examples of inconsistency (Cavendish, 1980, p. 8). The philosopher Karl Popper has written how his initial disgust with Freudian psychoanalysis for being able to incorporate all findings, however apparently incompatible, was tempered somewhat when he discovered that the majority of theories were similarly 'immunised' and impossible to refute (Popper, 1977).

What at times can be surprising is the enormity of the inconsistency. Belinda (see Chapter 3) held two distinct delusions, formed at different points in her life, which were actually mutually exclusive. One was that she was only a teenager and that the life experience she thought had been hers was all fed in using 'fancy computers and autosuggestion'; another belief was that during her life (i.e. the one she recalled as hers and the first delusion wiped out) she had been raped numerous times and had six children, each following a pregnancy of six days. Now while we might begin to understand the psychology of this split, and the important themes running through the two delusions, we should not be blind to the opportunity to weaken what was a towering delusional edifice by using the more important delusion to eradicate the other altogether.

Delusions Are Reactions to and Attempts to Make Sense of Specific Experience

We always construe a delusion as both a reaction to and an attempt to make sense of certain puzzling and often threatening experiences. It is an understandable and reasonable attempt to find meaning at a time when the individual is bewildered, anxious and all too often frightened. It carries the psychological force of having removed the sense of bewilderment, and given a focus to previously free-floating emotions. But, the delusion carries a cost in terms of distress and disturbance, which the individual might not otherwise experience. This is how we always portray delusions to clients (see Maher, 1988).

One of the advantages of this approach is that it reminds the individual how puzzling and bewildering the particular experiences were. It is important to explore this pre-delusional state of puzzlement from the ABC perspective. In our experience, two common reactions are to think either that one is going mad, with associated fear, or that someone is playing a trick or worse, and feel wary and suspicious. It can be therapeutic to unearth concerns from this pre-delusional stage, such as the fear of going mad, and to work therapeutically with them. What this also re-awakens is the sense of urgency and the search for meaning which existed; delusions carry the considerable psychological force of having eased this sense of anxiety and confusion, and perhaps allayed fundamental fears of going mad.

So far the therapist has begun the process of challenging the delusional belief, reframed the delusion as an attempt to make sense of certain experience (e.g. primary symptoms, trauma) and raised the idea that the delusion is psychologically motivated (i.e. eases puzzlement). The therapist and client may now pursue this last idea further by considering other possible psychological functions the delusion may serve. The evaluative beliefs associated with the delusional (inferential) beliefs, as we saw in the previous chapter, hold the key to the psychological function of the delusion. The therapist therefore proceeds to once again connect the evaluative and delusional beliefs, second, convey the nature of this connection in terms of a psychological function (e.g. delusion defends against negative self-evaluation), and third, dispute and test the associated evaluative beliefs. This process actually extends the redescription of the delusion offered above—a reaction to and attempt to make sense of certain experience—in that it attaches a further psychological motivation.

Assessing the Delusion and the Alternative

Finally the client and therapist would assess the delusion and alternative in the light of the available evidence and previous discussion, and the therapist may spell out advantages of the alternative interpretative framework. In this vein, for some clients the possible function of a belief is discussed by relating it to the client's experiences.

In order to illustrate the process so far, a case example follows of the process of weakening a delusion through verbal challenge.

Larry

One of the beliefs held by Larry (see Lowe & Chadwick, 1990) was that he had been Jesus Christ in a prior life. He reported having first realised this while he was in hospital over the Easter weekend, when he was undoubtedly acutely disturbed. There had been a prior admission to hospital two years earlier. By the second admission Larry already believed that he had been Leonardo da Vinci in a past life.

Two examples follow of the inconsistency and irrationality inherent in the belief. First, Larry said that while he was in hospital his mind was being read by millions of people and he claimed that a similar thing had been exerienced by Jesus. In support of this claim Larry pointed to Jesus's foreknowledge of both his subsequent betrayal by Judas and his being denied three times by Peter. However, the researcher pointed out that, if anything, these examples suggested that Jesus was reading other people's mind, or at least predicting their behaviour; they did not suggest that his own mind was being read by others. A second example centred on Larry's belief that Jesus had been a schizophrenic. The realisation that he had been Jesus was accompanied by the realisation that Jesus had suffered from schizophrenia. Larry held that by the time of his crucifixion, Jesus had completely lost his sanity. His contention was that Jesus's claims to have performed miracles were like the claims made by people who had been diagnosed as schizophrenic whom Larry had met when in hospital. However, it was pointed out that in the New Testament a key element to the miracle stories was that they were witnessed. As such, the biblical stories were quite different from the unsupported claims made by those people Larry had met in hospital.

The thrust of the alternative explanation put forward to account for Larry's belief that he was Jesus was that it arose in response to and as an attempt to make sense of his experiences leading up to and during the Easter weekend. He described these experiences, which included feeling that 'his head was on fire' and that he was being misunderstood and persecuted, similar to being crucified. At that time he also believed that he had written a third bible (i.e. a sequel to the New Testament)—although he no longer believed this. A combination of the parallels he perceived between his life and the life of Jesus, and his acutely confused state, led him to make the inference that he had been Jesus.

The psychological motivation for the belief was hypothesised to be twofold. First, it helped restore a degree of stability and calm, after his traumatic experiences. Second, the nature of the associated evaluations indicated that the belief might be helping prevent negative self-evaluations concerning his worth as a 'schizophrenic'. On his first admission to hospital he had been told that he was suffering from schizophrenia but no one had attempted to explain what this meant. Although he had no insight into the link between his beliefs and illness, Larry did think that he had been ill and the label became part of his self-concept—he was a schizophrenic. The second breakdown was a threatening experience in that it signified Larry's problem had not been a one-off.

Using thought chaining the therapist and Larry clarified first that he believed many other people viewed him as a 'nutter', a worthless person, because of his illness. Second, when Larry was asked to temporarily believe that the delusion was false, it was apparent that he would then endorse the negative evaluation and judge himself to be a nutter, a flawed person. Believing that Jesus had been a schizophrenic helped Larry resist this negative self-evaluation, though the defence was only partial. This insight allowed him and the therapist to dispute the idea that being labelled as having schizophrenia lowered his self-worth.

The interpretation that the delusion served to check negative self-evaluation was strengthened by an independent line of enquiry. The therapist asked Larry what the realisation that he had been Jesus added to the earlier realisation that he had been Leonardo. The subsequent discussion revealed that it related neither to concerns about death, nor to a sense of self-enhancement, but that it did explain why he was schizophrenic—Jesus had been, and he had the same mind. (Larry was able to account for why Leonardo had not been schizophrenic by modifying his belief and introducing the idea that just as a mind 'became tired and ill', so to, it could recover, and therefore was ill only in alternate lives. This it did during Leonardo's lifetime.)

In support of the alternative the researcher drew upon the prior discussion of the evidence, and of the plausibility of the alternative. Also, a number of additional points were made. These included pointing to the way Larry had had to revise the belief in order to keep it consistent with his belief that he had also been Leonardo in a prior life. It also seemed strange that although a number of features of Leonardo's life had filtered through into Larry's consciousness (including sketches of a helicopter) not one aspect of Jesus's life had filtered through in this way. Again, it was pointed out that the notion that Jesus had been reborn twice in the shape of Leonardo and Larry went against the New Testament teachings. The idea of the Second Coming was a key one in Christian thought and was at odds with Larry's belief.

In fact Larry's conviction fell and he himself began to generate counter-evidence. Thus, he began one session saying 'About me thinking I was Jesus. Well did I tell you when I was born? I was born on Good Friday. I was ill, I was in hospital, I had my birthday, so I put it all together . . .'

Empirical Testing

It is an integral part of cognitive therapy that the belief or assumption under consideration be put to empirical test. Reality testing, as it is known, involves planning and performing an activity which validates or invalidates a belief, or part of a belief. Beck et al. (1979) call these activities 'behavioral experiments', conveying that they are performed in order to test a hypothesis. Although such activities can have direct therapeutic effects (e.g. passing a driving test), the primary purpose of a cognitive therapist using empirical testing is to gain *cognitive* change (e.g. weaken the belief that the client is a complete failure).

Fennell (1989) provides a very clear procedure for how the therapist negotiates a test with the client. This is:

1. specify the inference the test is assessing (If . . . then . . .)
2. review existing evidence for the predicted outcome
3. devise a specific experiment to test the validity of the prediction
4. note and learn from the results
5. draw conclusions from this specific test.

All we would add to this is that when working with delusions, we set up a clear alternative belief in opposition to the delusion and clarify with the client in advance precisely what has to happen for each to be supported and refuted.

Occasionally a client will suggest how he might prove his delusion was true; when this happens, the therapist can examine if this might be developed into a reality test. However, proving that something is true is not the same as testing it. Again, it is essential to point out to clients what they are *not* predicting, as well as what they are, and to agree that if this turned out to be the outcome then this would falsify the belief and support the therapist's alternative. Both predictions must be specific and definite— clients must be pinned down to a statement specifying that this will happen in that time period.

For example, Nigel claimed to have special powers, including being able to know what people were going to say before they said it and being able to make things happen by simply thinking it. Nigel thought the power might be something to do with God. He reported having held the belief for three years and having never once doubted it. He was preoccupied with the belief four or five times a day; at these times he felt some sadness and anxiety. On one occasion he said the power made him want to kill himself because it was interfering so much with his life; in particular his enjoyment of television was spoilt by his sense of knowing what was about to be said, and indeed, he often would not bother watching. Also it gave him a sense of certainty at the betting shop which his winnings did not justify! The test with Nigel was straightforward and was initially suggested by him as a way of proving his power. Several different video recordings were put on 'pause' at prearranged times, and he was then asked to say what was coming up next. In practice Nigel did not get a single one right, out of over 50, and he concluded that he did not have the power after all.

Another man, Daniel, believed that he was Elvis Presley and suggested several ways in which he could prove this, and these formed the basis of the reality test. One was to tape record him singing an Elvis song, to play it to ten people, and to ask each of them who the 'famous rock singer' was. Another was for him to provide the lyrics for any Elvis song and provide details about any aspect of Elvis' life. Once again this simple test proved effective in reducing conviction.

Testing is not always so powerful. The reality test agreed upon with Bette, the client who believed herself to be an evil person who contaminated others, was to discover whether those people whom she believed she affected adversely concurred with this opinion. To begin with Bette came up with a five-point definition of what she understood by the term evil. Those people whom Bette felt both would classify her as evil according to her definition and whom she affected adversely were then asked to classify her according to the definition. Not one of the five people agreed that Bette was either evil or a harmful influence on others. All five stated independently that Bette did satisfy one criterion out of the five—occasionally having bad thoughts about people—but added that in their opinion this was true of most people and was not a necessary hallmark of an evil person. This test produced a strong but transient reduction in conviction.

It is commonly held that a well-planned and executed empirical test is the most powerful way to induce a person to change a belief (e.g., Piasecki & Hollon, 1987). As Beck puts it: 'There is no easy way to "talk the patient out" of his conclusions that he is weak, inept, or vacuous . . . By helping the patient change certain behaviors, the therapist may *demonstrate* to the patient that his negative, overgeneralized conclusions were incorrect' (Beck et al., 1979, p. 118).

This has not been our experience. To begin with we find that when this type of empirical risk-taking test is used as an opening intervention it has produced little or no effect, or the effect is large but fleeting (Chadwick et al., 1994), perhaps because strongly held beliefs are 'immunised' against disconfirmation (Popper, 1977). The effects are less impressive than those observed when verbal challenge is used as a first intervention. If reality testing alone were the most powerful way to weaken beliefs this would not be the case. Rather, it is as if the client first needs the alternative conceptual framework that comes from verbal challenge in order to be able to assimilate and make sense of empirical refutation (Trower, Casey, & Dryden, 1988).

Another point against the claim for the potency of reality testing alone, or using it in the first instance, is that when one studies how individuals respond to it (and verbal challenge) one finds enormous variation. For one person reality testing might be a telling intervention and conviction might plummet; for another it might have absolutely no impact; for a third conviction changes, but does so very slowly. Generalities about the effectiveness of an intervention seem to us to ignore how outcome is a complex interaction of therapy, therapist and client.

It might be argued that the effectiveness of reality testing depends not on its relationship to verbal challenge, but solely on the adequacy of the chosen tests. This remains a possibility, but it is difficult to know *in advance* what constitutes a 'good' test of a belief because the literature contains very few pointers on the composition of the test itself. A rare clue is offered by Beck et al., (1979) who recommended that a 'significant other' be included. This seems sensible, but again the reader is warned against thinking that this will assure success; in our research reality tests involving significant others have at times produced a big change and at others no change. This difficulty explains precisely why reality tests are negotiated; it is the clients who establish the adequacy of the tests and this is why therapy is always trying to work from within the client's perspective.

A second type of test is shame-attacking, which is more about challenging evaluations than inferences (Ellis, 1962). In shame-attacking the individual attempts to directly confront his fears by deliberately failing, making a fool of himself, etc. (see Chapter 2). Shame-attacking can often be used to test evaluations associated with delusions. Steve, for example, believed that people were frequently discussing and referring to him and perhaps plotting to harm him because they evaluated him negatively for being soft, weak and homosexual. This experience was most acute when he was walking along the street because he believed that he had a 'strange walk' which provoked amusement and ridicule and revealed his homosexuality. The shame-attack discussed with him was that rather than try to disguise his idiosyncratic walk, he might actually exaggerate it and make it even more 'strange', and in this way discover that there was nothing crushing and terrible in people maybe thinking that he and his walk were funny.

In the final section of this chapter we describe Derek's experience of cognitive therapy for delusions, which combines all the components looked at in this chapter. Therapy lasted a total of 20 weekly sessions, lasting around 60–90 minutes each, with an additional three follow up sessions over a six month period. Eleven sessions were spent building rapport and on cognitive assessment and formulation, and nine sessions on intervention. The therapist was Paul Chadwick.

Derek

Derek was a man in his late twenties who was currently out of work. He was married for the second time and had no children. Discussion of his childhood revealed that he was particularly close to his father, but there were no obvious signs of a difficult relationship with siblings or parents. Indeed, childhood recollections were of a happy and ordinary upbringing.

Derek was a likeable man. He was popular at school and his sexual development was smooth. However, when he was 18 his father died suddenly and tragically in a traffic accident. His father had been alone in the car and it emerged during therapy that Derek felt a sense of guilt about not having accompanied his dad on the journey. Within a few months he and his first wife separated, and a few months after this he was admitted to hospital and given a diagnosis of paranoid schizophrenia.

According to case notes from that period Derek presented with experiences of reference and thought broadcasting, and claimed to have great power. His mood was also low. Approximately one year later he was admitted following an overdose; at this point notes indicated that he was 'preoccupied with his father's death' over which he felt a personal responsibility.

In essence the clinical picture was much the same when cognitive therapy began, except that the experiences of reference and thought broadcasting had diminished considerably in frequency and intensity. In addition it was clear from assessment that Derek experienced occasional auditory hallucinations. The delusion was that he could communicate with people from the past and thereby change the course of history; in particular he believed he could prevent unnecessary death, saying 'no one would die other than from natural causes'.

Conviction was total or near total at every assessment session. As to the slight doubt that Derek occasionally expressed about the truth of the delusions, he referred to his dad's death and said: 'It's because I saw his body, dead. And I felt his hand. And his neck was black. That's the 5% uncertainty. I saw his body in the coffin.'

Derek was very concerned to enquire if the therapist believed him, and in a good-natured fashion would say what he thought of the replies. On one occasion, referring to the thought broadcasting he asked:

C: Have you ever heard voices, my voice?

T: No, I haven't.

C: (Smiling broadly) Bloody liar. You're a bloody liar. It's against your job prospects to tell me, that's what it is.

Derek was having delusional thoughts many times a day and at these times he felt very anxious. His BDI score at assessment was 20, indicative of moderate depressive symptomatology. The behaviour associated with the delusion was to watch television and await news of tragedies such as accidents, wars and murders. On hearing of such an event he would concentrate very hard to transmit the details to people in the past in the hope that this would change history and prevent the accident ever occurring.

Each week Derek observed numerous examples of confirmation, many of which were ambiguous. Some of the evidence was very consistent with the belief. One week, for example, a child tragically died and the police were subsequently criticised for having received a lead and not followed it up properly. During assessment he never once reported an instance of disconfirmation in spite of the numerous failed attempts to change history.

Exploration of past doubt, and testing RTHC went as follows:

T: Derek, I know you said that when you recall seeing and touching your dad's dead body, you doubt that you can change history. Have there ever been other times when you have doubted that you can change history?

C: There was one time when two local people died in a plane crash. I tried damned hard on old repeats of programmes and videos but nobody listened, nothing happened. I doubted for a while then.

T: Is there anything you can think of which if it happened today, would then make you doubt the belief?

C: No.

T: Right. Is there any way you could show people that your belief is true?

C: Yes, by winning the football pools, by making a video and using my power to get rich.

T: If you did win the pools in that way it would be very strong evidence that you had this power. If the attempt did not win, would this alter your belief at all?

C: It would mean that whoever I did it with lacked the will or the receptive powers.

Challenging the Evidence
One of the firmest items of evidence Derek put forward was that during his various contacts with other psychiatric patients, many had told him that they heard voices. He had inferred that they heard his voice and therefore this proved that his thoughts were indeed broadcast to others. By way of questioning this interpretation the therapist presented Derek with examples of the typical content of voices, and of two individuals in particular (obviously protecting their identity). One voice threatened to kill the woman who heard it, and another told the woman to shave her hair and eyebrows and cut herself. It was abundantly clear that these women and other hallucinators were not hearing Derek's thoughts, and it was speculated that perhaps there might be a connection between these women's voices and things which had happened to them in childhood and later life. Derek accepted this interpretation and expressed a sense of relief that he was not responsible for people hearing voices, as it had been apparent to him in hospital that for many people it was a distressing experience.

Challenging the Delusion

Challenging the delusion involved two main themes. First, the belief that he was the 'key to history' was construed as an understandable but mistaken reaction to, and attempt to make sense of, the experiences of thought broadcasting ('I'd think of something and they'd copy it'), reference (advertising cornflakes when he was eating them in the morning) and voices ('I'd pick up a pint and John Wayne would say "He's picking up his pint"' or 'I'd hear "He's going to die" on the TV'). Second, these experiences were construed as being related to strong evaluative beliefs and feelings evoked in Derek by the traumatic death of his dad.

To begin with, the therapist highlighted instances of irrationality and inconsistency within the belief system. One example involved two claims made by Derek that were contradictory. The first of these was that the government was instructing the medical profession to give Derek medication in an attempt to subdue his ability to communicate with people from the past. Derek justified this claim by stating that the government was afraid of what might happen if he was allowed to exercise his powers, and explained that the government's fear was largely responsible for his remaining out of the public limelight. The second and conflicting claim was that at peak television viewing time Prince Charles had issued Derek with a personal warning not to attempt to change the course of history. Derek said that in the warning Prince Charles both referred to Derek by name and supplied information on the nature of Derek's abilities. The therapist pointed out that inconsistency inherent in these two claims, one of which described him and his power as unknown and the second of which meant inevitably that he was known to a large portion of the public.

Derek and the therapist discussed how the delusion might be thought of as a reaction to the puzzling and alarming experiences of thought broadcast and reference. These experiences were initially discussed in terms of being indications of a breakdown in psychological well-being following the death of his dad and the end of his marriage. As was shown in Chapter 3, the therapist was able to chart how Derek had progressed from puzzlement, through a number of delusional elaborations, to arrive at the full delusion. The therapist put forward this developmental account as a way of demonstrating to Derek that his belief could be seen as being both a reaction to and a way of making sense of his experiences of reference and thought broadcasting.

It was argued that part of what made the delusion seem so compelling was that it removed the overwhelming bewilderment and anxiety he was experiencing at that time. In the sense that Derek's new understanding lessened this confusion, the therapist indicated that Derek's belief might be thought of as functional. It was argued that the delusion was false because from Derek's own perspective it was neither internally nor externally consistent.

This account was offered to Derek as a plausible alternative interpretation of his experiences. The therapist pointed out that within the context of Derek's experiences at the time the belief was understandable. However, given that there was an alternative explanation, it was useful to weigh up the two in the light of the available evidence. It was argued that the alternative interpretation was both more plausible and better supported. To support this contention Derek's attention was drawn to a number of points, including the following. First, the multitude of occasions on which Derek had unsuccessfully tried to change history went against his belief and offered support for the alternative. Second, further support was provided by the multitude of people, including family and close friends, who over the years had said that they did not hear what Derek claimed to have heard said on the television and radio. It seemed inconceivable, for instance, had Derek's mother and sister also heard the television and radio talking to him, that they would not have said so.

Derek's experiences of reference and thought broadcasting were not denied; nor was he told that these behaviours were signs of schizophrenia. He was reassured that these experiences were 'real'—it was his interpretation of them that was under scrutiny. It was speculated that they, like the delusion, seemed to be connected to the trauma and loss that he had experienced shortly before their onset.

Thought chaining when the delusion was assumed momentarily to be true revealed evaluative themes and related emotions concerned with Derek's sense of guilt and self-blame for tragedies, and negative evaluations of others for not doing more to help him prevent them. These evaluations were explored in therapy. Thought chaining was also explored in relation to the delusion being false, and this revealed a strong sense of powerlessness and helplessness surrounding his loss. It was discussed how the formation of the delusion some eight years earlier might have been motivated by a need to avoid facing these themes at the time of his dad's death.

At several points late on in the therapy Derek expressed loss at the wasted years spent believing and hence trying to change history. The therapist reiterated that the belief may have been adaptive in helping him to cope with so much loss and such overwhelming feelings.

Reality Testing
Midway through the verbal challenge, at a point when conviction had dropped, Derek suggested the reality test and actually requested that it be done in order for him to get clear in his mind if he had the power to change history. The proposed test was to make a video recording of Derek speaking to different people on a Wednesday, and then on the following Sunday to play it back while reading out

the weekend football results. Derek believed that he would be able to transmit the information to himself, on Wednesday as it were, and become rich. In fact Derek's conviction increased during the unsuccessful attempts to win the pools and the experience was perhaps too uncomfortable. The nature of this discomfort was only partly the lack of success, and more to do with Derek's experience of discovering the impossibility of what he believed; how could he be at one and same time reading the results on a Sunday and receiving a message from the future on Wednesday?

Outcome

The aim of therapy had been to reduce Derek's distress and delusional behaviour and preoccupation. Also, to draw his attention to connections between his dad's death and the nature of his experiences, and to begin perhaps to ease distress and blocked grieving.

Derek took much from therapy. Overall there was a sustained fall in conviction of about 30%. He became far less preoccupied with his delusion, and was usually much less distressed by it—although there were times when it remained as distressing as ever. His sense of guilt also eased considerably, in that he no longer blamed himself when his attempts to change history failed, and indeed, these attempts became fewer. His BDI scores having been consistently in the range of moderate depressive symptomatology, fell steadily over the course of the follow-up period.

Comment

It is tempting when considering Derek to think that he might have been better served if therapy had gone straight for the evaluative beliefs. This was a possibility. One of the major developments in our practice over the past decade has been an increasing emphasis on evaluations in our work with delusional beliefs. However, it is only too easy to underestimate the force of delusional thinking, and in practice it is difficult to sidestep delusions altogether. In general, we would offer two pieces of advice. First, the question of where to begin. Our impression is that certain individuals are very much wrapped up in their symptoms, this is where their energy is, and that for these individuals the delusion represents the most promising starting point for cognitive therapy. We think Derek was one such person. Second, we repeatedly find that some clients work much better at a delusional (inferential) level during any stage of therapy, whereas others effect emotional change more successfully by working primarily with the underlying evaluations. We try to adapt our practice accordingly.

SUMMARY

In this chapter we have described in detail the conceptual and practical steps in cognitive therapy for delusions. This process rests on methods of weakening evaluative beliefs as well as delusional inferences, and emphasises the importance of gaining insight into likely psychological functions of delusions.

Chapter 5

VOICES: ENGAGEMENT AND ASSESSMENT

ENGAGING CLIENTS WHO HEAR VOICES

The process of cognitive therapy with voices is one of working in an atmosphere of 'collaborative empiricism'. The goal of the opening, or engagement stage is to encourage the client to view the distress as arising from beliefs about voices, not being an automatic product of the hallucination. To achieve this the therapist needs to work with the client to overcome a number of obstacles to engagement, in the form of beliefs and expectancies the client has about the therapist, the process of therapy, and the voice's likely reaction.

Engaging individuals who hear voices can be especially difficult, perhaps because they experience such an impressive activating event in the hallucination. Therefore in addition to those general problems and possible solutions to the engagement problem discussed in Chapter 2, in this chapter we cover additional aspects of engaging people with voices. Three central strategies for promoting engagement are weakening specific beliefs which threaten progress, encouraging awareness of and contact with other voice hearers, and enhancing useful coping behaviour the client already possesses.

Finally, we proceed to describe and illustrate with case material our cognitive assessment of voices.

The Process of Engagement

As ever, the relationship should be safe and collaborative and the therapist pushes the idea that she is committed to reducing the client's distress and disturbance and thereby of improving his quality of life. As we have shown (Chadwick & Birchwood, 1994; 1995), distress is not simply the product of 'hearing voices' but also of beliefs about those voices; but the task of encouraging a client to question and explore the nature of his voices can be very difficult. When a therapist in a collaborative way explores and empathises with a client's reactions to hearing voices, she is probably knowingly or unknowingly chipping away at a number of beliefs and fears the client holds about her (e.g. she will put me in hospital), about therapy (e.g. I am too stupid to do it), and about how the powerful voices are likely to react (e.g. they will seize their chance and take complete control). Certain of these are specific to voices, and it is to these that we now turn.

Blocking Beliefs

General concerns (e.g. a fear of being controlled) may assume an added importance for people who hear voices, and there are certain fears about therapy which are particular to such individuals (e.g. that a therapist cannot understand what it is like to hear voices, or will enrage the voices). Although we have in mind the ABC model, we do not set out to examine and dispute and test blocking beliefs explicitly. Rather we have found it more helpful to slowly and often implicitly offer a particular view of how we as therapists work, how we view people who hear voices, and how we view the process of therapy.

Therapist as Controlling

Clients are often concerned that the therapist will be controlling, perhaps by forcing the pace in therapy. Given that most clients are already struggling with powerful voices, this fear is especially important to address.

It helps to recognise the client's strength in living with voices, and how this experience makes him ideally placed to determine the pace of therapy. We routinely offer and even encourage the use of a 'panic button' to enable escape from therapy without penalty. This strategy has a paradoxical effect in that the more assured a client is that he may withdraw from therapy, the more likely he is to invest in the therapeutic endeavour. A therapist might say something like:

T: 'I'm certainly not going to make you do anything you don't want to, there's no point in that. What we usually do is to build on individuals' ability to deal with their voices and to suggest a number of ideas and ways of thinking about them that other people have found helpful. If you like the ideas and you want to give them a try, that's fine; if you think it is not for you just say so, there's no problem. What I would like you to do is to give the whole thing a chance. How do you feel about that?'

Therapist will not Understand What it is Like to Hear Voices

What is usually behind this belief is the idea that because a therapist does not hear voices, she is not going to be able to help the client. Although we do not agree with this premise, we do acknowledge that it is entirely reasonable to worry about a therapist's ability to help. We do not tackle this belief directly, in a defensive way, but seek to convey the impression that we understand a lot about the experience of hearing voices and that the cognitive approach helps certain people, although there are no guarantees.

We find the cognitive ABC approach very useful in this respect because it clarifies which parts of an individual's experience the therapist is and is not able to understand intuitively. It may be that many therapists are unable to understand what it is actually like to hear a voice (the A) in the same way that they might understand anger, depression, anxiety. Certainly we do not feel able to do this and we acknowledge this to our clients. But what seems to us very understandable are the ways our client's make sense of their voices (the Bs) and the associated emotion and behaviour (the Cs).

We think it is critical that a client emerge from the engagement phase feeling that the therapist appreciates these aspects of his experience of voices. Therefore when working with voices it helps us greatly to draw on our research on voices (Chadwick & Birchwood, 1994; 1995; 1996). In particular it is important to be aware of the concepts of omnipotence and omniscience, the connections between malevolence and benevolence and affect and behaviour, and to use this knowledge to anticipate how a client may be feeling or inclined to behave, or what he may believe.

Omnipotence. The belief that a voice is very powerful and usually inescapable leads many individuals to feel 'caught in the voice's power' (Bauer, 1979). They also often feel depressed and ultimately helpless. The prospect of challenging omnipotent voices is risky and clients often feel anxiety about it.

Omniscience. This refers to the knowledge a voice is inferred to possess about an individual's thoughts, behaviour, fears, experience and self evaluation. Such beliefs can render the individual exposed, vulnerable and in awe of the voice. One client heard the voice of 'two old school friends' deriding and tormenting her about a minor peccadillo and urging self harm. The following observations were made:

T: 'I imagine that like many voice hearers, you have been amazed by what they seem to know about you . . . Have there been times when the voice told you to do something that you didn't want to do and you thought "they seemed to know so much about me, they must be powerful, I'd better do as they ask, just in case?"'

Compliance. Compliance with imperative voices is a complex issue. People who evaluate their voices as benevolent are well disposed to comply with commands, but feel conflict when these commands become life threatening. Those who believe their voices to be malevolent are ill-disposed to comply with voices, but they do so at times either through exhaustion or fear; this creates a different type of conflict. Therapists might say 'I expect there may have been times when you've reluctantly gone along with the voices to stop them nagging' or 'Some voice hearers say that when they do give in to the pressure to comply, they later feel guilty and cross with themselves'.

Losing confidence. 'Benevolent' voices evoke a positive affect which is not itself problematic; few benevolent hallucinators present to services (Romme & Escher, 1994). However, disempowerment, dependence and loss of confidence are common in this group. In our series there have been many who hold secret fears about the impact of their engagement and involvement with their voices.

Let us consider the case of Alice who hears voices she believes come from the Islamic prophet Masuuia. The voices were imperative in nature and covered every aspect of her day-to-day routine e.g., 'change his nappy'; 'he does not like pizza, do curry'. In fact much of her day-to-day behaviour was voice-driven. Although she believed the voice had 'chosen' her and she felt honoured, she was nevertheless aware of a steadily diminishing loss of confidence and increasing dependence on the voice.

Blocking Beliefs About Voices' Reaction To Therapy

One indication of clients' unease with therapy and the therapeutic relationship is comments about the therapists by the voices themselves. Our earliest experience of drop-out from cognitive therapy was that it was linked to voices expressing anxiety about treatment or about the trustworthiness of the therapist. Examples given by clients have included,

'don't listen to that bastard', 'remember your faith, don't put your t
her', or direct threats 'if he doesn't kill you we will (laughter)'.

Our initial experience, was that once such comments had been madc, uie
therapeutic relationship was already in jeopardy and sometimes difficult
to salvage—it was as if clients were externalising and therefore rationalis-
ing their own decisions. Anticipating that voices may comment adversely
about the therapist is one method of prevention against this and can
enhance therapist credibility. Alice, a woman we refer to frequently in
this chapter heard a voice she believed to be an Islamic prophet, Masuma.
In the following dialogue the therapist does just this and it leads to an
important disclosure:

T: Many people have said that their voices don't like people like me
discussing them. Has this happened with you?.

P: Well right through today's sessions the voices kept on saying 'remember your faith, remember your faith'.

Voices Are Too Powerful

One of the key findings in our research on voices has been the regularity
with which people attribute great power to voices. It follows from this
that assessment and therapy needs to be sensitive and gradual. As individuals begin to glean that therapy would involve a change in their
relationship with voices, many express concern that voices are too powerful to be challenged.

Challenging the belief that voices are omnipotent is a major test in cognitive therapy, and even in the assessment stage the therapist begins to chip
away at this. One particularly useful and comfortable way to begin this
process is by encouraging the client to stand back and use knowledge of
everyday behaviour to reconsider voices' behaviour. To the extent that
the normal construct is accepted, then an apparently mysterious and
unpredictable force becomes commonplace and understandable. Armed
with such understanding, the individual can begin to develop an intellectual mastery, the start of a process whereby the omnipotence or mystique
of the voice is challenged.

The notion that relationships with voices are to a degree interpersonally
normal (Benjamin, 1989) provides further opportunities for 'normalising
the abnormal'. Likening voices to a nosy neighbour is an analogy used by
Romme & Escher (1994), one which depicts the voice as an unwanted
intruder driven by curiosity and envy. Let us return to Alice for whom
this analogy proved fruitful.

T: Let me put the situation to you, it's the kind of thing that everyone will have experienced. Just suppose you had a really nosy neighbour who was forever poking his nose into your business. Let's imagine that you have tried to avoid this person at all costs; you rush indoors when he's not looking, you know the sort of thing?

C: Ah ha.

T: Let's suppose you wanted to make the nosy neighbour even nosier and more intrusive . . .

C: Worse you mean . . . you'd invite them in once or twice, then you'd really have trouble getting rid of them?

T: And if you wanted to stop the neighbour being so intrusive?

C: You'd have to put your foot down, say you're busy, maybe come back when you've more time, that sort of thing you mean?

T: Would it be easy?

C: No, because you wouldn't want to upset them, you'd have to say it in a kind way, but stick to your guns.

T: Voices behave like a nosy neighbour I think: they come in when they're not wanted even if you're busy doing something else. One can get apprehensive in case they appear; avoids doing things that 'invite them in' . . . sounds familiar? One client we know gets fed up with the interruptions, she sometimes shouts at them and sometimes she gives in and does what the voice asks. If this was just like a nosy neighbour what would you advise?

C: You say that she has to put her foot down again.

T: How could she do that, what comes into your mind?

C: She could say, 'I'll talk to you later when I have got more time', that kind of thing.

T: Should she avoid going places to avoid bumping into the neighbour?

C: No, she'd never be able to relax or be at ease.

T: Say the voice/neighbour got upset?

C: That's the neighbour's problem . . . but it won't be nice not getting on with your neighbours, you want a quiet life.

This type of discussion also raises the important point that voices have a voracious appetite for attention and unless the individual is able to impose strict limits he will gradually lose control and autonomy.

One of the main sources of a voice's power is its presumed intimate and exhaustive knowledge about the client (Chadwick & Birchwood, 1994). A further useful stereotype with which to liken such voices is a blackmailer, in that voices use this knowledge in a threatening way which encourages conformity and subservience. This conveys that what is required is to resist falling into this role.

There are further ways of gently normalising voices by making the client more aware of how they are predictable and understandable. Many of the situations that trigger or exacerbate voices are ones which clients find stressful. Establishing a connection between stress and voice activity begins to question the view of voices as powerful and superhuman, and portrays them as spiteful and weaker and as getting at people when they are at their most vulnerable. Clients are usually quick to recognise how voices feed on insecurity and vulnerability, and thereby to see that if they were less vulnerable and insecure, the voices' ability to control and frighten would be greatly reduced.

A good way to introduce this is to check if voice activity is greater on days with a therapy session, because for most clients sessions are stressful.

T: Are your voices worse or better at any time of the day?

C: As I go to sleep and first thing in the morning.

T: Did you get any this morning?

C: Yes they went on at me all morning.

T: Are they still at it?

C: They've died down now.

T: Is that usual?

C: Happens occasionally.

T: I recall it happened last week when we met. Is there a link? Going to appointments for many people can be quite stressful; do you get a little on edge?

C: A little. I don't sleep much.

T: Do you think it's possible that the stress might have made your voices worse?

C: Could be.

T: Have you noticed if the voices are more active at other times when you are feeling stressed or vulnerable?

Similarly for certain individuals it is helpful to make explicit that they are calling up their voices, and therefore in this respect are in control. The following is abstracted from session 5 of therapy with a client Billy who believes his voices are from his 'real' mother and father who will eventually reveal themselves and make him wealthy.

T: You say the voices are more frequent when you are on your own, is that right?

C: When I fall asleep in my flat.

T: They are less frequent on the bus when you come here . . . what about right now, are you getting them now?

C: I've not had them for a while.

T: Last night in your flat the voices came?

C: Yes.

T: What were you doing at the time?

C: I was sort of half watching TV.

T: And they came? Think back to last night, why were you only half watching the TV?

C: It was a crap programme.

T: Were you thinking about your children again?

C: (Nods) Yes, I was upset.

T: Is this one of those occasions when you call the voices up?

C: (Nods)

In this instance the loneliness and despair about this client's estrangement from his children is a setting condition for his voices. It sheds light on a possible psychological motivation behind the voices and reveals a central psychological concern for the client.

Coping Strategy Enhancement (CSE)

We use CSE as in essence another engagement manoeuvre which connects to the idea of empowering clients and weakening the voice's omnipotent grip. It involves developing a coping repertoire and over-rehearsing it to facilitate an automatic coping response (Tarrier, 1992). From the perspective of this book, we use it in the following ways:

1. to underline the strength of the individual's attempts to cope with their voices;
2. as a means of underpinning the therapeutic alliance;
3. to develop an understanding of factors that 'cue' the voices;
4. develop an awareness of the abilities that the person may have to deal with them.

Several examples follow.

Katie hears mutiple voices that threaten to convert her to Buddhism. She feels that they are a threat to her baby and is frightened and anxious and wants them to stop. Assessment revealed that they are worse as she goes to sleep or when she has difficult decisions to make; when engaged in conversation during the interview there were no voices and subsequent questioning revealed that when in company the voices were 'in the background'. Again, in the session merely asking her to think about voices brought them on; discussing other topics subsequently diminished them.

For Katie CSE first involved congratulating on her endurance—her ability to withstand the voices' incessant activity over the years. Second, bearing in mind that when she was with others she heard no voice activity, it was advised that whenever she was feeling overwhelmed by her voices she should seek the company of the hostel workers whose co-operation was gained. Also, in order to help her to sleep, she was encouraged to experiment listening to music using a personal stereo with a 'sleep function' which turned off after a period of time. Both strategies proved helpful.

Jenny has a ten-year history of psychosis. Analysis reveals that her voices are worse in the morning but ease in the afternoon when she tends to be more active (however she was not aware of the link). It was suggested that her afternoon activity was helping considerably to lessen the voices. Thus on those days when she felt exhausted by them and wanted some relief, she was encouraged to be more active in the home: in particular engaging fellow residents of her hostel in conversation, shopping and so on. It was agreed to try the new strategy on one particular morning and to observe carefully whether it brought relief.

Note that it was not suggested that she use this strategy all the time but only selectively, as it was felt that over-use of this procedure would be tantamount to a form of avoidance and thus exacerbate fear. Against this, the strategy was helpful and was used later as 'evidence' that she could indeed exert control over a voice she has previously thought of as omnipotent.

Universality

One of the most demoralising aspects of hearing voices can be the sense of being isolated and alone and facing a unique problem. Clients rarely talk even to one another about their voices, for fear of being judged or criticised in some way. Engendering a sense of commonality with other voice hearers is an important aspect of engagement, one that is pursued in a variety of ways.

The pioneering work of Romme and Escher (1994) in setting up first in Holland and subsequently in the United Kingdom a Hearing Voices Network has shown how voice hearers find the experience of meeting one another to be empowering, reassuring and to reduce stigma. An important part of this group process—indeed, of dynamics in much of group psychotherapy—is universality (Yalom, 1970), that is, the recognition that other people struggle with the same or similar problems.

For these reasons we encourage voice hearers to listen to fellow voice hearers describing their experience either in person or on video. We too encourage clients to participate in groups for voice hearers, and we use this format to introduce the basics of the cognitive approach. These groups are either structured and symptom focused or looser and concerned more directly with issues of low self-esteem.

COGNITIVE ASSESSMENT OF VOICES

In the remainder of this chapter we describe the ABC assessment of voices and illustrate its use with a number of cases. Throughout we emphasise the distinction between the form of the voice (topography, locus, cues), content (commands, insults, commentary) and the individuals relationship with the voice (beliefs, affect, behaviour). We have argued and demonstrated the value of the ABC model in relation to voices by revealing how emotional and behavioural responses to voices reflect beliefs about those voices, and are therefore not direct products of the hallucination. The meaning ascribed a voice shapes the relationship with it.

Thus assessing the personal meaning a voice has for a person is the defining feature of the ABC cognitive approach to assessment. The delusional beliefs we have found to be most significant are those relating to a voice's identity, purpose, power, knowledge, and about the consequences of compliance and resistance. We have developed a semi-structured interview schedule (Appendix 2) to guide the exploration of As, Bs and Cs, and in the next section we look at each in turn.

Activating Events (As): Content

Very often clients confuse content with what they believe about the voice. In other words they are describing Bs as As—a common problem discussed earlier. For example, Howard believed the meaning of his voices was to announce when he would meet his real father whom he believed to be a famous rock star. When asked what the voices said, he replied, 'They keep telling me that I'll receive my true inheritance; that it will be announced in the future and asking me to be patient'. Close questioning revealed the voice actually to have said merely 'It won't be long Howard'. Also, clients sanitise what the voices say (e.g. omit swearing) and convert utterances into sentences; we try to get a verbatim account of content.

Some authors suggest the use of a diary method to monitor *in vivo* what the voices have said. Our experience with diaries is that they prove a major chore and have rarely been completed and if pushed too early in therapy can provoke disengagement. This may partly be the result of fear of the voice.

Voices usually speak with clarity and at normal volume, they are repetitive and their words have emotional force. Voices are brief (four to five words per utterance) and usually repetitive in nature. Most voice hearers report hearing more than one voice. Sometimes voices speak together, commonly in conversation or argument about the voice hearer, although individual voices may be experienced in distinct episodes. The majority of voices are perceived as male (Juninger & Frame, 1985); there is no connection to the sex of voice hearer, although there is some evidence that voices are more likely to be attributed an age comparable to that of the hearer. Some three quarters of voice hearers believe their voices to be from a different, usually superior, social class from their own. (The suspicion that voices are imbued with authority is one we develop at length later.)

There have been many systems offered for classification of voice content. Yet how a voice is classified often is determined by how an individual perceives it; in other words, an element of interpretation exists. For example, the statement 'go to London' may be perceived as a command or mere advice, or 'be careful' a threat or considerate warning.

The content of voices is nevertheless immensely variable in style, intonation and delivery, yet the majority of content can be allocated into a limited number of categories and this is the approach taken here. For a cognitive assessment specific examples of the clients' voices should be elicited; our semi-structured interview schedule (Appendix 2) provides some general categories to explore. The category probes are useful as clients find recall difficult particularly if the content is unpleasant or embarrassing, and we briefly discuss each one here.

The distinction between a command and suggestion rests on the client's interpretation and is not always clear cut. Perceiving a statement to be a command may reflect the tone of the voice or may stem from beliefs about the voice. The key thing is to record exactly what the voice says and clarify why the client interprets it in the way he does. We find it helpful to gauge the severity of commands and therefore distinguish between commands that involve harm to self or others (e.g. 'kill him'), are antisocial ('smash that window'), or minor imperatives ('make the tea').

Examples of suggestions include, 'the green shirt looks best', 'I wouldn't trust him, he's shifty', 'leave college, they've got it in for you'. As before, whether a voice is experienced as offering advice rests partly on interpretation. Comments interpreted as predictions tend to be of the following form: 'bread's cheaper at Tesco's' or 'your husband's coming home S, you'd better get up'. What characterises a prediction in the mind of the client is that it is capable of falsification and is not something that the client thinks he or she believes or already knows.

It is very common for voices to comment on clients' thoughts, behaviours or weaknesses, for example 'He's thinking about his money', 'What was the point of smiling at the milkman' and 'Yes, well done, you showed him the door alright!' A commentary is often characterised by a recurring theme, perhaps a client's appearance or sexuality.

The most commonly encountered utterances are brief terms of abuse or vulgarity, usually experienced as isolated insults (Juninger & Frame, 1985). Insults are easily understood and universal: swearing, laughing, sexual insults etc., are embedded in the culture and are rarely perceived differently by the client (e.g. as a compliment!).

Criticism by contrast is more personal and has subjective meaning. For example a voice saying 'He hates spaghetti' was interpreted as critical by Katie, who had just prepared this for her husband whom she was anxious to please. Criticism of this type often points towards the nature of the client's negative self-evaluations.

Bizarre and humorous voices are relatively unusual. Examples have included: 'Monster crabs claws for you old boy', 'He's not liked but he's well liked' and 'Seismic sex'.

Locus

There seems to be agreement that equal numbers of individuals report voices coming through their ears (externalisers) as originating inside their heads or minds (internalisers). If external, they are located either centrally or to the right; movement towards this locus does not make them louder. Internalisers usually identify the forehead as a locus and are able to separate this from the source of their thoughts; this challenges the traditional concept that internal voices are 'pseudo hallucinations' not definitely distinct from other thoughts.

Concurrent Symptoms

Although hallucinations may occur in a number of modalities, including visual, tactile and olfactory, in a review of 15 studies of people with a functional psychosis Slade & Bentall (1988) noted that on average auditory hallucinations were found to be present in 60% of patients. This compared with only 29% experiencing visual hallucinations, generally considered to be more often associated with organic brain syndromes (Goodwin, 1971).

Other auditory hallucinations frequently accompany the experience of hearing voices, including music (often choirs), banging doors and footsteps. Many describe a sense of 'presence' around them and this often has its origins in other hallucinations which typically include visual, olfactory, visceral and tactile modalities (Chadwick & Birchwood, 1994).

Cues and Contexts

Initially most voice hearers do not recognise that their voices are 'triggered' by events or feelings. It is an important aspect of assessment to clarify that this is so, and to explore the psychological meaning of the trigger.

Most commonly we find that voices are cued in settings where an individual perceives a psychological threat and feels distressed. This may for one person be isolation and loneliness. For many it is anxiety preceding and following therapy sessions. Similarly, voices can be active during uncomfortable silences in sessions. Thinking about voices is another common trigger, or being reminded of events that arouse guilt or anger. For example, for one man remembering being homosexually raped was sufficient to trigger a long period of voice activity.

Also, as with intrusive thinking in obsessional disorders, attempts to neutralise voices are almost invariably associated with increased activity. For example Jenny developed a neutralising strategy which involved saying the exact opposite of what her voice commanded, but she found that saying this to herself merely increased voice frequency or loudness. Perhaps no one thing is so commonly perceived to be a threat as other people. Strangers on a bus or in a shop, having to challenge authority, formal occasions are but some of the many such encounters associated with voice activity because it is these settings that expose clients' interpersonal vulnerabilities.

A minority of voice hearers are able to initiate contact. Keith, for example, simply calls out to his voices in his mind; another individual described entering into an 'altered state of consciousness' akin to a trance-like state. A number of individuals reported they could get in contact with their voices by listening to a particular radio or TV station and in one case by phoning the speaking clock! Sadness or dysphoria (but not fear) is mentioned by voice hearers in several studies as preceding voice activity, Hustig & Hafner, 1991. An intention to perform certain behaviours or acts is reported to precipitate voices of the commenting or critical variety. Nayani & David note that the intention to eat was cited as a trigger of voices in 50% of their sample. Watching television seems to be a particularly strong cue: clients typically report that a person on television was staring at them and the voice seemed to speak through the TV presenter as if talking about the individual.

Voice Topography

The majority of voice hearers experience numerous hallucinatory episodes every day. These episodes last no more than a few seconds or minutes in a third of people, up to one hour in some 50%, and are continuous in about a fifth. By and large, more frequent voices use a greater variety of words. The frequency, audibility, clarity and volume of voices can only be measured by self-report and several methods have been devised (see Garety, 1992). The self report measure we favour is the one devised by Harry Hustig from the University of Adelaide in Australia and is reproduced in Appendix 4 with permission. The scale measures frequency, audibility, clarity and affective response.

Assessing the Behaviour and Affect (Cs)

Coping Behaviour and Distress

There has been much research interest in the coping strategies used by voice hearers. Coping behaviour and distress varies greatly between individuals, and traditional approaches have struggled either to account for this variability or to identify universally good or poor coping behaviour and there is disagreement about whether it is generally better to have many or just one coping option (see Tarrier, 1987). However, one very helpful distinction was drawn by Slade and Bentall (1988) between strategies which focus attention on the voice, and those which divert attention.

Romme et al. (1992) report that successful copers tend to listen to their voices, do not tend to use distraction and view their voices as a positive phenomenon. Thus they urge people should accept their voices and invest in them. Similarly, focusing on a voice seems to be associated with less distress in the long term than distracting oneself from it (Haddock, Bentall & Slade, 1993; Slade & Bentall, 1988).

Our research on voices has established that behaviour and affect (Cs) associated with voices do indeed reflect the beliefs held about them. In particular those who regard their voices as malevolent tend to resist them (argue, shout back, avoid cues that trigger voices, use distraction, drink to excess or sleep), and those that believe them to be benevolent, engage with their voices (listen to them, call them up and willingly follow advice). Resistance goes with negative feelings of fear, guilt, anger, anxiety and depression; in contrast, engagement goes with an affect akin to reverence, elation.

Coping behaviour only becomes understandable, we believe, when it is connected to clients' beliefs about their voices. However in cases where clients have no overriding beliefs about the power or purpose of their voices, there seems to be a greater variety of behaviour or strategies and these are associated with the sense of the voices as irritating or unpleasant, in the sense for example that a tinnitus sufferer might construct his experience (Chadwick & Birchwood, 1995). This is in keeping with a cognitive perspective, because a clear and consistent behavioural and emotional disposition would be expected only when voices had a clear meaning to the individual. In those instances where a voice was interpreted as either malevolent of benevolent, and individuals either engaged or resisted, voice hearers still recognise the way certain behaviour may bring temporary relief (e.g. distraction) where others exacerbate the voices (e.g. shouting back). Identifying individual's strengths when dealing with his voice and enhancing them (Tarrier et al., 1993) is an important engagement manoeuvre and is included in our semi-structured interview schedule (Appendix 2).

Assessing Beliefs (Bs)

As in Chapter 3, we shall address the issue of assessing the delusions—in this case, beliefs about a voice's identity, meaning, power and control— and also the client's evaluative beliefs about himself and others. This information is essential to the cognitive approach and it is the prime focus for effecting emotional change.

Individuals interpret voices not as their own thoughts, but attribute them to others. Consequently it is possible to view an individual's relationship with a voice as interpersonal, and indeed the relationship shows many of the dynamics common in ordinary relationships (Benjamin, 1989). While it is known that a common first reaction to voices is puzzlement (Maher, 1988), individuals evolve different ways of interacting with their voices. Romme and Escher (1994) helpfully describe the process of belief formation in terms of three stages. These are the initial starting phase, characterised by uncertainty and fear. Next, during the organisation phase, voice hearers accept the experience and begin to determine the nature of the relationship with the voice. This flows into the stabilisation phase, when many people find a more consistent and less disruptive co-existence.

Beliefs about Voices

Power

The presumed power of voices is summarised by two core beliefs concerning compliance and control. Compliance beliefs come in two forms. The first concerns the inferred consequence of disobedience and obedience to imperative voices. For example, a client may believe 'If I don't do what my voices say, I will be harmed' on the basis of the evidence that in the past when he resisted commands something went wrong at home (father hit me, my dog died, the house was burgled).

A second compliance belief, that may operate in the absence of commands refers to presumed consequences of failure to listen or take the voice seriously. Clients typically believe things like 'If I ignore my voices I will miss something really important' or 'If I ignore them they'll get angry and they may harm me'. Typical evidence again is either voice behaviour (they shouted or threatened me) or an event which is attributed to the voices ('after I ignored the voice I could not talk and stood immobilised in the corridor for over an hour'). Nevertheless, like all delusional beliefs, these are not always seen by clients as being inferences which may or may not be true. The therapist is at pains to separate the As, B, and Cs when clarifying beliefs and evidence, as follows:

T: You were saying that when you refused to do what the voices told you yesterday you felt pains in your body and were anxious and thought this was a punishment for disobedience. Is that right?

C: Yes.

T: And because this pattern has happened a few times you are thinking to yourself that the voice might do it again if you disobey it in the future, and this makes you feel afraid?

More generally around 80% of voices are believed to be omnipotent, or very powerful. This appearance rests on four types of evidence. First, individuals report collateral symptoms that contribute to the sense of omnipotence. One man, for example, was commanded by his voice to kill his daughter; he recalled one occasion when she was standing by an open window and he experienced his body being moved towards her. A second man heard a voice telling him that he was the son of Noah, and occasionally when he heard his voice he experienced con-current visual hallucinations in which he was dressed in a white robe and walked on water. Second, individuals give examples of how they attribute events to their voices, and then cite the events as proof of the voices' great power. Thus, although two individuals cut their wrists under their own volition, both subsequently deduced that the voices had somehow made them do it. Similarly, one man attributed respon-sibility for his having sworn out loud in church to his satanic voices. Third, the majority of voice hearers are unable to influence either the onset and offset of their voices or what was said, once again suggestive of the voices' power.

Finally, very many voices give the impression of knowing all about people's past histories, their present thoughts, feelings and actions, and what the future holds—that is, of being omniscient. Frequently voices would refer to behaviour and thoughts of a highly personal and emotive nature, such as a criminal act or personal weakness, which the individual feared others knowing. Alice, for example, believes her voice to be a prophet and to possess superhuman knowledge about her, the past and the future. Her evidence for this is that the voice predicts the arrival home of her husband; tells her what page to read in the Koran to find an important meaning and knows about her concerns, particularly about her competence as a wife and mother.

Perhaps because of this lack of privacy, individuals often attribute more knowledge to the voice than the content actually displays; for instance, general statements like 'we know all about you', are thought to refer to specific actions. Understandably, this appearance of omniscience leaves many individuals feeling exposed and vulnerable.

Identity and Meaning

It is definitional to an auditory hallucination that the individual believes the voice to originate from someone of something other than himself. That is, clients make external attributions about the sources of their voices (Haddock, Bentall & Slade, 1993). Evidence for this external attribution might be 'the voices come through my ears', 'it's not my voice', 'it says things I would never say (e.g. swearing)', or 'I don't make it happen'. In our research we have been very keen to explore beyond a general external attribution to look at specific types of beliefs about a voice's identity and also its purpose or meaning—in effect, answers to the question: why am I hearing this particular voice?

Beliefs about identity and meaning, like those about omnipotence, usually reflect a combination of fact (Activating event) and inference (Belief). In particular, the same major sources of evidence are at work: voice content (the voice may have disclosed its identity); omniscience (the voice may reveal personal knowledge available to only a very few people), predictions (the voice may reveal superhuman attributes), and other symptoms (concurrent visual hallucinations perhaps of an angelic form).

The thought that the voices are omniscient and possess intimate personal knowledge about the individual's personal weaknesses, fears or worry of the moment, is an especially powerful piece of evidence for many clients' beliefs about identity and meaning, as are derealisation, experiences of control, visual and somatical hallucinations.

Malevolence and Benevolence

In a large majority of cases, an individual voice is believed to be intent either on harming the person (malevolent) or helping him (benevolent) and this distinction is of profound importance to assessment and therapy for voices.

Indeed, such is the importance of these two beliefs that we have devised and standardised a self-report questionnaire to assess them and their connection to emotion and behaviour. This measure, The Beliefs About Voices Questionnaire (BAVQ: Chadwick & Birchwood, 1995), which is reprinted in Appenix 3, accurately classifies 90% of individuals' voices. The BAVQ includes a simple rating of power, and our data indicate that the dimensions of power and malevolence/benevolence are orthogonal. Thus it is possible for a voice to be regarded as malevolent in intent but powerless; or powerful but of uncertain purpose. Clients' emotional distress may be eased by changes in beliefs about power, or malevolence/benevolence, or both.

Beliefs in malevolence are of two types; either the voice is an undeserved persecution, or a deserved punishment (Trower & Chadwick, 1995: these themes are developed fully in Chapter 7). An example of persecution is Keith whose voice swears and criticises him. He believes the voice to be Satan trying to get his scalp and drive him mad. An example of punishment is Maisie who hears a voice instructing her to commit suicide and to murder her family. She believes the voice to be God punishing her for an abortion.

Beliefs in benevolence are more varied, but include themes such as the voice protecting, guiding, or being especially interested in the client. In Table 6 we present the key points of the cognitive assessment of 12 people with voices, giving six further examples of benevolence and malevolence and distinguishing content, beliefs and evidence, distress and behaviour.

Assessing Evaluative Beliefs

When looking for evaluative beliefs associated with voices, we find it most helpful to begin with beliefs about a voice's identity and meaning— in particular the judgement about malevolence or benevolence. Beliefs that voices are malevolent or benevolent are formally speaking secondary delusions, one paranoid the other usually grandiose. Conceptually we follow others in viewing both as psychological defences of the self (Bentall et al., 1994; Neale, 1988) although we conceptualise paranoid beliefs related to either persecution or punishment separately because we think these are defences to fundamentally different threats to self (Trower & Chadwick, 1995: and see Chapter 7).

We believe that by using thought chaining it is possible in effect to go beyond the delusional defence and reveal the defended negative self-evaluations. As

Table 6 A Cognitive Assessment Of Six People's Voices Believed To Be Malevolent (1-6) And Six Benevolent (7-12)

Patient: sex, age, diag. and duration	Voice content	Beliefs: identity, meaning and effect of compliance	Evidence: content, symptom, attribution, influence	Affective response to voices	Behavioural response to voices
1. M 49 Schiz. >20 yrs	Imperative Told to rape and kill	I. Voice of Devil M. Being punished for killing someone C. Devil will drive me mad if don't obey	C. Content is evil and knows my thoughts and past S. Delusion of control I. None	Frightened Angry	Shouts back and swears (covert) Compelled to listen No compliance
2. M 43 Schiz. >20 yrs	Imperative 'Be careful' 'Try harder' No control over voice	I. Powerful witches who used to be neighbours M. Punishment for being noisy and stopping study C. If I con't obey they keep on at me	A. Recognise voices C. Read thoughts and know past I. None	Exhausted Tormented Scared	Shouts back and swears (covert) Compelled to listen and complies unwillingly
3. M 31 Schiz. 10 yrs	Imperative 'Be untidy' 'Don't wash'	I. First and only employer M. Controlling me and holding me back in life C. My intelligence is better than his so I don't obey	C. Reads thoughts and knows my past S. Delusions of control A. Voice gets worse if I make progress I. None	Irritated Depressed	Listens and argues with voice No compliance
4. M 29 Schiz. 10 yrs	Imperitive 'Kill yourself' 'Hit him' Abusive 'He's a rapist' 'He's a queer'	I. God and unknown woman M. Punished by God because done evil things C. If disobey will nag me and harm me	S. Thought insertion Experience of reference and control A. Voice knows all about me I. None	Tormented I hate it	Listens, argues, swears and shouts Some unwilling compliance

Table 6 (cont.)

Patient: sex, age, diag. and duration	Voice content	Beliefs: identity, meaning and effect of compliance	Evidence: content, symptom, attribution, influence	Affective response to voices	Behavioural response to voices
5. F 32 Schiz. 12 yrs	Imperative 'Eat raw meat' 'Take a bath' Abusive Sometimes can influence content	I. Five members of family M. Persecuting as they don't like me, and I killed a nurse C. They continue until I obey	C. Knows all about me A. Recognises voices Family ignores me S. Deluded I. Sometimes voice answers questions	Angry Irritated	Listens and argues Complies unwillingly
6. F 29 Schiz. 11 yrs	Critical 'You're a fat bitch' Imperative 'Kill yourself' 'Slash your wrists' 'Don't listen to MB'	I. Two men from my past M. Punishment for complicity in incest C. If I resist they will kill me	S. Seen dark silhouettes C. Know my history, thoughts and actions A. Made me cut wrists many times I. None	Fear	Argues Partial compliance (cuts to wrist never serious) Drink eases voices Distraction
7. M 29 Schiz. 10 yrs	Critical Abusive and swearing Imperative Tells him to blaspheme	I. Voice is from Satan M. Trying to get my scalp C. If I stop hearing the voice, Satan has won; if it continues I cannot go to heaven	S. Thought insertion (swear words); Delusions of reference (TV) S. Voice made me swear out loud in church I. None	Fear Confusion	Shouts back Reluctant compliance Sleeping, music and talking helps
8. F 38 Schiz. 4 yrs	'This is God' 'She is chosen' Says she is attracted to men, suggests sexual acts Advises prayer and worship	I. An evil force M. Punishment for my fantasies about other men C. If I stop listening it will make me do things I don't want to	C. Voice wants to make love to me, so can't be God. Knows my thoughts and my attraction to other men S. I caressed my body sexually and couldn't stop I. None	Fearful Exhausted	Shouts back ('leave me alone') Talking out loud helps Tried prayer and exorcism Listens reluctantly

Table 6 (*cont.*)

Patient: sex, age, diag. and duration	Voice content	Beliefs: identity, meaning and effect of compliance	Evidence: content, symptom, attribution, influence	Affective response to voices	Behavioural response to voices
9. F 41 Schiz. 10 yrs	Imperative 'Infinite power rise in inflation' 'Negative power output' Prediction 'They've gone up by infinity'	I. The devil M. Using me to transmit messages to Prime Minister to ruin the economy C. If I resist the economy will be saved but the voice will nag me	A. Any adverse economic news is my responsibility I. None C. Voice used to say evil things	Anxious and agitated Foreboding Guilt	Anxious listening Resists (says opposite), but sometimes gives in and complies Reads financial news Distraction
10. F 34 Schiz. 3 yrs	Imperative Most day-to-day tasks Comment on her intention and behaviour	I. Voices are from prophet Masuma M. They are her to help me through a personal illness C. If I resist I will fail as a mother and will be defying my god	C. Know what I think Give good advice (recipes) Say 'remember your faith' when resist Make accurate predictions I. None	Calm Reassured	Willing and full compliance Listens carefully
11. F 32 Schiz. 8 yrs	Imperative Voices give marvellous advice	I. Voices from God and have his power M. To protect me and develop my powers C. If I obey bad things will not happen	C. Know thoughts and history A. Their advice stops conflict S. Experience of control I. No influence	Strong Confident Happy	Elective listening and compliance
12. F 24 Schiz. 3 yrs	Imperative 'Kill yourself' 'Give up smoking' 'Don't go to church today'	I. An ex-girlfriend, who is a goddess M. She protects me. I hear because I've great power C. She keeps on at me if don't comply	C. Know thoughts and past A. Grandoise delusion I. Can call up voice and influence content	Interested Some irritation	Elective listening Selective compliance

was discussed in Chapter 3, there are only two ways to advance a thought chain—to assume that the delusions are either true or false, and in both cases to proceed to explore the implicational meaning of this. With voices believed to be benevolent, a type of grandiosity, thought chaining is advanced most effectively by assuming the beliefs are false. This is because assuming the truth of a grandiose delusion will likely lead to a thought chain which ends in a view of self which is (excessively) positive. With benevolent voices the threat to self occurs if individuals *lack* the omnipotent and benevolent voice; to defend against this is, we believe, its psychological function.

For example, Bernice heard a voice telling her she was the daughter of a princess and was soon to be reunited with her royal family. If one assumed that this was true and began thought chaining, the view of self revealed would not be the psychologically feared one, but the wished for one. When Bernice considered that this belief might be false, the thought chaining revealed that she viewed herself without a royal connection as a nothing and her life as a waste.

Again, let us consider Maisie, who heard two voices exhorting her to commit suicide and kill her family. She believed one voice to be god and the other her dead daughter. She believed both to be benevolent, offering her a way to atone for an abortion, in that if she carried out their commands she and other family members would be reunited with her aborted daughter.

Her evaluative beliefs clearly related to her sense of badness and unresolved guilt and grief following a terminated pregnancy. This was revealed by thought chaining, and asking the question, 'Let us suppose that this voice is not the voice of your daughter, how would this make you feel?' She said this would make her feel terrible, her daughter would be dead and she would be eternally damned and bad. The evaluations together with the inferences were used to construct the formulation—that the voices and visual hallucinations were defences against unresolved grief and guilt, with associated negative self-evaluations, surrounding a termination. In practice, this insight was addressed gently and after 12 sessions (see next chapter).

Having identified the self-evaluation, through thought chaining, the therapist is then able to use this theme to seek psychological meaning in other areas of the hallucinatory experience—notably, voice cues and content. So in the case of Maisie, her voices were triggered by her thinking about the termination and also by reading about abortion and related issues.

With individuals who believe their voices to be malevolent the picture is more complex because of the fundamental psychological differences between punishment and persecution paranoia. We strongly urge the reader to refer to Chapter 7, where we explore fully these differences and their implications for assessment and treatment. For now, suffice it to say that if the delusional theme is one of punishment, the self-evaluative theme is easily and directly accessed by assuming the truth of the belief and clarifying first the other-self negative evaluations, and then the related self-self evaluations. If the theme is persecution then in order to clarify the nature of the other-self and self-self evaluations, we believe that thought chaining needs to examine the implications of the delusion being both true and false.

SUMMARY

In this chapter we have presented our ABC assessment approach to voices. Assessing Bs rests on first clarifying central delusions about a voice's identity, purpose and power, and eliciting the evidence for each. The therapist is then able to use thought chaining to pursue related evaluations and to use this information in combination with full psychological history to formulate the case.

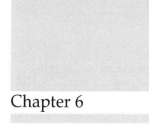

Chapter 6

DISPUTING AND TESTING BELIEFS ABOUT VOICES

INTRODUCTION

In this chapter we consider the key elements of cognitive therapy for voices. There are many points of overlap with the earlier chapter on delusions. This is no accident but follows logically from our analysis which holds that it is the beliefs or delusions (Bs) about voices that drive the disturbed emotions and behaviours (Cs) and not the voices themselves (As). The central concern of cognitive therapy for voices therefore is not the elimination of voice activity, but the weakening of the beliefs that sustain distress. The cognitive interventions used focus on ways of changing individuals' inferences about the meaning of their voices (e.g. 'I am being punished for my failure') and the associated evaluations (e.g. 'I am totally useless').

This chapter is divided into two sections. The first looks at those aspects of cognitive intervention that are unique to working with voices and do not occur in work with all types of delusions. The peculiarities relate to: the fact that there are always multiple delusions, which should be tackled in a specific sequence; the process of engaging clients in disputing and testing; the use of hypothetical contradiction and disputing; to methods of empirical testing. In the second section we present two detailed case illustrations of the complete process.

FEATURES UNIQUE TO WORKING WITH VOICES

Although the conceptual aims and methods of change used are similar to those described in the chapter on delusions there are unique considerations that go with working on voices. We shall consider each conceptual step in the process and indicate points of uniqueness.

Therapy Targets Multiple Delusions

We view beliefs about voices as reasonable attempts to make sense of what is a puzzling and emotionally provocative experience. Beliefs about voices are formally speaking either partial or full delusions. When working with voices a therapist is always interested in multiple delusions. In particular our research (Chadwick & Birchwood, 1994; 1995) has identified four beliefs to be of paramount importance. These are the voices' inferred identity, purpose, power and omniscience, and the effects of compliance and resistance. Cognitive interventions are aimed at changing all these central beliefs. Nonetheless it is still common for individuals to change only one or two of their core beliefs, but such an outcome is still beneficial in terms of reduction of distress and disturbance.

Delusions Are Tackled in a Specific Order

We strongly believe that beliefs about voices are best tackled in a particular order. For two reasons we recommend working initially with beliefs concerning the power of the voice (and the powerlessness of the individual)—especially those about *compliance* and *control*. First, challenging them arouses less anxiety than those about identity and meaning. If successful, voices come to be seen as less powerful and individuals as more so, and distress is eased somewhat. Also, clients often see implications for other beliefs about identity and meaning (e.g. 'If I can control the voice, can it really be the devil?'). In practice beliefs about identity and meaning are often so closely related that they may be challenged as one.

Developing a Rationale for Collaborative Empiricism

Having completed assessment, a transitional point is reached. The client should be feeling more secure in the therapeutic relationship, be more aware of his strengths in dealing with his voices, and have achieved at least some understanding. Specifically, before proceeding to disputing and testing of beliefs a client and therapist need to have a shared understanding of three points. First, that beliefs about voices are not facts but hypotheses, inferences, which may or may not be true. Second, that beliefs and not voice activity underpin the client's distress. Finally that the reason for ever questioning and testing beliefs in a collaborative way is to ease distress and disturbance, and that in the particular case of this client there is good reason to think that he would be better off. We shall take each point in turn.

Delusions are Beliefs, not Facts

Most voice hearers will have doubted their beliefs and many will even have changed them over the years, often from benign to malevolent view or vice versa. The therapist draws out any such doubt and belief change and helps the client to see it as evidence that ideas about identity and meaning are *interpretations* and are neither definite nor immutable. Howard, for example, believes that a famous rock star is soon to declare him as his son and that upon this announcement he, Howard, is to be given a position in the record industry. His evidence is a voice promising him his 'rightful inheritance'. Although Howard does not doubt that he is the rock star's son, he has begun to doubt that he will ever gain his rightful place. Indeed, this concern has led him recently to employ a solicitor to write to the record company. The therapist might explore this as follows:

T: How long has the voice been promising to give you your 'rightful inheritance'?

C: For a long time.

T: You were saying the other day that you were feeling a bit down about it all.

C: I am really wondering whether it is ever going to happen—my solicitor's got no reply from the record people.

T: Right, so for many years you have believed you will be instated in the record industry, but recently you have begun to doubt this will ever happen; how does this doubt make you feel?

C: Disappointed, let down.

Another client, Jane hears voices that seem to originate in household objects—kettles, hairdryers and so on. Although she fully believes that the voice is trying to drive her mad, she well remembers having been wrong about one aspect of the belief which at the time had seemed significant.

T: I remember you saying that right at the beginning of all this you thought that your house was haunted by a poltergeist.

C: Yeah that was scary. The lights went on and off, I was gripped. Well I spoke about it with my mother and she remembered it—the lights did go on and off.

T: Wasn't it lightning or something like that?

C: Everyone in the street had the same thing, I mentioned it to my neighbour and he remembered it as well.

T: So that was one thing you believed totally, and felt frightened about, but was actually wrong.

C: Absolutely, silly idea.

Connecting Distress to Beliefs

Having established that beliefs are mere possibilities, the therapist now wishes to show that the client's distress and disturbed behaviour is tied to this one particular meaning the client has given to his voices, and is not an automatic feature of hearing voices. To achieve this clients are asked to imagine for a moment that their beliefs about the voices are false and to consider the impact on their distress. So as to make this exercise safer, we do not always ask clients to imagine temporarily that their voices are their own thoughts—this can be too direct and threatening—but perhaps instead that it is an impostor, or some such. This may seem a collusion, but we find it necessary very often at this stage of preparing the way for subsequent challenge.

A case example illustrates the process. Maisie is a 60-year-old woman who hears a voice she believes to be from God compelling her to kill herself, her friends and her colleagues' friends.

T: Just suppose for a moment that the voice you hear is not in fact the voice of God, but an impostor; would that make any difference to the way you feel?

C: Well my worries would be over wouldn't they.

T: How would that be?

C: Well if it's not God then I don't have to obey the commands to hurt people. I'd feel a lot happier.

Building Motivation to Change

What the previous two points are doing is showing that the beliefs about voices carry a cost, that they may or may not be true, and that beliefs do change. This point is made explicitly when the therapist and client agree a rationale for collaborative empiricism. Here the therapist needs to draw out the client's motivation to question his beliefs by considering the advantages and disadvantages of their being true or false. As we have seen already in this chapter, the consequences of acting on beliefs about voices are often extreme—castration, murder, etc. However, it is important to consider what advantage they confer, too. Having established firmly that the client would be better off if the beliefs were false, the therapist suggests that it would therefore make good sense for her and the client to explore the beliefs together in the safety of therapy.

Reaction to Hypothetical Contradiction (RTHC)

RTHC was initially constructed as a measure of the susceptibility of a belief to change by examining a client's response to hypothetical evidence or occurrences that contradict the belief (Brett-Jones, Garety & Hemsley, 1987). In essence, the client is asked to consider how, if at all, a specific hypothetical and contradictory occurrence would affect the belief, were it to occur. For many clients RTHC not only taps into openness to change, but also begins the process of attending to disconfirming evidence, and prepares them for subsequent empirical testing. Again, we find that the most effective use of RTHC is to imagine a change in one of the client's central beliefs about identity, meaning, power and compliance.

In the case of Maisie the RTHC drew on her own difficulty reconciling strong religious beliefs with those about her voice. She was asked, 'Just suppose a Catholic priest said that God would never command anyone to sin, would this alter your belief that God is commanding you to murder?'

Jayne, who many years earlier had studied Latin, hears a voice talking in Latin announcing that it is a Roman soldier. There are many grammatical errors in the voice's speech. She was asked, 'I want you to imagine you wrote down exactly what the voice said and took it to a Roman historian, and he or she said the ancient Romans would not have spoken in this way. If this happened, would it affect in any way your belief that the voice is a Roman soldier?'

Disputing Beliefs about Voices

The thrust of the therapist's challenge is that the beliefs are reactions to, and attempts to make sense of, the auditory hallucinations (Chadwick & Lowe, 1990). They are described in therapy as reasonable and understandable attempts to achieve this and as having been driven by a psychological motivation to ease anxiety by making sense of what was happening. However, the beliefs are interpretations, personal meanings, given to voices, not facts of the hallucination. The therapist reviews evidence and inconsistency, and plans tests, with the aim always of evaluating these two possible meanings: that the beliefs are true, a discovery, or that they are reasonable and understandable, but mistaken. As ever it is vital that the therapist really practises Socratic questioning and works collaboratively. This involves drawing out clients' own doubt, puzzlement, double-awareness, critical faculty, etc., rather than forcing a contradiction upon them.

The major piece of evidence for the delusional beliefs is always the actual voices, especially content—these are, after all, the activating events (As) which the delusions (Bs) are invoked to explain. The role of beliefs is critical because individuals usually attribute voices with a power and knowledge that goes well beyond what they have actually said. Several examples of challenging follow.

Compliance Beliefs

It is really quite common for beliefs about compliance not to fit a client's experience, and it is perhaps only their emotional impact which prevents clients from abandoning them. Kate, for example, believes 'If I drop my guard the voices will kill me', but in fact she has dropped her guard on many occasions without consequence. This might be pointed out as follows. 'Kate, you say that the voices have the power to kill you and you must be on your guard constantly. I certainly appreciate the fear that this must create. What puzzles me, though, is that your guard is often down, like when you are asleep. How is it that they have not succeeded in all these years?'

David's voices instruct him to inflict harm upon himself. He believes 'If I don't do what the voices say they will nag me and nag me until I do'. Yet when David has complied, the voices continue to pressure him. 'David, we have found that you comply with the voice at times of extreme pressure and only then because you believe this will bring you some peace. Yet our discussion shows that in fact you get no respite even after cutting yourself. This means the belief may be wrong in which case perhaps we can find ways of helping you to really gain respite and without cutting yourself.'

Omniscience

The appearance of being all knowing (omniscient) is a vital aspect of many voices (Chadwick & Birchwood, 1994) and often features as a key piece of evidence that the identity of a voice is superhuman. It leaves individual's feeling exposed and vulnerable and very prone to guilt and shame. Omniscience might be in the form of an ability to predict the future, offer novel insights and ideas, or a voice might reveal or hint at knowledge of the individual's thoughts, fears, weaknesses, etc.

Alice believes that her voice is a prophet endowed with the ability to foretell the future. In particular, the voice anticipates exactly the arrival of her husband home from work each day. To begin the process of questioning she was asked: 'Let's suppose for a moment that the voice cannot foretell the future; can you think of other possible explanations for last night's prediction?' One such possibility was that the voice was making a very safe guess. This was further explored as follows. 'Alice, as your husband comes home between 5.15 and 5.30 nearly every day it could be argued that the voice is making a prediction anyone might make, particularly you. If the voice is guessing on the basis of past experience, and not foretelling the future, then we might find it did not predict those few occasions when he comes home at other times, for example when he goes into town shopping or out sailing. How well has it done this?'

Maisie's voice gave her detailed instructions on how she was to kill members of her family. However, under close scrutiny the plan crumbled and did not appear likely to have been drawn up by an omniscient and omnipotent being.

T: Tell me about the plan the voice has given you to complete this mission.

C: I have to go to the hotel, kill Ann; then go to Wolverhampton and kill Brian, Carl and Donna.

T: I see; how would you get to Wolverhampton?

C: On the bus.

T: You don't drive?

C: No I can't afford it.

T: Let's just imagine for a moment that you had killed Ann, what would happen then in the hotel?

C: There would be mayhem, blood everywhere.

T: Then what?

C: They would call the police I suppose.

T: How long would it take them to come?

C: A few minutes I suppose, something like that.

T: And where would you be by then.

C: At the bus stop (laughter). It's not going to work is it?

T: If this is the voice of God then shouldn't the plan be absolutely fool proof?

Voices are known to be common following sexual abuse, bereavement and other forms of emotional trauma, and occur in several diagnostic groups (e.g. schizophrenia, manic depression, psychotic depression). We find it helpful to think of them as a response to an extreme psychological threat. This view is not original, nor does it rule out the influence of biological factors because we have no explanation for why only certain people who experience these threats and traumas experience voices.

In therapy we work with individuals to try to make psychological sense of what their voices might mean. In particular, we seek first to understand the individual's psychological vulnerability, in terms of fears about loss of autonomy (self-definition) or attachment and related evaluations of self and others, with associated emotional distress. This is achieved through history taking and exploring the implicational meaning tied to voices through thought chaining. We then use this knowledge to try and discern patterns running through various features of the experience of voices. For example, was first onset triggered by a psychological threat to either self-definition or attachment.

As was discussed in Chapter 5, we find that voices believed to be benevolent most commonly function by masking negative self-evaluation—for example, advising a woman on how to care for her family, so hiding her own sense inadequacy. It is also common for benevolent voices to be interpreted as would-be sexual partners, again perhaps offsetting concerns about unlovability. Malevolent voices relate most commonly to themes of punishment for personal badness, or persecution motivated by jealousy, spite, etc. (see Chapter 7 for a full account of the punishment-persecution distinction).

Empirical Testing of Beliefs

In cognitive therapy with voices, we use two approaches to testing. The first is the general approach to belief testing (see Chapters 2 & 4); the second centres on the ubiquitous belief 'I cannot control my voices'. All tests must include the following:

1. be precise and realistic,
2. incorporate an agreed, foolproof way of knowing when it is complete and what the outcome was,
3. provide an opportunity to support or disconfirm two beliefs—the client's delusion and the alternative generated in therapy.

Alice believed her voice to be a prophet and fully versed in the Koran. Her evidence was that it instructed her to turn to certain pages and read it, after which the voice would comment wisely on what she had read. Earlier when discussing evidence for the belief the therapist had queried why the voice never commented in advance upon the significance of the chosen text. The reality test picked up this theme and required that Alice ask the voice what was written on certain pages. Alice said that if the voice succeeded this would support the delusion; if not, it would weaken her certainty that the voice was a prophet.

Alice further believed that her voice made all her day-to-day decisions for her, and that if she took these decisions instead, these would lead to failure. To test these two points two further tests were agreed and carried out. First, it was agreed to assess if the voice did indeed take all daily decisions. Alice made a detailed record of everything she did in a single day from making tea, deciding what to eat, deciding what to have for lunch, when to change her baby's nappy and so on. Alice indicated whether each decision had been her own or the voice's, and the outcome of each one. Over three consecutive days her records revealed that 58% of decisions were voice driven and 42% were self-determined; this latter figure included 10% which represented a rejection of the voice's advice. There was no evidence that Alice's decisions fared any worse than the voice's. This test therefore supported the alternative explanation she and the therapist had generated, namely that her voice was actually her own thoughts and that the experience was driven by her fear of inadequacy and failure. Through further gradual behavioural testing and discussion Alice felt more and more autonomous and less and less dependent and incapacitated by her voice, thus further weakening her negative self-evaluations.

Testing Beliefs about Control

In our research 70% of those who believe their voices to be 'very powerful' could neither start nor stop their voices, compared with only 20% of those not making an attribution of omnipotence. For this reason we have developed a specific test for the belief 'I cannot control my voices', which we operationalise as being able to influence voice activity, especially onset or offset.

In effect the client and therapist learn to engineer situations to start or increase the probabilty of hearing voices, and then to stop or reduce them. In this way the client gains a surprising degree of control over the voice.

The initial assessment provides information about cues that provoke voices for a particular individual (see Chapter 5); concurrent verbalisation is known to stop or diminish voices temporarily. This information is combined in the following five steps:

1. Identify cues that increase or decrease voices.
2. Practise the use of 'increasing' and 'decreasing' strategies within a session.
3. Propose the notion that 'control' requires the demonstration that voice activity can be turned up/on and down/off.
4. In sessions encourage the client either to initiate or increase voice activity for short periods then reduce or stop it.
5. Once the client has achieved some fluency, consider the implications for beliefs about the voice's control and power.

The major difficulty conducting this type of test is infrequent voice activity. With low frequency voices it is sometimes impossible to increase activity to such a pitch that concurrent verbalisation may be used to diminish them. However, it is still possible to start voice activity in the way described, and for very low frequency voices this may have to suffice.

In the final two sections of this chapter we describe therapy for two individuals who hear voices, to illustrate the overall process of intervention. The cases were chosen to try and reflect the diversity of this type of work. The first, David, was seen by Max Birchwood and heard a voice that was connected to a traumatic experience of being raped. The second, Jenny, was seen by Max Birchwood and Paul Chadwick, and experienced a voice which was hypothesised to connect to issues of personal inadequacy, though the connection was less immediate than in David's case.

David

David is a 33-year-old man with an eight-year history of psychosis which has received many diagnoses mainly affective psychosis. David described childhood as an unhappy period. He never knew his father and he felt his mother had no time for him. He felt much closer to an aunt who lived with them, but she died when he was 11 years. He describes this loss retrospectively as a source of great distress, though at the time he did not really acknowledge this, still less express it. David and his mother agree that after this he became withdrawn, truculent, moody, played truant from school and got involved in petty crime. His mother felt she could no longer cope with him and he was taken into care in a local care home, where he was sexually abused by a care officer. He felt too afraid and guilty to report this, and felt anger towards his mother for placing him there and towards the abuser. In his early twenties he was imprisoned for a serious crime and developed psychotic symptoms in prison.

David experienced a strong interpersonal conflict. Throughout adolescence and adulthood he felt wary of people and 'built up a wall'. He was sensitive to criticism and recalled always having been prone to evaluating himself as worthless and unlovable (thus making him more susceptible to the attentions of the abuser) and others as bad and untrustworthy. The episode of rape confirmed these evaluations. Yet insufficient attachment left him tending to agree with others and seek dependent relationships.

As well as experiencing psychotic symptoms he experienced periods of depression, with numerous incidents of self-harm. At the time of referral he was in hospital and regarded as a high risk for self-harm and suicide. He was receiving Chlorpromazine and Lithium, with little effect.

Assessment of the Voice

David heard one voice inside his head. Most of the time the voice commanded him to cut his genitals ('cut off your penis you dirty bastard'; 'cut it';) and less commonly passed insults ('you shit') and comments ('he loves it'). The voice had been active daily for five years. The voice was triggered by thoughts of the rape, or any media reference to child abduction, paedophilia, gay issues, or conversations about badly behaved children.

David was disposed to resist his voice. He argued and shouted at it and used distraction methods. He partially complied with commands when the pressure became extreme by cutting his penis, usually only superficially. He believed the voice to be that of his abuser, Mr X, because it sounded like him and also he, David, would not say the things the voice said. He believed the voice to be a punishment for having disclosed the rape. His experience was that when he resisted the voice, it got louder, and he believed this to be generally true. Also, he believed that if he stopped listening, he would be vulnerable and might be seriously injured. He perceived himself to be powerless, and unable to control the voice, saying 'I want to stop it, but I can't'.

Formulation

The formulation seemed straightforward; that David's voice was a reaction to the trauma of childhood rape. The beliefs about voices were reactions to, and attempts to make sense of, the hallucinatory experience. The associated evaluative themes related on the one hand to David's own badness and guilty sense that he deserved punishment, and on the other to anger at the abuser, whom he saw as abusing trust.

The approach to therapy was less straightforward. It may seem tempting for therapy to concentrate on the abuse, with little or no focus on the voice. However, three reasons militated against this. First, David had consented to having therapy for his voices—he had not discussed with his referrer, still less agreed, to looking at the rape. Second, it is easy to lose in writing about David the extent to which he was cognitively, behaviourally and affectively caught in the voice's power (Bauer, 1979). It is doubtful whether side-stepping the voice would have worked. Third, it was thought that David might find an approach which targeted the rape as too threatening.

However, the rape was obviously central to understanding the voice and associated beliefs, feelings and behaviour. The approach therefore adopted was a standard one for delusions; namely, to focus on the beliefs using the formulation to give the process meaning and force for the client. David and the therapist slowly developed rapport prior to any intervention. Then the process of working through the individual beliefs was begun, and the therapist tentatively and gradually offered the insight that the voice might not be Mr X speaking today, but a psychological reaction to the traumatic rape, a kind of reliving of the experience.

However, although aspects of the rape are addressed indirectly in this process, and most strongly in relation to challenging the negative self-evaluative beliefs, this is not the same as offering therapy for the rape. Rather the rape is brought out from behind the shadow of the symptom and the individual is strengthened psychologically; the individual is then invited to consider focusing on the trauma in therapy. (Regrettably David declined this offer.)

Engagement
David was desperate for the voice to stop. Hitherto his experience of the voice had not been explored in detail and his dissatisfaction with the illness model as an explanation for his voices only increased his despair. David's experiences and concerns were listened to carefully over a number of sessions. His strength in resisting the demands of the voice was acknowledged, and his occasional self-mutilation was redescribed as temporary exhaustion on his part, rather than a testament to the voices irresistible power.

When invited to talk about the rape, he described what he had suffered as a child and his feelings of anger to the perpetrator, and his mother for placing him in the hostel. He also admitted feeling guilt for having neither said no nor sought help at the time. At this stage in therapy David did not see the voice as a psychological reaction to the abuse, but a genuine punishment by his abuser for having revealed it to others.

The coping strategy that helped to suppress the voice calmly—talking and thinking about relatives—was selected for enhancement. The therapist recognised the value of this strategy, and it was practised in sessions.

Omnipotence

His distress about the voice was extreme, and the beliefs he held regarding the power of the voice (implicit in compliance and control beliefs) were driving much of his day-to-day distress. David was concerned that if he did not go some way towards full compliance, then the voice might become so loud and forceful that he might castrate himself. The therapist explored this fear more: at a rough calculation, the voice had commanded castration over 15 000 times: on the vast majority of occasions he had resisted, and at other times he complied only partially, apparently with no adverse consequences. Full resistance was therefore practised in the safety of therapy, in order to bring home that it was really possible and did not make castration more likely.

Since he appeared to have some power to resist, the question was raised, who was in control of the cutting, David or the voice? David said that he felt he had 'no choice' on many occasions, but acknowledged that it was indeed he who initiated any cutting (not the voice itself) and that the voice drove him to it with its constant nagging and insistence. In other words the voice influenced him not by power, but persistence. The voice did not possess sufficient power to inflict harm itself, or force him to comply. David's own capacity for control was reviewed at this stage. Using the analogy of learning to drive a car, control was thought of in terms of an ability to start and stop the voice:

T: If you were driving a car and you needed to prove to yourself and to others that you are in control of the car how would you do it . . .

C: I would be confident about my driving and not show fear of the car.

T: How would you do that?

C: Hold the steering wheel confidently.

T: What about stopping the car?

C: Of course, when I'm ready.

T: I guess the same for moving off when your ready?

C: Right.

T: So part of feeling in control of the car involves stopping and starting the car when you're ready; agreed?

C: Ah hah.

T: I wonder if the sama analogy works with your voices. If you can show that you can start as well as stop them that sounds like real control. What do you say?

It was known from earlier assessment period that events associated with the rape he suffered in childhood, or flashbacks and direct memories of it, activated his voice. Items in the newspaper and on the television were especially provocative and David avoided both. Using a relatively innocuous newspaper item, David found he was able to activate his voice within a session. By then talking about relatives (i.e. using concurrent verbalisation) he was able to stop them. This technique was practised regularly.

David felt slightly concerned that if he relied exclusively on concurrent verbalisation to diminish voices, he may become more fearful of them. A 'focusing' strategy (Haddock, et al., 1993) was therefore used, involving shadowing the voice's speech in his own mind. Once he had synchronised his own voice with that of the 'other' voice, he was instructed slowly to reduce the volume of his own voice to see if he was able to bring the 'voice' volume down in turn; he could.

Regular practice of both techniques was undertaken, initially in the presence of the therapist and subsequently alone. David achieved good control and his fear of the voices reduced. The implications of this ability to control the voice were discussed; if the voice was so powerful, how could he control it? It was suggested that the testing techniques, allied to his own ability to resist commands, indicated that he was more in control of the voice than vice versa. At this point David still believed that the voice was Mr X, but now viewed him as less powerful. His anger towards Mr X eased temporarily , and was supplanted by a powerful feeling of being 'in control of Mr X'. David had reached this stage in six formal sessions and with considerable support from a nurse on the ward where he resided. By this time David had become curious about the link between the means by which he initiated his voices and the onset of voice activity itself. This curiosity was pursued further by a means of opening a dialogue about the role of anger and guilt as a mediating state and, by focusing on voice content, to determine whether it might reflect his own occasional feelings of guilt about the rape.

The range of cues that triggered his voices was therefore reviewed. As part of the on-going process of developing control, David had been using as cues stimuli of increasing potency to bring on the voice. The rationale at this stage was to enable him to tackle 'real life' cues that were continually triggering the voices. He experienced many bad days that were linked to the media coverage of a baby who had been abducted from a hospital.

T: Can you read this item again about baby Abbie. Tell me exactly what is going on in your mind.

C: It's awful. How could anyone do something like this (tears). I know how this child must be feeling. It's disgusting.

T: How does she feel?

C: Painful. I have pains in my backside.

T: Does this remind you of experiences in the children's home?

C: I try not to think about it, it makes me feel really shit.

T: Is this what you are fighting now, thinking about these events in your childhood?

(David found habitually that the more he tried to ward off intrusive thoughts and images, the more they occurred)

T: When you can fight it no longer and the memory intrudes into your mind, what do you feel?

C: Disgust, I feel fucking angry. I should have stopped him. I could have yelled out.

T: You didn't feel able at the time.

C: Because he was in charge I was only twelve. I was afraid.

T: When you say you should have stopped him do you mean that you feel guilty about it?

C: Yes.

T: You were only twelve, I guess self-preservation sort of overrides it, he was powerful—right?

C: He was.

T: And you were vulnerable.

Analysing each cue in this way underlined the common themes of anger and negative evaluation of others, and guilt with its negative self-evaluation. At this point (session 9) an interpretation was offered:

T: These events stir powerful beliefs and feelings about you and Mr X, and you seem to move between anger and guilt. It may be that these powerful feelings are causing your voices in some way. Also, this would make some sense of the commands. I wonder if this is a possibility that we should consider?

C: Is that what you think is causing my voices?

T: It's not impossible by any means.

Outcome
Following six months of cognitive therapy, David continued to hear the voice. It had reduced in frequency to the point where he was able to read tabloid newspapers, even though there were usually items about child abuse, etc., without triggering voices. He had not considered or completed any acts of self-harm for four months. He no longer believed the voice to be Mr X and felt he had power to control it. BDI scores had reduced from 28 to 14. He entered a training course but continued to find interpersonal contact stressful and with the exception

of a few people on whom he felt dependent, remained somewhat solitary. Guilt about the rape continued and he felt overwhelming anger. He decided not to pursue these themes any further in therapy, which ended.

Jenny

Jenny was referred by her psychiatrist for help in coping with her voices. She was a single unemployed economics graduate in her forties with a ten-year psychiatric history.

Assessment of Voices
For the last three years she had heard voices in half hour bursts, usually in the morning and at bedtime. The content was invariably to do with economics, such as 'infinitely power the rise in inflation', 'negatively power productivity a million, trillion times'. These and similar statements were usually perceived as commands and occasionally as predictions. Jenny also held a delusional belief that she could transmit her thoughts using telepathy. Therapy lasted 13 sessions spaced over six months. Meetings lasted one to two hours because Jenny had to travel a long way.

Jenny believed the voice to come from the devil, and that he was using her telepathic power to destroy the British economy. Specifically, the devil would give a command that in economic terms was disastrous, Jenny would be compelled to repeat this command and in so doing would unwittingly transmit it telepathically to the Prime Minister, who would act upon it. She believed that if she resisted, then the economy would be saved but the voice would continue to torment her. In practice, each time the voice began she would resist by saying exactly the opposite of the command, until she finally weakened and repeated the Devil's command, when the voice would stop. She monitored the economy religiously and felt guilt, anger and depression when it dipped. During the first two sessions time was spent listening carefully to her story and restructuring her account into a framework that distinguished what the voice said, what she believed and why she believed it. This stage of clarification and reflecting of her account was carefully documented for her and served also to question her interpretation of the content of the voice; for example, what did the term 'infinitely power' mean, did it refer to the mathematical notation or was it a descriptive term; and how might the Prime Minister choose to interpret it?

The distress occasioned by the voices was stressed repeatedly—they caused her to resist and to be on her guard almost without respite. Jenny's resolve was recognised by her therapists but it was plain to all that she was close to exhaustion. The principal engagement manoeuvre involved exploring with Jenny the effect the voice had on her life, both positive and negative, and considering how things would be both better and worse if her beliefs were mistaken. It was clear that although the voice gave a sense of purpose to Jenny, it did so at very considerable cost and she was close to exhaustion. It therefore seemed prudent to collaboratively examine the beliefs, and if necessary consider alternative ways of finding a sense of purpose. Jenny was reassured that she could withdraw from therapy without penalty, that it would be entirely up to her to evaluate, and if appropriate, act upon issues raised.

A second influential engagement step involved contact with other voice hearers. Jenny was lonely and isolated in her tussle with her voices. She was shown a video of a man describing his experience of voices and how he coped with them, and she felt much commonality. Also, Jenny began to attend a day centre for two days a week, where she was particularly interested to learn the views of other fellow voice hearers that their voices 'create an aura of power' and that others had found their voices dwelt on topics that were painful to the individual. Congratulated on her determination to cope with them, the experience of other voice hearers was conveyed to her and was of great interest to Jenny.

Formulation

Prior to hearing voices Jenny had experienced clinical depression, which had related to a sense of worthlessness and failure. Our hypothesis was that the voice related to these concerns, in that it both played out her sense of failure, worthlessness and guilt when the economy did badly, but also defended against full despair because there was the hope and control that went with attempting to save the economy and country.

Achievement had been highly valued by her parents and Jenny had pushed herself very hard to gain a university degree. There was a sense in which her self-worth was contingent upon her succeeding and achieving. This partially held out. Jenny was conscious of her failure to achieve and make use of her training as an economist, something that was valued very highly by her parents and this exposed a self-evaluation of having failed her parents. The need to feel she was worthwhile and repaying her parents' investment in her was driving her to 'save' the British economy at great personal cost, thus offsetting underlying depressive concerns.

Thus it was thought that the major block to Jenny internalising and accepting her voices was the risk of despair and negative self-evaluation. The strategy adopted in therapy was therefore to work on her beliefs about the voice, offering the speculation that the voice and beliefs related to concerns about failure and worthlessness, and to gradually shift the emphasis onto these concerns and her lack of purpose in life. The alternative psychological interpretation was offered to Jenny after five sessions at a point where she was searching for alternative ways of understanding the voice.

A second and related block to weakening beliefs about the voice was Jenny's fear of internalising the pernicious social stereotypes of mental illness, which she found unacceptable and shaming. In this respect, our therapeutic approach of seeking to understand voices as psychological reactions to events, perhaps motivated by threat to self, helped her to assimilate her voices without negative self-evaluation.

Intervention
The early phase of cognitive therapy focused on her beliefs about the power of the voice, compliance and control. The most obvious inconsistency in her beliefs was that most days she did, reluctantly, repeat the Devil's commands and yet the predicted economic disaster did not ensue. Also there were certain puzzling features in the account; for example, how was the Prime Minister to know that he was to act on the commands, and even should he know this, what does 'infinitely power' require? Again, why should the Devil, an omnipotent being, need to work through Jenny, as opposed to communicating with the Prime Minister directly?

Whenever the economic news was poor Jenny would feel depressed and guilty inferring 'it is my fault' and she would take the news to be evidence for her beliefs. She was encouraged to generate and examine an alternative view of events which was that the main economic indices went up and down regularly and bore no particular relationship to the transmission of messages. This exercise not only led her to her question critical evidence for her beliefs, but also to recognise that beliefs are possibly mistaken and how they influence behaviour and feelings.

Two hypothetical contradictions were put to Jenny. First, she was asked if her belief would be altered if she met with the Prime Minister and he assured her that he did not hear her messages. Second, she was asked if her belief would be altered if she went out of her way to comply with the commands and the economy was unaffected. She thought that both these events would weaken her conviction that the beliefs were true.

Following Maher (1988) the alternative explanation offered to Jenny was that her beliefs arose in response to, and as a way of making sense of, her voices. The beliefs were not labelled as delusions, but were discussed as being a reasonable and reasoned attempt to understand what must have been a puzzling and alarming experience.

Jenny first tested the belief that she could not control the voices. She found that either reading about economic affairs for a short time, or neutralising typical commands (i.e. saying the opposite to what the voice wished) led to an increase in voice activity. Subsequently reading aloud material unrelated to economics (i.e. concurrent verbalisation) decreased voice activity. In other words, simple changes in her own behaviour meant that she was able to increase and decrease voice activity—an ability to switch them on and off—and this helped her believe that she had some control over her voices.

Subsequent testing of beliefs about identity and meaning began. Testing began with the command which was deemed least threatening by virtue of having the smallest potential for economic disaster ('infinitely power the price of milk'). It was agreed a confirmation of her belief required that the price of milk should at least double, and also it should do so within two weeks. The implication of the prediction not holding up was agreed in advance. This process began with comparatively innocuous commands (increasing bus fares and the price of milk) and progressed to the more central (taxation levels and interest rates). Also with each command the principles of systematic desensitisation were applied to reduce Jenny's anxiety; thus she would repeat the chosen command several times, then rate her degree of distress, relax for a few minutes, and then repeat the procedure again until her distress was negligible. In all cases the test did not lead to the supposed consequence and this weakened Jenny's beliefs about the consequences of compliance.

Her belief about personal inadequacy rested essentially on her sense of having failed and disappointed her parents. It was as if in order to accept herself, she required their acceptance first. Her mother was experiencing failing health and Jenny was spending a great deal of her time helping and supporting her. Jenny raised her feelings of failure directly with her mother and they were able to discuss these issues for the first time. Her mother expressed her pride in Jenny, not least because she had an illness that was not of her making, yet she had battled hard to rise above it, and had succeeded. Contrary to Jenny's view of her illness as a shame to be hidden from public view, her mother disclosed that she always discussed her daughter's illness in a positive manner. The support that Jenny had shown her mother won great admiration from her sister, mother and father.

Outcome
Conviction in all four beliefs fell significantly and Jenny reported feeling less fear, guilt and depression. Her voice activity is now far less frequent and she is no longer resisting the voice by saying the opposite to the commands. Some few months after the changes in her beliefs about voices, Jenny experienced a surge of dysphoria and despair and felt life held little challenge or meaning. The intensity of this ennui did ease and Jenny began steadily to construct a life which held more of both.

SUMMARY

In this chapter we have isolated the unique adaptations to cognitive therapy required when working with individuals who hear voices. As we have seen, the connection between the process of therapy and psychological formulation is complex. David's experience is particularly informative. In therapy the childhood rape was connected to the voices, thereby rendering them more understandable to him, and this process revealed the extent of his need to address the trauma. He was so involved with his voices that we considered the strategy of weakening this link and imparting insight the correct one. Yet in no way could this process be said to be a therapy for the rape. It was not, it was a collaborative attempt to weaken the distressing impact of voices on his life, in part by understanding their possible psychological meaning. Cognitive therapy might have proceeded to look at the rape, or an alternative therapy could have been used, but David declined both.

Chapter 7

COGNITIVE THERAPY FOR PARANOIA

INTRODUCTION

The cognitive approach to paranoia—as with other symptoms—differs in important ways from traditional psychiatric approaches, and these theoretical and conceptual differences are important to understand before commencing assessment and therapy. Therefore we begin this chapter by discussing the pioneering ideas of Zigler & Glick (1988) and Bentall (1994), which concentrated our own interest in this area. We next discuss what we believe to be an important and original isolation of two distinct types of paranoia—persecution and punishment (Trower & Chadwick, 1995) and consider the clinical implications of this separation for assessment and treatment, using case material. Finally, we offer our own theoretical ideas about the origins of the two types, and in particular how this relates to breakdowns in the self-construction process.

THEORETICAL, CONCEPTUAL AND EMPIRICAL ISSUES

Contemporary cognitive theories of paranoia cut across diagnostic boundaries and are built around the concept of self, and the related issues of threat and defence of the self. In particular, there is currently much debate about the connection between paranoia and depression. In a seminal paper Zigler & Glick (1988) proposed that paranoia might be a defence against low self-esteem and that certain forms of paranoid schizophrenia might be a defended depression. This theory appeals because it seeks to connect paranoid disorders to the layman's ordinary explanations of behaviour (Antaki, 1981). Most people have a tendency to blame someone else for their shortcomings, and to take credit for their achievements; this 'self-serving bias' (Miller & Ross, 1975) enables us to feel indignant and angry where we might otherwise feel low and deficient.

Zigler and Glick's theory might be taken as an account of how paranoia either *emerges* or *persists*. However, there are three problems with this theory. First, depression and low self-esteem are not the same thing; so if paranoia defends against low self-esteem, it does not necessarily defend against depression. Second, even if paranoia is a defence against threatened low self-esteem or depression, this in itself does not explain why this particular defence should *emerge*. Thus, while threatened low self-esteem or depression may be a necessary condition for the emergence of paranoia, it is unlikely to be sufficient.

Third, the possibility that paranoia *persists* because it defends against depression has been refuted. Individuals with paranoid delusions are typically depressed (Bentall, 1994). In addition, hallucinating individuals with paranoid secondary delusions are both significantly more commonly and more severely depressed than those with nonparanoid secondary delusions (Chadwick & Birchwood, 1996). Again, the weakening of paranoid delusions does not precipitate increased depression, but on the contrary is often associated with a fall in the depression score (Chadwick & Lowe, 1994).

There is substantial evidence for the possibility that paranoia persists because it defends against low self-esteem rather than depression. In our own research on voices while 'malevolents' were found to be more commonly and more severely depressed than 'benevolents', their self-esteem as scored on the BDI was no worse; they had significantly higher scores for mood and vegetative symptoms, but there was not a significant difference on those items for self-denigration. Also, Bentall and his colleagues have shown that in paranoia the self-serving bias is exaggerated and that although commonly depressed, paranoid people typically display *high* self-esteem (Bentall, 1994). What is more, Bentall and his colleagues have used subtle and indirect methods of assessing self-concept, and found that paranoids actually respond as do depressed people—that is, they attribute failure internally (see Bentall, Kinderman & Kaney, 1994). In other words, it seems that while superficially paranoids are able to blame others and retain positive self-esteem, there is a depressive self-schema which is comparatively easy to access. The paranoid defence seems to operate as this part of Zigler and Glick's theory predicts, but we are still left with the question of why.

The picture emerging so far certainly supports a theory of paranoia as a defence against low self-esteem. Individuals who are depressed, often very depressed, show an exaggerated form of a self-serving bias which protects against self-denigration and low mood, and usually have high self-esteem.

Bentall, Kinderman & Kaney (1994) have recently proposed an integrative theory of paranoid defence which pulls together many of these strands of evidence. Bentall and his colleagues' model points to an exaggeration of an ordinary tendency to reject responsibility for negative events at the heart of this.

In Bentall's model the motivation for an exaggerated self-serving bias is thought to be the attempt to limit the discrepancy between ideal and actual selves (see Higgins, 1987), and Bentall raises the interesting idea that the origins of this exaggerated interpersonal defence lie in early childhood.

Our own preliminary research (Chadwick & Trower, in submission) on paranoia was based on a model derived from the fundamentals of the cognitive ABC model (see Chapter 1), and it shared many features with Bentall's model. To recap, cognitive theory asserts that extreme and disabling emotion is associated with different kinds of negative evaluation (Trower, Casey & Dryden, 1988), and with negative person evaluations in particular; these may be other-to-self, self-to-self, or self-to-other and are defined as stable, global and total condemnations of the entire person. Furthermore, a wealth of evidence from diverse theoretical perspectives indicates that evaluative beliefs may relate to one of two central motivations, namely, relatedness and autonomy (Blatt & Zuroff, 1992). The core evaluative beliefs are those of being unlovable, weak, worthless, bad, a failure, and inferior.

From this cognitive perspective, we argue that the paranoid defence is like a form of the angry attributional style—individuals perceive interpersonal negative evaluation and construe it as being unjust, a form of persecution, and they reject the criticism and condemn the persecutor. Our view differs from Bentall's emphasis on a self-serving bias in paranoia, in two important ways. A first point of distinction is that we narrow down the possible sources of threat to interpersonal negative evaluation. Bentall's model is primarily an attributional one dealing with how people make inferences about the likely cause of success and failure. Although he mentions evaluations in his discussion of the work of Higgins, Bentall neither states explicitly that evaluations are a necessary part of his own analysis of paranoia, nor has he measured them in his research (see Bentall, Kinderman & Kaney, 1994). A second point of distinction is our stipulation that the paranoid defence, like the threat, is an interpersonal negative evaluation of the other person; again, Bentall's model argues only that an external attribution is made to explain a failure (i.e. someone or something was responsible). At this point in our own theorising we believed that it is only when the evaluative as well as inferential processes at work in paranoia are explicit and central that the essence of paranoia is caught—an angry, negative evaluation of a persecutor.

Thus, in a recent study (Chadwick & Trower, in press) we tested our reformulated cognitive theory of paranoia. We used the EBS (Chadwick & Trower, 1993: see Appendix 1) to compare a group of paranoid and depressed people on their responses to a list of statements which measure the three types of negative person evaluations: 'other-self', 'self-self' and 'self-other'. All three predictions derived from the model were borne out; the paranoid and depressed groups perceived similar amounts of negative 'other-to-self' evaluation (i.e. threat); the depressed group reported significantly more negative 'self-self' evaluations (i.e. the individual agrees with the other's negative appraisal); and the paranoid group reported significantly more negative 'self-other' evaluations (i.e. they condemn others).

ARE THERE TWO TYPES OF PARANOIA?

So far we have shown that there is conceptual and empirical support for the notion that paranoia defends against low esteem. However, we now wish to turn to emerging evidence that there are in fact two fundamentally different types of paranoia (Trower & Chadwick, 1995). The account of paranoia so far presented describes and explains only one type of paranoia, which we are calling 'poor me' or persecution paranoia. Poor me paranoids tend to blame others, to see others as bad, and to see themselves as victims. This is the pattern exemplified in the research by Bentall, Kinderman & Kaney (1994). In the second type of paranoia— which we are calling 'bad me' or punishment paranoia—individuals tend to blame themselves and see themselves as bad, and view others as justifiably punishing them. We draw this conclusion on the basis of recent empirical work, extensive clinical practice of applying cognitive therapy to paranoid delusions, and existing distinctions in rational-emotive behaviour therapy.

Evidence for the Bad Me Paranoid Subgroup

The first piece of evidence for two types of paranoia comes from the Chadwick and Trower (in submission) study cited above. Although the three hypotheses were all confirmed (paranoid and depressed perceived similar degrees of threat but the depressed condemned themselves, the paranoids condemned others) three of the 11 paranoids responded more like depressives. That is, they had poor self-esteem and they did not condemn others. The implication of this is that a minority of paranoids do not fit the Zigler & Glick (1988) model.

A second piece of evidence comes from our recent development of a cognitive approach to understanding and managing voices (Chadwick & Birchwood, 1994; and see Chapters 5 and 6). As we have discussed, beliefs about the malevolence of a voice are of two fundamentally different types: either the voice is a deserved punishment for a previous misdemeanour, or an undeserved persecution. This crucial distinction colours the whole phenomenology of the hallucinatory experience, thus giving us further evidence for two types of paranoia. 'Poor me' paranoids would clearly have a tendency to interpret threats, including voices, as persecutory, since they blame others, while 'bad me' paranoids would have a tendency to interpret threats as punishing, since they feel guilty and blame themselves.

A third source of evidence that there is a form of bad me paranoia which differs phenomenologically from the well-recognised poor me paranoia, comes from extensive clinical experience while developing cognitive therapy for delusions (Chadwick & Lowe, 1990; 1994; Lowe & Chadwick, 1990). We have become increasingly aware that certain individuals with paranoid delusions have very poor self-esteem, and that this poor self-esteem is inextricably linked to the paranoia. For these individuals we have developed a unique approach within which we work systematically with the paranoid delusions and the negative self-evaluative beliefs (Chadwick & Trower, in press). We illustrate cognitive assessment and therapy for both types in this chapter.

The Conceptual Distinction—Poor Me, Bad Me

These different strands lead towards a reformulation of existing cognitive models of paranoia. Our distinction between on the one hand the paranoid who sees himself as bad and blameworthy, and on the other the hapless and angry victim, follows a well-established conceptual distinction made in cognitive psychotherapy. Wessler & Wessler (1980) when discussing depression make a distinction between discomfort disturbance, which derives from a demand that one gets what one wants and 'deserves', and ego disturbance, which derives from a demand that one is successful or approved of in order to be worthwhile. The belief 'poor me' and associated beliefs of self-righteousness and self-pity, come from dis-comfort disturbance in which the person receives some perceived injustice, such as being ignored or rejected or not being appreciated and believes 'I don't deserve that . . . it's awful that I don't get what I deserve'. 'Bad me' and associated beliefs of worthlessness comes from ego disturbance in which the person receives disapproval or criticism and concludes, 'If they think I'm bad, worthless, then I am and that's awful'.

We suspect that this distinction is fundamental to many disorders besides paranoia and depression. In Table 7 we summarise the main differences between our two types of paranoia, and these points help to give structure to the process of ABC cognitive assessment of the two types, to which we not turn.

ABC ASSESSMENT OF POOR ME AND BAD ME PARANOIA

In preceding chapters we have detailed the standard features of cognitive ABC assessment. In the present chapter we shall presume this knowledge and draw out those elements which are peculiar to assessing paranoid delusions. We begin this section on assessment considering what a paranoid delusion is, and then for each type of paranoia offer a case example and look at the central issues of ABC assessment.

The central task facing the therapist, as ever, is first to engage the client in the process of cognitive therapy, and second to isolate both the delusional inferential beliefs, and the evaluative beliefs about self and others. This task is easier with punishment paranoia because the other-self and self-self negative evaluations are conscious and comparatively easily accessed. With persecution paranoia the therapist needs to tease out both the other-self negative evaluation beliefs implicit in the client's delusions, and also explore for possible negative self-evaluations which are not conscious all the time.

Yet bearing in mind the general problems defining delusions, and given that certain cognitive models view paranoia as an exaggeration of ordinary thinking, it is worth first considering a general question: what is a paranoid delusion? Let us consider a man who believes that he is unpopular, that people at the office are talking about him and poking fun at him, and that they would like to get him to move office. Is the belief a paranoid delusion? At this stage, no. For a start he could be right. This possibility must always be taken seriously because strictly speaking a paranoid delusion is an inference and therefore, however improbable, it may be correct.

What if our imaginary client goes on to say that he has noticed little signs in the office relating to him, such as a copy of a travel book left conspicuously on a desk in order to give him a message to 'travel'. This idea is paranoid in the everyday sense of the word, but do we yet have a paranoid delusion? The answer, we think, is still no. Individuals who are depressed or socially anxious commonly misinterpret everyday objects and behaviour in just this way. There is a sense in which most social phobics and many depressed people may be called paranoid.

What if he goes on to say that he thinks they are hatching a plot; that is, not merely wishing that he would leave and maybe making his life uncomfortable, but conspiring to have him sacked. Well, if he does not have good evidence for saying so then this would constitute a paranoid delusion. Again, if he introduced the idea that they were reading his mind, or putting thoughts into his head, or bugging his flat, or having him watched at home, or controlling him—all of these would be clear examples of a paranoid delusion.

An important part of assessment is therefore to determine if indeed the individual has a paranoid delusion. As we have indicated, the therapist is looking for a belief in either punishment or persecution, and is furthermore looking for certain tell-tale features—a plot or conspiracy, and one or more of the other symptoms listed. An additional feature in many paranoid delusions is the strong likelihood of the person being attacked and killed, rather than being damaged psychologically; however, on its own this does not distinguish the paranoid, but does so only in terms of how and why he is to be attacked, in which case we are back to those criteria already mentioned.

Persecution (Poor Me) Paranoia

It is our experience and belief (Trower & Chadwick, 1995) that the psychological motivation for persecution paranoia is to defend against a sense of being ignored, neglected and insignificant, with associated feelings of emptiness and despair. Where a persecutor in reality leads his life as if the client did not exist or was of little significance—the persecutor ignores him, or makes noise and disturbs him, or throws rubbish in the garden and spoils his view, and shows the client neither interest nor respect. In the delusional reconstruction, everything the persecutor does relates to the client; every noise, gesture and action is a provocation and the client is the focal point of the persecutor's life. The motivation for this interpretation is captured in the old saying: 'If there is one thing worse than being talked about it is not being talked about'. The central challenge for the therapist is to get the client to go beyond the delusion and to consider and work on any such enduring vulnerability which may emerge. This move is achieved through thought chaining and Socratic dialogue, and especially by focusing on the negative person evaluations.

It is helpful at this point to consider a case example. For several years Charlie has believed that her neighbours have been persecuting her by pumping poisonous gas into her house. She often feels queasy and nauseous after smelling the gas and gets a gastric pain. She thinks the gas is pumped through using a heavy iron machine which she can hear often 'banging and being dragged around'. She struggles to understand why it is happening to her—she has done nothing to merit it—but she thinks a particular man, who is envious of her and would perhaps like to marry her, might be implicated. She gets very angry about the persecution and often telephones the police, who have paid many visits to her and to the neighbour. She is also very angry with the police and others for the unwillingness to do anything constructive. She bangs on the adjoining wall and has confronted her neighbours several times, often 'armed' with a broomstick. She too has experiences of reference and misinterpretation.

We believe Charlie illustrates the central features of persecution paranoia. The focus is on herself as hurt, not bad. Her paranoia has a specific *focus*— a few named and known individuals. She is a victim, wronged and *persecuted*. She does not deserve to be treated in this way and she therefore has the moral high ground and feels *righteous indignation* and there is a trace of grandiosity in her thinking. Consequently she is very *angry*, and she seeks to *confront* the other. She enlists powerful others whom she hopes will believe her and help her have *revenge* by exposing the other's badness. She seeks to be free of the other's malign influence and to be treated in the way she deserves.

It is our experience that individuals with persecution paranoia are more difficult to engage in therapy. This is in part because of the prominence of anger but also the absence of conscious negative self-evaluation. We now turn our attention to this central challenge of drawing out the evaluative beliefs—other-self, self-self and self-other—that are associated with the delusion. A quick example to convey the point might be Charlie believing that her persecutor is a totally evil bastard who spites her through envy (a conscious self-other evaluation). The hidden negative other-to-self evaluation might be that he treats me with contempt, like I am a complete nothing (negative other-self evaluation). The defended self-self evaluation, which is rarely conscious, is that she is completely insignificant, a nothing. If the therapist is able to uncover all this, then she and the client are well placed to gain insight into the psychological function of the paranoia and begin easing her own vulnerability to negative self-evaluation, with associated emotional distress.

We shall now consider this process in more detail. Dick believed that staff from the polytechnic where he had been a student were persecuting him and 'holding him back in life'. In particular, he believed they send spies into the family post office to spy on him. The following dialogue relates to Dick's belief about articulate customers in the family shop being spies, and illustrates how the therapist may move from a surface paranoid inference to draw out implicit evaluations. To ease comprehension we have indicated in brackets the As, Bs, and Cs.

C: It happened again this morning, I was in the shop (A) and some articulate man was hanging around trying to provoke me (B).

T: You think he was trying to provoke you?

C: Yeah, smiling to himself and checking up on me. Treating me like shit. Letting me know, like, that he was watching me (B).

T: How were you feeling when he was hanging around in the shop.

C: Bloody angry, I wanted to go and let him have it (Cs). You know, take him down a peg or two. I didn't though, I just served him.

T: You didn't confront him because it upsets your mum? (Dick nods.)

[At this stage the therapist has two paranoid inferential Bs and the emotional and behavioural Cs. The task now is to probe for the implicit other-self evaluations to which Dick was responding angrily. The clue lies in Dick's comment about being treated like shit.]

T: So, you thought the man had come to spy on you—had been sent by the lecturers—and you felt angry and wanted to express that. You were angry that he and others might be persecuting you. It sounds as if you were also angry about the *way* in which he spied; that he was treating you like shit and that he was also being superior, you know, needing taking down a peg or two. What did you mean by being treated like shit?'.

C: Well, you know, looking at me like I'm just a shop assistant and he's something better. Like he knows why I'm just a bloody shop assistant.

T: Right, just a shop assistant. And how do you think he views shop assistants?

C: Dirt. Shit. Nothing.

[Here the therapist has drawn out an implicit other-self negative person evaluation. The therapist now goes on to try and convey that the anger relates to the inference about being persecuted and the other-self evaluation.

T: And that's what he conveys to you in his behaviour, that he sees you as dirt?

C: Yes.

T: Supposing he wasn't part of the conspiracy, just a shopper. How would you feel if just an ordinary shopper treated you like dirt?

C: I'd be bloody furious. Who does he think he is?

T: So, this morning in the shop two things made you angry about this man, one was that you thought he was spying on you, the other was that he treated you like dirt.

[At this point there are options—explore the anger more and clarify the self-other negative person evaluation, or, as the therapist actually goes on to do, explore for a defended negative self-evaluation. To facilitate this he explores Dick's own feelings (Cs) about being a shop assistant]

T: And how do you, Dick, feel about being what you called a bloody shop assistant?

C: Well, it's degrading isn't it, I feel useless (B). Selling make-up. The shop's not my scene at all. It's not what I should be doing. I can't seem to get anything right. Sometimes I can't even look at people when they come in the shop and I go out back and leave it to dad (C). I feel so ashamed to be seen there (C). It's not what I wanted from life, not by a long chalk.

Now the therapist is in to the self-evaluative Bs ('useless, can't do anything right') and Cs (ashamed, disappointed) which the anger and paranoia served to defend. Having made this breakthrough the therapist is able to pursue two general ends. First, she seeks a common formulation, or insight; namely that the paranoia may be a defence against negative self-evaluation. To do this she specifies the delusional and evaluative Bs and Cs more clearly and explores with the client how the angry sense of persecution and self-other condemnation serves to mask the sense of degradation, negative self-evaluation, despair and shame. If this insight is common, the therapist and client will understand that a more adaptive defence for the client is to work on understanding more fully and weakening the negative self-evaluative beliefs, and this can be pursued in the standard cognitive manner.

So, in persecution paranoia thought chaining is advanced in three steps. First, clarify the delusion. Second, clarify the other-self evaluation. This is most easily achieved by *temporarily assuming that the paranoid delusion is false.* In the dialogue above the therapist asks Dick to imagine the person is not a spy, just an ordinary shopper, and look for the other-self evaluation. Third, look for a self-self evaluation.

Punishment (Bad Me) Paranoia

The task when assessing bad me paranoia is to conduct a standard ABC assessment and to go on to establish the negative self-evaluation, which unlike in poor me paranoia is conscious. Once the therapist has identified clear negative self-evaluation, then she is free to follow the standard steps outlined above, namely, identifying this belief and associated affect and behaviour as a problem and exploring how it connects to the paranoia, to early childhood, and how it might be worked on in cognitive therapy.

In our experience this task is relatively easy to achieve in bad me paranoia because the client is usually very preoccupied with his badness. The following dialogue with Barry (see above) illustrates the process.

T: Barry, has anything happened in the past week to alter your belief in any way?

C: I couldn't sleep last night, just lay in bed tossing and turning, and I started thinking about what I'd done. Then there was a lot of noise outside and a car horn sounded, then it screeched away. (As)

T: What did you make of that?

C: That they had been outside monitoring what I was doing and thinking (B). When I began to think about what I'd done, the horn was a signal and they went off to get the others. I was terrified (C), I thought they were coming to get me (B).

T: So you thought they were able to read your thoughts, and that once they noticed you thinking about the bad things you'd done in the past they decided to come and get you. Is that it? (Barry agrees.) What I'm wondering Barry, is when they caught you thinking about those things, what sort of person do you think they thought you were?

C: A pervert, bad, that I might do those things again.

[Here the therapist has an other-self negative evaluation. He next clarifies if it is a proper person evaluation—a stable and global rating of his entire worth.]

T: Right, so they would condemn you as bad, a pervert. And would they be condemning your behaviour, just one part of you, or would they be condemning the whole of you—you as a person are bad and perverted?

C: Me as a person.

T: One other thing I wondered Barry, you were saying they would get you because you might do it again. When they condemn you as a person for being bad, do they think that you could change, you know, leave behind the badness?

C: No, they think I'll always be bad. Even if I never did another bad thing in my life, I'll always be bad because of what I've done.

T: Barry, just for a minute let's imagine that what you have said is true, that's exactly what happened that night. How would it feel to have them condemn you as totally and forever bad?

C: Terrible. I'd feel so bad, I'd hate myself.

T: You would hate yourself?

C: Yes, for being like that.

T: You'd see yourself as totally and forever bad.

So, with punishment paranoia the therapist advances thought chaining in three conceptual steps (Chadwick & Trower, in press):

1. assuming the paranoid delusion is true,
2. clarifying the nature of the other-self person evaluation,
3. clarifying the self-self negative evaluation.

In temporarily accepting the client's delusion, it is temporarily put to one side and other, evaluative personal meanings are explored. In our experience clients find this a surprising and revealing manoeuvre, and also feel reassuring because it conveys understanding.

INTERVENTION FOR POOR ME AND BAD ME PARANOIA

In the next section we give a fuller case description of cognitive therapy. We return to Dick and discuss intervention with his persecution paranoia, and discuss intervention with Billy, a man with punishment paranoia.

Dick

Conceptually the process of intervention for Dick's persecution paranoia comprises three related stages (many other clients do not progress as far through this sequence, but any progression is likely to have beneficial effects). These general stages of intervention with persecution paranoia are:

1. Dispute and test the persecutory delusion, casting it as a reaction to and attempt to make sense of certain experiences (activating events).
2. Connect the delusion to the other-self evaluation: that is, convey that the client perceives an implicit evaluative threat in the behaviour of others, and responds angrily to this as well as the inferred persecution.
3. Convey the insight that the defensive self-other negative evaluation is a defence against possible self-self evaluation.
4. Dispute and test the self-self evaluation.

Background
Dick's psychiatric history went back nine years, beginning soon after he left a postgraduate training course prematurely. Dick presented with a clear paranoid delusion about being persecuted by certain lecturers from his old polytechnic. This delusion involved the key features of a conspiracy to hold him back in life, with associated delusions of mind reading and reference. At assessment he scored 25 on the BDI (moderate depressive symptomatology) and expressed suicidal ideation. His hopelessness was linked in part to his delusion and in part to his general malaise. Dick had never felt able to socialise, even though he would have 'loved to', and described himself as 'too shy'—he had never had a sexual relationship.

Dick reported that his persecution began as an undergraduate. He was not quite sure why the lecturers chose to persecute him; he is sure they could read his mind and thinks they may have judged him to be 'immature' and 'impulsive'. Dick believed he was deliberately given a poorer degree class than was merited, and that since graduating from polytechnic the lecturers had been going to great lengths in order to prevent him from finding employment, even to the extent of having him fired from a post graduate training course after only a few weeks. Dick contended that the persecution would continue until such time as they decided that he had matured sufficiently, at which point they would help him to find suitable employment. He held that in order to carry out their plan, the lecturers were sending people into the family post office, where he worked frequently, to check up on him by reading his mind. Thus, when working in the family shop Dick viewed articulate customers whom he did not know as 'spies'. Many times he had shouted and sworn at those customers whom he suspected of being sent by the polytechnic; he recalled as typical a time when he angrily told on one customer 'Get out. Fuck off. I've had enough of you'.

Conviction was very high at the start of the study, and Dick reported never having had more than a fleeting, slight doubt in the delusion. Preoccupation was high; his belief played on his mind many times each day and he felt very distressed at such times. He was very angry about the way he was being treated.

The delusion was formed soon after Dick was asked to leave a postgraduate nursing course, some three years after completing a first degree. Apart from feeling disappointed by his class of degree, Dick experienced no paranoid ideas about his lecturers while actually attending polytechnic. Following graduation Dick spent over two years working abroad in America. While there he was advised that his career prospects would be enhanced if he acquired a recognised nursing qualification, so he returned to England and enrolled on a postgraduate course. However, during the course Dick appeared to find the course pressure, added to the anguish of still not mixing or finding a partner, too much. Although he could recall shouting until his throat was sore, still he thought that he had been dismissed unfairly and had not been given an adequate chance to prove himself. He contacted staff at his old polytechnic and asked for help to earn a reprieve, but even though he thought the staff had telephoned as requested a second chance was not granted. He returned home and the paranoid delusion was developed.

Dick spoke very little about his parents. He identified strongly with his father, who died some years earlier. He had wanted to enter his father's profession but had not done well enough academically. There was a sense of Dick trying to achieve and be like his father, but failing in this process. In particular, the failed postgraduate nursing course had been a way, he hoped, of gaining a sense of importance and significance. Dick's mother was very supportive and loving, although Dick appeared to have found the relationship stifling.

Formulation
The delusion was reformulated as a reaction to, and way of making sense of, a number of experiences of reference and mind reading which occurred on his return home. The delusion was conceptualised as being motivated by a need to avoid an overwhelming sense of personal inadequacy and unimportance with associated shame and despair. This sense of shame and inadequacy was most forceful with lecturers from his old polytechnic, who now saw him as a shop assistant, and this may explain why they became the focus of the paranoia.

Intervention
Challenging the delusion worked well. Using the insight gained during the assessment period, the therapist and Dick assessed two central and opposing ways of making sense of his experience. First, that the delusion was accurate. Alternatively that it was a reaction to, and way of making sense of, a number of experiences of reference and mind reading which occurred on his return home, and was motivated by a need to ward off a sense of personal inadequacy and unimportance with associated shame and despair.

Discussion drew out a number of aspects of the delusion which were internally inconsistent or irrational: two examples of this are given here. First, it was pointed out that Dick's spell abroad was inconsistent with the delusion. He stated that on leaving to take up the post in America he had no intention of returning to Britain. Furthermore, he felt absolutely certain that the staff at his polytechnic had played no part in his decision to return to Britain. On his application form for the post abroad Dick gave the names of two of his polytechnic lecturers as referees. Thus, these two members of staff had actually been instrumental in Dick getting the job and leaving the country: yet subsequently it was these two lecturers in particular whom Dick believed were at the heart of his persecution. It made no sense for the two main protagonists of Dick's persecution to have assisted him to leave the country to work, possibly for good. (A similar argument was forwarded in relation to Dick's entry to teacher training, where again a reference was sought from the polytechnic.)

An example of irrationality concerned the fact that for the entire three years Dick spent in close contact with his lecturers he remained unaware of their special interest in him. By his own admission, at no point during his degree course did Dick have an inkling that his lecturers were reading his mind or that they viewed him as impulsive and immature. At the time Dick felt that his relationship with his lecturers was mutually satisfactory; only almost three years later did he 'realise' that this impression was mistaken.

A developmental account that looked at the setting conditions for the formation of Dick's belief was put forward in support of this alternative. Dick admitted to having been under a considerable strain at the time he entered postgraduate training: his lack of an adequate social life and his continued failure to find a partner had prayed on his mind over a number of years. Also, his sense of inadequacy and failure were becoming more acute. Dick first developed his ideas following a significant life event—his premature departure from the course—during a period he described as one of great confusion, anger and despair. He also felt enormous shame. He was a polytechnic gradudate, he had worked abroad, he had started to train to be a nurse but had been asked to leave—and all this was known by staff from his old polytechnic, who now occasionally saw him back home with his mother and in the family shop working as a 'shop assistant'.

The polytechnic lecturers were perhaps primed to be a focus for the paranoia because of their occasional actual involvement in his progression, and their high status position. The dawning 'realisation' that his old polytechnic teachers had written to the course to have him sacked brought relief from confusion, self-blame and shame. He was able to abnegate responsibility for his class of degree (as a student staff read his mind, first discovered his shortcomings and the persecution began) and the subsequent long-term failure to find employment (staff were preventing this). Chance meetings with the lecturers became episodes of spying, and this generalised to all articulate people.

As the delusion weakened the therapist and Dick were able to explore other ways of understanding the experiences of reference and mind reading. The therapist suggested that Dick's level of shame, anger and confusion at the time were associated with these experiences. Dick was able to recognise that shame and self-consciousness lay behind his sense of being spied upon, and that the anger and fury defended against this. This was consistent with the fact it occurred only with articulate shoppers. Similarly he found a veiled reference to himself in the walk and bearing of only those people who looked educated and well-dressed—they were 'rubbing his nose in it'.

Dick also came to realise that at the time the paranoid interpretation was probably a necessary one because by externalising, or projecting, responsibility for his plight the situation became tolerable, just. However, the therapist suggested that it was the threatened negative self-evaluation (I am inadequate, unimportant) and associated feelings of shame and despair which were the motivation for the delusion being formed. The therapist and Dick made some limited progress and weakening these self-evaluations about inadequacy and insignificance.

Outcome
Dick reported finding therapy helpful, and valuing what he found to be a good, supportive therapeutic relationship. Dick did become less certain of his belief over the course of therapy, although at those times when his affect was high he was temporarily once again totally sure of the belief. This outcome was accepted by both Dick and the therapist as preferable to permanent certainty. His mother reported that he seemed less distressed and more insightful, but she too recognised that some days were as bad as they ever were.

His preoccupation was unchanged, and his anxiety at such times fell, if at all, only slightly. As therapy progressed and Dick became more open he did face up to much disappointment. He spontaneously came to recognise that while the lecturers were probably not persecuting him and spying on him, they were largely *indifferent* to him and his circumstances (in fact there were indications that one had tried to help him). And at times he spoke of feeling hopeless, saying on one occasion: 'Am I a write off, Paul? Is there any hope? I don't feel any hope most days. I feel very depressed. It's beyond crying.'

He had felt depressed and suicidal for many years in spite of the paranoid delusion being extremely strong. Depression scores recorded at assessment, intervention and the first three months of follow-up all indicated a moderate level of depressive symptomatology. At the six-month follow-up the BDI score was down to 9, once again indicating an association between reduced delusional conviction and depression. Thus in spite of confronting painful emotions and negative self-evaluations, and in spite of weakening his delusional conviction, the highest BDI score was recorded at initial assessment and the lowest (and asymptomatic) six months after therapy.

Billy

In this section we describe the process of intervention for Billy, a man with punishment paranoia. Assessment for this type of paranoia reveals the client's core negative self-evaluation and paranoid (punishment) delusion. Conceptually cognitive intervention involves three further stages:

1. The therapist disputes and tests the client's central negative self-evaluation of badness.
2. The therapist conveys to the client the insight that it is this sense of badness which drives the paranoia.
3. The therapist disputes and tests the paranoid delusion.

Background
Billy was seen 21 times by Paul Chadwick; 6 times for assessment, 12 intervention sessions, and several follow-up appointments spread over 12 months. All sessions lasted 60 minutes and took place weekly.

Billy's life had been extremely traumatic. He was told by his mother that he was conceived when his father had raped her, and that this had effectively marked the end of the marriage, which broke up some five years later. On the separation Billy went at first to live with his father, then his mother—however, she remarried and he did not get on with his step-father who physically abused his mother, though not him. For lengthy periods during his late childhood he slept in the same bed as his mother, and many of his early memories of sex and sexuality were associated with her. In his late teens Billy sexually molested a girl on one occasion, and on three occasions had sexual contact with animals.

Billy presented with a number of symptoms. He described clear paranoid thinking, with associated delusions of reference and mind reading. Also, he heard occasional abusive voices (usually male) in the third person when outside, calling him names like 'pervert'. Billy was depressed, scoring 25 on the BDI at assessment (moderate depression). Also, he described being troubled by intrusive thoughts and images. The thoughts were either blasphemous ('damn Jesus to hell') or abusive ones directed at other people ('she's a slut', 'he's a wanker'). Billy would try and neutralise both types, saying for example 'she's not a slut' or 'don't damn Jesus to hell'. Also, Billy experienced intrusive images of his sexual behaviour with the girl and animals.

Billy held two distinct paranoid beliefs and one depressive self-evaluative belief. The first paranoid belief was that he was being punished by members of the public for his sexual misdemeanours. Specifically, Billy believed that others could read his thoughts, including the obsessional ones, and therefore knew about the sexual acts; hence they tormented him (i.e. the voices and references) and were planning that he should be exposed and ultimately attacked. The second paranoid delusion was that God was punishing him; this belief was distinct in that it rested on separate evidence and was developed much later than the first. Specifically Billy experienced frequent and severe pressure in his head, which he attributed to God physically punishing him for blasphemy (the intrusive thoughts) and for having broken a promise to God to attend church.

Intervention
The negative self-evaluative belief was that he was a totally bad and perverted person, and this belief rested on his sexual behaviour. This belief caused Billy most distress and was challenged first. Conviction during baseline was in the range 75–99%, but at the close of the first intervention session was rated only 40%. Billy identified two aspects of the session as being particularly significant. First, he had never before connected the circumstances of his conception with his sense of badness. Second, he found the distinction between condemning certain of his actions (which both he and the therapist did) as opposed to him as a person, to be persuasive and relieving—also, rating his behaviour, not himself, as bad gave him a sense of optimism that he might avoid future indiscretions. The agreed homework was that Billy would list those of his acts which he considered to be both good and bad; this would both further test the notion of total badness, and also help to define the nature of his vulnerability to behaving badly. This drew Billy's attention to the fact that all his perceived badness related to sexual behaviour, and this again was connected to the circumstances of his conception. Conviction fell steadily over the course of therapy and remained low at follow-up.

The belief that people who could read his mind were tormenting him and planning to attack him was challenged second. Conviction, which had been high and stable throughout baseline, fell at the first intervention session (week 8) to 50%, where it remained for the subsequent three weeks before falling to only 30% at the concluding session. The alternative put forward by the therapist was that the paranoid belief was a reasonable but mistaken reaction to and attempt to make sense of two puzzling experiences—his experience that others knew about the sexual indiscretions and referred to it directly (hearing voices) or indirectly (references), and the sense of 'transparency' that accompanied intense embarrassment and guilt when intrusive thoughts occurred in company. In support of the alternative Billy noted that these were the occasions when he thought his mind was being read, no-one had ever challenged him or hurt him, and the only people he thought could not read his mind were those who knew of his sexual indiscretions. Two tests were used; first, and least difficult to accomplish, Billy agreed to think thoughts such as 'If you say "pink flamingo" I'll give you

£50'. The test was carried out repeatedly over two weeks with those people Billy thought could definitely read his mind and use the money! The subsequent, more difficult test involved Billy not neutralising his intrusive thoughts about other people ('he's a wanker', 'she's a slut'). In both instances the outcome was consistent with the therapist's belief and at odds with Billy's.

The second paranoid belief, that God was punishing Billy for blasphemy, was tackled last. Conviction was erratic week-by-week but there was a clear downward trend over the course of the 11 weeks of baseline. The belief was interpreted as an attempt to account for a strong and painful pulsating Billy began to feel in his head soon after he began experiencing intrusive and blasphemous thoughts. It was argued that the belief was driven by guilt, but also anger at his very difficult life history. Also, the therapist gave Billy information about the number of people who experience automatic intrusive thoughts (see Salkovskis, 1989), which helped both to normalise the experience and differentiate effortful thinking from thoughts that flash across one's mind. The agreed tests were that Billy would read the Bible in order to discover if the Christian God punished people in this world and in this way, and subsequently talk about his belief to a local vicar. In fact Billy did only the first of these, as he said after the first test that the belief no longer troubled him.

Outcome
The BDI was given regularly during assessment and intervention. Prior to intervention BDI scores indicated a depression of moderate intensity; however, the third BDI score was markedly lower and fell in the mild range—this fall corresponded with a fall in Billy's conviction that he was a bad person. The following two BDI scores were slightly higher, but probably still within the mild depression range (Beck & Steer, 1987). Over the follow-up period BDI scores fell steadily, and the final score was in the asymptomatic range.

Billy had been on stable medication prior to the onset of the study. At the one month follow-up assessment he reported that his psychiatrist, who was unaware how the study had progressed, had reduced the Stelazine by 50 mg on the basis of a clinical improvement.

THE THERAPEUTIC RELATIONSHIP

It is our experience that individuals prone to punishment paranoia on the whole respond better to cognitive therapy, although there are exceptions to this rule. In particular we suspect this differential outcome results from two features of bad me paranoia. First, the individual presents with strong negative self-evaluative beliefs, and in our experience is always anxious, avoidant and depressed. This allows the therapist to emphasise the standard cognitive approach of being concerned to reduce the individual's distress and disturbance. Both therapist and client wish to reduce the latter's depression, self-condemnation, anxiety and avoidance, and there is surprisingly little scope for conflict. In our work we prefer to begin therapy by disputing and testing the depressive self-evaluation, and only subsequently to challenge the paranoid beliefs (Chadwick & Trower, in press).

The second point is that in confessing his bad deeds the individual with bad me paranoia is exposing his badness to the therapist and thereby running the risk of being condemned and rejected. In other words he is doing the thing which he most fears, and this in itself may be a powerful shame-attacking exercise. Although the therapist strongly condemns certain behaviour (e.g. abuse), she does not attack or reject the individual. In this way the client does not experience the predicted attack and over-whelming shame, but sees that it is possible for others to accept him in spite of what he has done.

In contrast, with the poor me paranoid it is more difficult for the therapist to express his concern for the client. The client usually demands that the therapist say if she believes his story and frequently has a strong expectation that he will once again be misunderstood and mistreated. In our experience the opportunity for conflict is considerable and with many such clients there is risk that they might either reject contact altogether or drop out early on during assessment.

Indeed, transference is often rife in paranoid ideation. For example, Barry felt much guilt about having attempted anal sex with a woman and in one session he interpreted the therapist's rubbing his eye to be an oblique reference to this act. In fact Barry even developed a paranoid delusion involving his therapist, namely, that the therapist had a team of 30 whom he charged to follow Barry around in public and provoke him. The therapist's response to this was three-fold. First, to recognise the importance of the accusation—that the therapist was breaking confidentiality in an appalling way. Second, the therapist decided *not* to challenge the content of the delusions, but merely to observe that Barry felt particularly vulnerable straight after sessions (this was when the belief was most strong). Third, the therapist tried to engage Barry in discussion of the meaning of his new delusion. An obvious theme was that Barry found it very difficult to trust others; even though he attended regularly and reported feeling safe in sessions, there still was a need to construct a critical and punishing therapist figure. The ensuing discussion revealed that without fail, every person Barry had trusted in his life had let him down in a major way. Another possible meaning, not discussed with Barry, was that perhaps he found it easier to imagine that the therapist's interest in him was constant, rather than recognise that it was limited.

One of the most interesting features of both types of paranoia is that each presents the therapist with a striking, but different, paradox. In bad me paranoia the client on the one hand says that others can read his thoughts and already know all about his badness, yet on the other he fears nothing so much as others discovering his badness and punishing him. We find that this inconsistency can be used effectively to reduce conviction in delusions of mind reading. The person with persecution paranoia states that he *really* is being persecuted, with the implication that what he needs is a policeman or a lawyer; but many attend their appointments with a psychotherapist. We gently reflect this paradox and speculate that perhaps one part of the client recognises that somewhere tied up in the delusion is a psychological vulnerability with which he would like to help.

PARANOIA AND THE SELF

So far in this chapter we have looked at the psychological assessment and treatment of our two types of paranoia. In the concluding section we offer our own theory to account for their emergence.

We believe that the pioneering work of Zigler and Glick (1988) and Bentall (1994) offers the basis for an adequate understanding of persecution paranoia, but that they do not fit the second type we have isolated, punishment paranoia. Most significantly, the self-serving bias does not appear to operate in bad me paranoia. In relation to evaluative thinking, for example, if individuals used a strong self-serving bias then they would show a tendency towards negatively evaluating others, but not themselves—the reverse is actually the case.

Therefore a new theory is required which takes account of both types. We believe Bentall and Zigler and Glick are right to argue that the concept of self is central to paranoia, and furthermore that paranoia is a defence of the self. Our own theory of two paranoias (Trower & Chadwick, 1995) is a theory of how a sense of self is ordinarily constructed, and what happens when the process is threatened and breaks down. In the remainder of this chapter we shall briefly outline this theory.

What is the Self?

Following a long tradition of post-Cartesian thought on the self (Levin, 1992) we take the position that there is no such 'thing' as the self, but rather the self is continuously constructed and is never secure. We propose that there are three necessary and sufficient conditions for the construction of self, namely an objective self, a subjective self, and the other.

The objective self. The objective self is the product—the self that is constructed. This, the most familiar aspect of self in everyday life, refers not to some mysterious inner entity, but to the observed, behavioural, public self, or what James (1890) called the phenomenal 'me'. The substance of the objective self is the self-presentation behaviour of an individual, but as we shall see, requires an observer—the other—to make this self-presentation 'objective'.

The subjective self. The subjective self is the self as agent (Harré, 1979), who chooses the actions—the self-presentation behaviour—that constitute the objective self, and monitors (i.e. observes and judges) those behaviours, and also monitors the feedback from the other. The self as agent not only has the power of action but the cognitive processes of observing, interpreting, inferring, attributing, evaluating, recalling etc. This appraisal function is complex, and entails not only the direct appraisal of the agent's own action, but the appraisal of the other's appraisal of the agent's action.

The other. The other is of course simply the other person with reciprocal subjective and objective aspects. For our present purposes, we emphasise the other's role and function as observer, thereby providing the 'public' objectivity of an audience which transforms the presentations of self into the objective self.

The Making of the Self

The making of a self is widely acknowledged by a number of eminent authors to be a, perhaps the, fundamental human passion and need (e.g. Rogers, 1961; Maslow, 1954; Kohut, 1977).

How does this self-construction process work? The model we develop draws on Goffman's seminal book *The Presentation of Self in Everyday Life* (1959) and the self-presentation literature that this has spawned (e.g. Schlenker & Leary, 1982; Jones, 1990). Goffman's idea draws on the metaphor of drama—a person constructs his self by means of self-presentation performances before an audience, and the self in this sense *is* the behaviour-before-an audience i.e. people are (via the objective self) primarily the parts they play.

It is possible to operationalise the process of self construction as a sequence of stages. In a simplified way, the process begins with self-presentation behaviour for others. Self-presentation is defined by Schlenker (1980) as the attempt to control images of self before real or imagined audiences, and thereby to influence how audiences perceive and treat the actor. The second stage is the perceived, anticipated or imagined evaluation by others of the self so presented—in brief, other-to-self evaluation. There are two possible third stages. One might be the evaluation of self by the actor him- or herself, consequent upon the other's evaluation—in brief, self-to-self evaluation. The other might be the evaluation *by* self *of* the other.

We have already met the key players in this drama of everyday life. These are the objective self which is the product, the subjective self which is the producer, and the other which is the objectifying audience. Next we shall try to analyse these functions and roles in more detail, examining the components of self and other as they might operate for two individuals, A and B. The interaction of the components and processes of self (individual A) and other (individual B) are interdependent and will be analysed together as a system.

Let us begin with individual A. As we have seen, the main role of A's subjective self is as an agent for action and appraisal. In this role it has two processing dynamics. First, as agent for itself individual A has the power to produce/perform various self-presentation behaviours/actions, and then evaluate those actions.

The second processing dynamic of A's subjective self is as agent for B. In this role A has the power to identify, reify (make real) and appraise B's objective self (I see your self-presentation behaviours, make them 'real' (i.e. the public, objective 'you') by providing this audience or mirroring effect, and appraise 'you'). Reciprocally, the same pattern follows for B.

Threats to the Self

In this section we outline two major forms that could threaten the construction of self. First, the insecure self in which the agent can produce the appropriate self-presentations but the other is habitually neglectful or absent and therefore the agent cannot achieve the status of *objective self*.

Second, the alienated self in which the other is *too* present, and the status of objective self is achieved but is imposed by the other.

Insecure self. The first threat to self-construction of an objective is a lack of the attentive, 'objectifying' or 'mirroring' other. According to the theory, the agent is in dire need of the other in order to *be*—to be an objective self in the real world. If the other is absent or severely neglectful, then the agent may fail to be an objective self in the world. This state may be experienced in its undefended form as abandonment, emptiness, insignificance, worthlessness, unlovability, unwantedness, and emotionally as anguish or depressive *ennui*.

The prototypical insecure self has his subjective self, his agency, intact—indeed he may have a surfeit of it, almost excessive freedom—whereas he lacks an objective self. He may have a clear sense of the self he wishes to construct—his desired or ideal self. His mission is to find an other (specific or generalised) to objectify his desired self and his failure and ultimately his despair is to be ignored or rejected and thus experience existential nothingness. The most prominent defence is narcissistic rage (Kohut, 1972).

Alienated self. The second threat is due to the other being excessively present and intrusive—of not only mirroring the objective self but of taking possession of it (Sampson, 1993). We can explain this as follows. To be *my* objective self, *I* as agent must construct the self presentation *for* the other, and the other must emphatically recognise and value this self as *my* self, freely constructed. But if the objective self is controlled and indeed constituted by the other, then it is not my self but an alien self imposed upon me. A *feels* like an object labelled by the other (as bad, dirty, useless, or even wonderful) and experiences shame and self-consciousness.

In summary, the alienated self senses that he has lost his freedom, and experiences his subjective self, his agency as overwhelmed by the other, and his objective self, while secure, is possessed by the other. His mission is to escape his entrapment, and his despair is his enslavement.

The Two Types of Paranoia and Threats to Self

We propose that poor me and bad me paranoia exemplify the two types of threat vulnerability and the consequent defences described. In Table 7 we list what we believe to be the major differences between the two types.

The Poor Me Paranoid

We propose that the poor me paranoid exemplifies the *trait* of the insecure self and shows that vulnerability and defence. He is dispositionally disposed, mainly through early learning, to experience the self as insecure. The need that the poor me paranoid seeks to secure is the guarantee of recognition of this grandiose self by the other. If he fails, then he has not achieved an objective self, a presence, in the world.

Here we are talking about more than the ordinary self-ideal discrepancy, where the degree of discrepancy is generally moderate, and people can

Table 7 Major differences in symptom presentation between persecution and punishment paranoia

Delusional theme	Punishment	Persecution
Focus of paranoia	Very wide (e.g. general public, people on the bus)	A few named and known individuals or organisations
Delusional conviction	Unstable	Stable and total
Susceptability to change	Open to hypothetical challenge	Resistant to hypothetical challenge
Grandiose element	Absent	Strong
Affect	Anxiety and guilt	Anger
Behaviour	Avoidance/escape	Confrontational
Motivation	Hide own badness from others	Have persecutors revealed as bad

usually realistically see their way to at least approach the ideal, and the 'real' self is one which ordinary people can certainly live with. Here we are talking about self-ideal discrepancies which are huge—between the espoused grandiose self which is not an ideal to aim for but which the person completely identifies with (Jacoby, 1994/1991), and the unconscious actual self which may not be an objective self at all but a failed, i.e. non-existent self because of the lack of the objectifying other.

It is likely that an unconscious level of processing (Brewin, 1988; Dowd, 1994), there is an awareness of the dangers of this collapse (Bentall, Kinderman & Kaney, 1994), but what *defence* does the poor me paranoid have? The solution is to explain the other's withholding of recognition, expressed in the form perhaps of indifference or more strongly as rejection or criticism, as *persecution*, and thereby magically, i.e. delusionally, transforming and indeed *reversing* the meaning of the other's communication. Now invalidation becomes endorsement of his specialness. *This* is the strategy of the poor me paranoid.

Construing others as persecutors is a way of blaming others for one's own lack of success and 'presence' in the world. The poor me paranoid is able to choose this attributional style to defend his grandiose self-image because his subjective-self is intact. The act of judging others necessitates having a sense of autonomy, i.e. sense of agency, of freedom to choose and judge. In addition the poor me paranoid is other-focused rather than self-focused, because there is no objective-self to be self-focused upon. He puts the other in the role of object to be labelled, attributes causality to the other as object, and finally blames the other as the cause of his demise—a form of the self-serving bias seen in ordinary people except more so. The outcome will be a set of other-blaming beliefs and demands—he should not treat me this way! He is a worthless rat! He should be condemned! etc. So long as the poor me paranoid can maintain his strategy, he will retain a *high* self-esteem. He will be motivated to go to great extremes to maintain this, for example by amplifying the enormity of the conspiracy against him—as would be warranted to persecute an immense talent. He will construe himself as superior and the other as inferior. One of the main bases of his superiority will often be a moral one—implied in the idea of labelling others as persecutors, which implies evil intention.

The Bad Me Paranoid

The bad me paranoid is predisposed to experience the self as alienated and bad or flawed, and the paranoia is a defence against this subjective self being revealed through self-presentation behaviour and being objectified by the other. The fear is not of an absent other, but an intrusive and controlling one. The self is not in danger of disappearing into nothingness but of being controlled by the other. Unlike the poor me paranoid, the bad me paranoid is in danger of losing his agency, his autonomy, because his objective self is constructed and controlled by the other. He is prone to interpret others as enormously threatening and powerful, and himself as weak.

A sharp difference from the poor me paranoid is that the other is not persecuting him but *punishing* him. The difference is due to the fact that the bad me paranoid 'knows' (in the sense of experienced as a fact not a belief) himself to be bad, indeed totally and irrevocably bad, and therefore deserves to be punished, and conversely is undeserving of being treated with respect. The person believes the other is good, worthy and superior (even grandiose and omnipotent) and *I* am bad, morally inferior. We also have a reversal of the self-serving bias, for here the person attributes blame for bad outcomes to self, and responsibility for good intentions and outcomes to the other.

The *threat* to the bad me is having his bad subjective self made real by the other. Before recognition of the bad subjective self by the other the person experiences more or less continuous low self-esteem, inferiority and powerlessness, high trait anxiety (driven by the ever-present danger of being recognised) and of guilt for intrinsic badness, inadequacy etc. However, after recognition the person experiences in addition high public self consciousness and intense shame, a desire to escape, and depression, marked especially by helplessness and hopelessness. Once he is recognised and exposed through some aspect of his self-presentation, he experiences himself as becoming metamorphosed into a bad object, constituted and controlled by the other. The anticipation of such a fate creates a fear close to terror, and to fall to such a fate creates a sense of alienation, and of despair and inevitable depression.

What *defence* does the bad me paranoid have? He does not believe he can turn and denigrate and disempower the other in a self-to-other negative evaluation, like the poor me paranoid, because he experiences himself as fatally flawed and in the wrong, and his will as paralysed. It is clear from the foregoing that the defensive need of the bad me paranoid is not to seek out the other to present a grandiose self, but at all costs to *hide* the flawed subjective self-in-embryo from the other lest the other takes over and *constructs* this bad self. Thus where the poor me paranoid defence is to expose and gain recognition of the grandiose self, the bad me paranoid defence is to conceal the bad self.

It follows that the bad me paranoid defence is principally one of anxiety-driven avoidance. This person is hypervigilant of others, in order to be always ready to take avoidant action. The 'bad' self-schema ensures that, through various cognitive biasses such as selective abstraction and the reversal of the self-serving attributional bias, much if not most of the other's behaviour will be perceived as a critical other-to-self evaluation. Avoidance may take the form of literally hiding away, of seeking 'asylum' in a safe place, away from the 'pressure' of others. The paranoid fantasy is that others are forever discovering the hidden badness and plotting a punishment.

Another more subtle form of avoidance is to present what Winnicott (1960) called a false self—the person presents a self that conforms to whatever they imagine the other desires them to be. Thus a client, Alf, says 'I just have to do what others expect, like when I'm playing billards, I mustn't look too flash, nor on the other hand too modest. If I get it wrong I just feel terrible, so ashamed . . .' The person needs to monitor not only his behaviour but even his thoughts.

Origins of the Two Types of Paranoia

We pointed out earlier that the theory of self, threat and defence offered here needs a developmental framework which can show how early learning can shape the two types of self-schema which underlie poor me and bad me paranoia, and become a vulnerability factor for later precipitating events. Given that paranoia may be considered a type of affective disorder (Zigler & Glick, 1988), in that depression is a key part of the phenomenology, it seems appropriate to look to the depression literature for a possible developmental model that might fit our two types. Blatt and Zuroff (1992) point out that a number of theories stress the importance of differentiating a depression focused on interpersonal issues such as dependency, loss and abandonment, and a depression focused on issues of self-definition such as autonomy, self-criticism and feelings of failure and guilt. There are clearly similarities here with the insecure poor me paranoid and the alienated bad me paranoid that we have described above (there are also important differences, though these need not concern us here).

Blatt and his colleagues have discussed the developmental origins, predisposing personality characteristics, clinical manifestations and unconscious conflicts of 'anaclitic' (or dependent) and 'introjective' (or self-critical) depression. We will focus here on one aspect of this broad picture—the childhood antecedents of the two types. Briefly, parent-child interaction research shows that depression centred around issues of dependency is characterised by a parental style of being psychologically unavailable, uncaring, neglectful, and if affection was given, this was inconsistent. As a result the individual intensely and chronically fears being abandoned and left unprotected and uncared for—the picture of anxious insecure attachment. The child finds it difficult to assume that interpersonal relationships can be maintained in the absence of the other, or that that experience of love and care can continue beyond the immediate moment.

The parallels we would draw here are between the dependent depressive and the poor me paranoid on the one hand, and the self-critical depressive and bad me paranoid on the other. Clearly a programme of research is needed to establish whether the two types of paranoia are indeed associated with the two types of parental styles as suggested, and to show that these in turn lead to the development of self-schemas which leave the person vulnerable to the types of threats to self we have predicted.

SUMMARY

In this chapter we have argued for two psychologically distinct types of paranoia and have discussed the implications of this distinction for assessment and intervention. Finally we have offererd our own speculation about the nature and origins of the two types, as we think current cognitive models do not extend to punishment paranoia.

Chapter 8

CHALLENGING CASES AND ISSUES

CHALLENGE 1: WHEN CLIENTS DO NOT CHANGE

One of the most common challenges we have witnessed in ourselves and others occurs when clients do not change. All too often this leads therapists to do one of two things; make either an internal or an external attribution. Thus, therapists might question if they, or their therapy, are up to the task. Or they might succumb to the temptation to label all clients who do not change as challenging or difficult people, with an implication that the clients in some awkward way wilfully resist the therapist's best efforts. The latter attribution is a clear example of the self-serving bias, discussed in relation to paranoia (see Chapter 7), whereby a person externalises responsibility for what he or she perceives to be a failure experience. In this instance, a therapist blames a client for not improving. However, the threat is the same in both cases, though in making a self-serving attribution it is defended: if clients do not change this may be because of my inadequacy.

Comment

However, this view seems to us to be a distortion, for two main reasons. First, it presupposes that all clients should respond to cognitive therapy and therefore if one does not someone or something is at fault. Second, it asserts that in those instances where someone is at fault, it is always the client.

Research and clinical experience show that it is unreasonable to believe or, worse still, demand that all clients will respond to cognitive therapy however well it is done. In the case of unipolar depression, for example, clinical wisdom suggests that about three in four carefully selected depressed people respond to cognitive therapy (Piasecki & Hollon, 1987); and research has begun to identify therapist and client variables predictive of either good or poor outcome (Williams, 1992).

Our view is that outcome in cognitive therapy for delusions reflects an interaction between the therapist, the therapy and the client (Chadwick & Lowe, 1994). This is not to imply that therapists and clients do not have a responsibility—of course they do, always. Both have a responsibility to behave professionally and co-operatively, but this is not sufficient to guarantee clinical improvement. Nor are we implying that we as therapists never perform poorly and adversely affect outcome—regrettably this does happen. And some clients do not co-operate with therapy and do not recognise the need to respect boundaries. And so on. But on the whole we are arguing that outcome is determined by an interaction of numerous variables, some to do with a client, some a therapist, and some their relationship. Moreover, outcome is a very complex matter; in relation to delusions, for example, an individual might become less sure of a belief, less distressed by it, less disturbed by it, less preoccupied by it, less prone to act on it, less depressed or anxious generally, etc. Any and all these changes might be said to constitute positive change.

Obviously if too few clients responded positively, or if there were no empirical evaluation of cognitive therapy for delusions and voices, this would constitute a considerable challenge. However, there is now a substantial and coherent body of evidence to show that cognitive therapy is an effective treatment approach for some people with delusions and voices (see Chapter 9).

Therefore, from this perspective we define a challenging case not as a client who does not change, but one who leads us to question one or more of the main features of our understanding and use of cognitive psychotherapy. In fact in some of those instances we shall discuss the outcome was good. We now proceed to consider a further five challenges:

2. when 'symptom substitution' occurs
3. when therapy seems to make the client worse
4. when a symptom is not a problem
5. when an alternative therapy is implicated
6. when the therapist feels overwhelmed.

When discussing each we shall adhere to a common format, namely to define the challenge posed to the theory or therapy, to describe an illustrative case, to discuss related practical and theoretical issues, and finally to consider a possible resolution.

CHALLENGE 2: SYMPTOM SUBSTITUTION

A definition

Symptom substitution may be said to have occurred when one symptom is lost and a second, new symptom emerges which is believed to be a response to the same threat as was the first. In relation to voices and delusions, the present context implies that one delusion is lost and a second emerges that is thought to be functionally similar. This is not to be confused with the idea of a 'defenceless' person becoming more depressed following the loss of a delusion, which we believe reflects different dynamics and is discussed below.

Larry: A Case Illustration of Symptom Recurrence

At the start of cognitive therapy Larry (see Chapter 4) held three distinct delusions; that he was to be married to a woman, Amanda, with whom he had not been in contact for many years and who he believed was reading his mind and controlling many of the things that happened to him (one delusion), and that in prior lives he had been Leonardo da Vinci (a second delusion) and Jesus (a third). Over the course of 23 weeks of assessment and therapy, Larry came to reject all three beliefs and showed a number of predicted clinical benefits (see Lowe & Chadwick, 1990). However, at the one-month follow-up meeting the 'Amanda' belief was once again held with absolute certainty. Indeed it had returned as part of a new and more elaborate delusion; namely, that he and Amanda were no longer to be married because their relationship had been discovered by his brother who had screwed things up. Instead he was now betrothed to a famous sportswoman who was now reading his mind and controlling his life, in much the same way as had Amanda before.

The Challenge to Cognitive Therapy

The challenge to cognitive therapy is straightforward—why spend months working hard to remove one symptom, if another is going to emerge which is functionally similar. If this type of replacement were very common, it would be a real worry for therapists because it might imply that a lot of client and therapist time and effort and emotional energy is being wasted. (A second worry relates to the question of why the symptom is replaced, and one tempting answer is to say that the client *needs* the delusion or voice: this is discussed below.)

This ties in to a wider and popular challenge to working with symptoms—that is, why spend therapeutic time seeking to remove the product of the person's problem (i.e. the symptom), when one could use a different therapy to get at the 'real', or 'underlying' problem?

Comment

This challenge has its historical origin in Freudian analysis. In an elegant and masterful discussion of the changing face of psychodynamic psychotherapy, Judd Marmor (1992), a past president of the American Psychiatric Association and of the American Academy of Psychoanalysis, discusses the merits of working with symptoms. He says:

> In the early days of dynamic psychotherapy, dealing with symptoms directly was considered an inappropriate thing to do. The prevailing myth was that if you removed the symptom without solving the underlying psychodynamic psychopathology, the symptom would inevitably recur. The reasoning was based on a hydraulic conception of personality, as if the patient's symptom were a leak that had developed because of increased pressure within the system and would inevitably recur, if not in the same spot, then elsewhere, if the leak was sealed without reduction of the underlying pressure. However, experience has shown that this does not always jibe with clinical reality. When patients are relieved of symptoms, they not only feel better at the time, but often continue to feel better. The reason for this is that the human personality is part of an open biopsychosocial system, so that removal of a symptom not only increases inner feelings of well-being, but also can produce improved interpersonal relationships, with the resultant positive feedback that can modify the entire system beneficially. (p. 193.)

This quotation is clear and generous. We would add to it only three brief points. First, in our experience, symptom recurrence of the type experienced by Larry is very unusual. Second, modern cognitive therapy does much more than merely address symptoms—as we have seen in earlier chapters the process of case formulation and therapy seeks to connect symptoms to early relationships, to current interpersonal behaviour, and to unresolved fears, threats and defence. Undoubtedly the development of cognitive therapy along these lines owes much to the psychodynamic tradition. A final point is one made by Malan (1979) concerning the merits and demerits of psychodynamic versus symptom-based approaches. Malan rightly asserts that historically psychodynamic approaches have placed a stronger emphasis on understanding the person and his or her history, and in this sense have in the past had an added explanatory power. However, he also acknowledges that at times a psychodynamic formulation may fail to connect to the symptom at all—in other words, the client's presenting problem, a symptom, may not be understandable in terms of the case formulation. Thus it is clear that there are risks in placing too much or too little emphasis on symptoms.

CHALLENGE 3: WHEN A CLIENT SEEMS TO GET WORSE

Certain clients actually show higher levels of distress having had their delusions or voices weakened than they did at the start of therapy.

Jenny

In Chapter 6 we discussed at length the experience of Jenny, who became more depressed following the weakening or her beliefs about voices—those being that she was being commanded by the Devil to convey disastrous economic advice to the Prime Minister, who would be obliged to act on it. Conviction in these beliefs fell considerably, together with associated guilt and depressive delusional mood, and her delusional behaviour (e.g. assiduously tracking economic developments) decreased. However, she also became gradually more dysphoric and despairing and experienced a sense of life being less purposeful and of personal failure. Thus, while in terms of delusional conviction, distress and disturbance, she improved, her life seemed to contain less achievement and purpose and she was dysphoric.

The challenge to cognitive therapy may be stated plainly—is it unhelpful to remove delusions (including beliefs about voices) even when these delusions are associated with distress and disturbance? This possibility, that reducing delusions or voices might be harmful to a client, probably crosses the minds of most cognitive therapists, and warrants careful consideration. Certainly the idea that delusions are functional and beneficial has a long heritage, and in our experience is still a popular view. In the literature this notion originates from Jaspers (1962), who talked of delusions being of vital necessity to the individual, and said that without them the person would inwardly collapse.

Comment

It is very disconcerting to consider that therapy might be making people feel worse rather than better, so we have found it helpful to scrutinise the arguments carefully. We believe that the challenge collapses under this scrutiny and may be rebuffed on theoretical and empirical grounds.

1. The challenge seems to us to ignore the fact that when symptoms are formed, clients do not have clear options—they do not, for example, consciously consider whether to form a self-defensive paranoid delusion, or engage in supportive therapy to ease their interpersonal vulnerability.

2. We know of no strong evidence to show that weakening a delusion in therapy is harmful to most, or even to many, clients. Given that the majority of our clients are experiencing considerable distress and disturbance when we first meet them while they are deluded, it seems wrong to withhold a treatment (cognitive therapy) which would be routinely offered to people with neurotic disorders and which is known to ease distress and disturbance on the basis of an untested theoretical claim— that people would be worse off without the delusion or voice.

3. The theoretical underpinning of the argument is that delusions are a defence formed to prevent psychological collapse. Again, where is the empirical evidence for this assertion? And even if we grant the claim, that delusions are a vital defence, this does not imply that therapists should stop trying to weaken delusions. That is, even if there were persuasive empirical evidence that delusions are *formed* for essential defensive functions, this would not imply that delusions were maintained for this same reason. It is quite possible that some months or years after a delusion is formed, it no longer fulfils the psychological function which prompted its formation.

4. There is robust empirical evidence that for most people the weakening or loss of delusions, including those secondary to voices, is associated with an increase in psychological well-being (Chadwick & Lowe, 1994).

5. For the minority of individuals who do get worse (become more depressed, anxious, etc.) following the loss or weakening of a delusions, there need be no causal link between these two happenings. Alternatively it may be that as clients become less and less deluded they become more and more aware of how little society offers—this would be a very strong reason for improving living conditions of our clients, but not surely one for withholding therapy.

6. When a person does, for whatever reason, feel worse following the loss of a delusion this requires a considered and empathic response rather than a hasty call to stop such therapy. It is widely acknowledged that in many psychotherapies clients will often go through a period of feeling worse before they begin to feel better. Thus, we need to distinguish between feeling worse as a part of the process of therapy, and feeling worse

at its conclusion (this is regrettable, but still a risk in all therapies). In our practice we find that on those occasions when a client does feel worse following the loss of a delusion, if this is not temporary decline we raise it with the client and explore how it might be explored in therapy.

CHALLENGE 4: WHEN SYMPTOMS ARE NOT A PROBLEM

Broadly speaking when a client reports no distress or disturbance associated with a delusion or voice, the therapist has one of two initial hunches—either there is no emotional and behavioural distress (i.e. no severe and problematic Cs within the ABC framework), or the therapist believes that the client is distressed but is not reporting it. We shall consider each type.

Some clients initially say that a voice or delusion neither distresses nor disturbs them, but it emerges that this is not so. For example, it is common for clients who hear voices believed to be benevolent to say that their voices are not in any way a problem. A woman assessed by the author reported hearing voices, which she believed to be benevolent spirits who were guiding her through life and helping her avoid problems. She said at assessment that the voice in no way was a problem for her. However, although it was true that her beliefs about the voice did not distress her, she had surrendered independence such that she rarely acted without checking with her voice and also avoided doing many things she very much wanted to do. In this sense the voice was associated with a behavioural disturbance in the form of not doing things she desired.

During cognitive assessment it became clear that the client had a lifelong strong fear of negative evaluation by others and had always been fearful of upsetting others. The client became aware of a connection between this enduring cognitive vulnerability and her dependence on a powerful guiding voice. However, the client chose not to address these issues in cognitive therapy, but rather to tolerate her dependence on the voice and her fear of negative evaluation. The choice as to whether to engage in cognitive therapy was, as ever, the client's.

Many clients report no distress or disturbance when the therapist strongly suspects that both are present. For example, one man who heard voices racially abusing him stated that these did not trouble him in any way. However, his own voice was very heavy and sad when he spoke about the voice, and his assertion that things were going very well for him sounded hollow; furthermore, all his non-verbal behaviour indicated that he was deeply upset by the voice and by life generally. The first six sessions with this man began with the therapist (Chadwick) helping him to become more aware of his distress and despair; these six sessions involved much supportive counselling and drew on Gestalt techniques of increasing awareness—and although thought chaining was used, no disputing or challenging took place. Only subsequently did cognitive therapy begin.

If following a careful cognitive assessment the therapist concludes that the client is not experiencing any distress or disturbance, then in our opinion cognitive therapy is not indicated. This is because the rationale for therapy has gone—that the client and therapist work collaboratively to ease the former's distress and disturbance. Working merely to change beliefs is not an end in itself. Of course the delusion may be posing problems for others and this needs careful exploration and useful therapeutic options need to be considered, but not we think cognitive therapy for the client.

CHALLENGE 5: ANOTHER THERAPY SEEMS MORE APPROPRIATE

One of the main challenges facing a therapist is to know who not to take on for therapy. Such a decision might be taken because the client's problem is too close to something the therapist judges herself unable to work with at that point in her life, or because she believes the client to be better served by an alternative therapeutic approach. The former is a personal matter, one for the therapist and her supervisor to bear in mind, the latter is a topic about which we can offer some guidance.

To do cognitive therapy—any therapy—well is a significant achievement and one that relies on hard work. Cognitive theory and cognitive therapy are both constantly changing and drawing on other areas of clinical and general psychology. It is our view that to hope to master two or more therapies is a considerable aspiration and one that is perhaps beyond most of us—certainly none of the authors has so far managed it! Some will view this as regrettable, arguing that therapists should be able to respond to the clients in a truly flexible fashion (Lazarus, 1992); we are sympathetic to this opinion, but in practice it is very difficult to achieve. This means that many of us are, by necessity, one club golfers. We will incorporate ideas and techniques from other schools of thought, but we are unlikely to be equally and highly skilled in skilled in formulation and therapy from a range of therapeutic perspectives (cognitive, psychodynamic, behavioural, etc.).

Therefore we need to be clear what our particular approach can and cannot realistically be expected to achieve and be aware of when to use alternatives, and why. As yet cognitive therapy for delusions and voices is not sufficiently well established for clear inclusion and exclusion criteria to be known. However, two general rules of thumb shape our decision not to offer a client cognitive therapy for delusions or voices—the client may be offered cognitive therapy for a different difficulty, for example a personality disorder (Beck et al., 1990), or may be offered a different therapeutic approach altogether. First some clients show clear delusions and voices, but their energy and affect seem to lie elsewhere, perhaps in troublesome family dynamics. Second, certain clients seem to use voices or delusions for what may be called conscious defence. We shall consider each in turn.

Naomi: A Woman Better Suited to a Family Therapy?

Naomi heard voices she believed to be a collection of immediate and distant relatives, some alive and some dead. She lived at home with one parent and three siblings. The first two sessions were spent on cognitive assessment. In brief, her voices were critical and abusive in content, and gave many commands. Other than being clear about their identity, her beliefs were vague: perhaps they, the voices, were trying to harm her in some way, or perhaps not. She felt very dependent on the voices. Sometimes she was distressed on hearing them, at other times she felt detached. On the whole, she did not present as being 'caught in the voices' power' (Bauer, 1979). When her family was discussed she seemed to the therapist to display considerably more energy and affect.

The client agreed to her family being invited to sessions 4 and 5. On meeting the woman and her family the themes in their interaction were resonant of those in the voices; the family controlled the client and took responsibility for her, she felt dependent on them, and she was unsure of their motives. If she behaved in a passive and submissive way, the family was loving, almost smothering; when she resisted they were critical or patronising. In the interaction Naomi displayed none of her intelligence and autonomy.

At sessions 5 and 6 the client explored her options. One was to proceed with cognitive therapy for voices. However, this was rejected in favour of family therapy (with a different therapist) for two main reasons. First, Naomi's energy seemed to the therapist, and on reflection to her also, not to lie in the symptom, the voices, but in the family interaction. Second, what she really wanted to change was the way in which she related to her family: cognitive therapy for voices was unlikely to achieve this. Although cognitive therapy is being developed for work with families, in Naomi's case the available therapist was from a different theoretical orientation.

Surrinder: A Case for Exploratory Psychotherapy?

Surrinder believed that at the turn of the century she was to be transformed into a god who was to end all suffering in the world, and also that she was communicating with Elvis Presley, who wished to marry her. Surrinder was of South Asian origin; however, neither belief was culturally based—neither her family nor her mosque accepted her beliefs, and both had urged her to seek help.

The first assessment interview revealed that she was distressed by her belief that she was to become a god, but not by the belief about Elvis. However, the early assessment interviews were unusual in several respects. First, conviction that the beliefs were true wavered substantially between and across sessions. In itself this is unusual, but what was further peculiar was the sense that Surrinder was deliberately encouraging optimism in the therapist—so at the first session she went from saying one moment that her delusions were definitely true and factual, to a few minutes later smiling and saying that maybe these were all just her thoughts, what did the therapist think? Second, Surrinder displayed no affect when discussing either belief; indeed, she displayed no real distress at any point during assessment. Third, there seemed to be an element of flirtation in her interaction with the therapist; sexual frustration was a very strong issue in the client's life at this point, and in the past, sexual promiscuity had featured large.

Over a period of four sessions the therapist reflected these points to the client, along with his own uncertainty as to whether cognitive therapy for her beliefs and voices was sensible. The client and therapist agreed not to proceed with cognitive therapy for voices and delusions but rather to pursue exploratory individual therapy.

CHALLENGE 6: THERAPIST THOUGHTS AND FEELINGS

An important task facing all cognitive therapists is to attend to their own thoughts and feelings during therapy. Our experience of working with delusions and voices, as with other clinical problems, is that at times we can be overwhelmed by our own thoughts and feelings about the client, our ability as therapists, or both. In other words, being a therapist is a challenge in itself.

One of us (Paul Chadwick) interviewed a man who heard malevolent voices. He had heard the voices over a number of years and was still completely caught in the voices' power. This man's description of hearing voices was vivid and the extent of his distress and disturbance was extreme. At times, for example, he was literally frozen with terror, petrified. After a cognitive assessment interview, the therapist experienced a strong sense that cognitive therapy was insufficient to deal with the client's distress and felt anxious to avoid offering therapy.

Supervision suggested this doubt had at least two origins. First, it reflected a reasonable thought that the degree of distress encountered was extreme and that it might therefore be difficult to progress; severity of depression, for example, is one of six factors known to influence outcome in cognitive therapy for depression (Williams, 1992). The therapist may have been using an internal gauge drawn from clinical experience with this client group, and in this sense the doubt was legitimate. Second, supervision revealed that the interview stirred in the therapist a strong sense of responsibility for the client and this felt like a heavy burden and one which provoked anxiety and an avoidance impulse. In supervision an ABC analysis was carried out of the therapist's own anxiety in response to this client's helplessness; the therapist's implicit fear was of letting the client down, of failing as a therapist. Through the supervision process these concerns were understood and disputed and although the therapist retained a sense of concern for the client, the anxiety and avoidance did not recur with this client.

The Importance of Supervision

It is our firm conviction that supervision is essential for all therapists. It helps us to expose our own thoughts and feelings about therapy with a client; about ourselves as therapists, and to understand and thereby restrict how these might influence therapy. Indeed, there is a sense in which all six challenges discussed in this chapter might be addressed more usefully in case supervision. And these are but some of the benefits of supervision. It also can help correct, or at least show, our own blind spots. Again, by considering our reactions to a client, we can learn much about the client and his interpersonal behaviour; for example, it is our experience that many clients who evoke a strong sense of responsibility from their therapists use subtle interpersonal behaviour which draws care giving and protective responses. And so on. We view case supervision as an essential component of cognitive therapy for delusions and voices.

SUMMARY

Over the past ten years we have frequently been challenged by particular problems in therapy for delusions and voices, and have noticed that often these difficulties were related. In particular, we spotted that there were certain recurring challenges to the way we thought about and used cognitive psychotherapy for delusions and voices. In this chapter we have addressed six challenges which have led us to think critically about our own assumptions about cognitive psychotherapy for delusions and voices, namely: clients who do not change; symptom substitution; when a client seems to get worse; when a delusion or voice appears not to be a problem; when an alternative therapy seems more appropriate; when a therapist feels overwhelmed by a client. The resultant deliberations help us to be clear about what cognitive psychotherapy and we as cognitive therapists can reasonably be expected to achieve. Undoubtedly some clients will not improve, and certain others would be better served by an alternative therapeutic approach. However, we think that by being open to challenge of the kind discussed in this chapter cognitive therapy will become a stronger therapeutic option for our clients.

Chapter 9

FROM A SYMPTOM MODEL TO A PERSON MODEL?

INTRODUCTION

This book began describing the reasons for a paradigm shift from studying syndromes to symptoms and proceeded to describe our use of cognitive therapy as an assessment and treatment approach for delusions and voices and paranoia. As we hope to have shown, the move from a medical model to a symptom approach has considerable merit. In this final chapter we summarise some of the key features of the symptom approach, and then proceed to argue that the next decade of psychological research and practice may require a further paradigm shift from a symptom model to a person model, and that in fact this shift is well underway as can be seen through our own work. We discuss how this further paradigm shift would allow the advances seen in the understanding and treatment of delusions and voices to be extended to other psychosocial interventions for psychosis (e.g. family and EE work, early signs intervention).

THE SYMPTOM APPROACH

As we argue in the opening chapter, we believe the move away from studying schizophrenia as a syndrome, towards study of individual symptoms liberated and energised psychological research and practice. In particular we would draw out four central themes which permeate the symptom approach generally and this book in particular. These themes are a focus on symptoms, personal meaning, collaboration, and treatment. We shall consider each in turn.

Symptoms

For practical reasons the book has addressed separately three symptoms: delusions, paranoia, and voices. In fact from a psychological perspective the three are not independent and our approach to all three has focused on weakening delusions as a means to ease distress and disturbance. A key feature of our work on these symptoms has been an assumption of *continuity* between psychotic and nonpsychotic phenomena, and a rejection of the traditional assumption of discontinuity (see Strauss, 1969). Once the delusion concept was unshackled from the hypothesised syndrome, it became far easier to consider how delusions were like other beliefs. For example, in strongly held beliefs of any kind a confirmation bias is usual, conviction tends to be high and stable, change is difficult, logic is frequently absent, beliefs once formed tend to guide future behaviour. One of the main achievements of the cognitive approach to symptoms has been to reveal how the assumption of discontinuity between ordinary experience and psychotic experience was imaginary—there is considerable commonality between delusions and strongly held beliefs, and what differences exist are often subtle and represent variation on common themes.

To this extent our cognitive approach may be described as seeking to *normalise* an individual's experience. However, it is important to be clear about what is being normalised. We take the view that in cognitive therapy for delusions and voices the important task is to normalise psychological processes, but we are cautious of advocating this for content too. So, we would empathise with a client who believed people could read his mind and were plotting to kill him, and convey how these beliefs render his fear and avoidance understandable. We might empathise with the client's sense of transparency (see Chapter 7). We might further illuminate how his life experience made it understandable that he should be fearful of others and expect to be hurt. Indeed, if one takes a cognitive developmental perspective the formulation process is itself an exercise in normalising experience, making it psychologically understandable. But we would stop short of saying that perhaps people really can read the client's mind and perhaps there is a plot to kill him because to do this would seem to confuse the issue of what requires an explanation. Is it how an individual comes to believe, in a distorted way, that the world is threatening, hostile and unsafe, or why other people should come to be reading his mind and planning to kill him?

Personal Meaning

The focus of the cognitive approach is on an individual's personal meaning. The B within the ABC framework is the key to formulation, assessment and treatment. Historically the achievement of Kelly (1955), Ellis

(1962) and Beck (1976) has been to place the individual's (conscious and unconscious) search for meaning at the heart of the process of formulation and therapy. This is the component that is largely absent or neglected in the medical and behavioural models, and indeed in most lay models of explanation.

Collaboration

In order to understand an individual's belief system, we believe that a therapist has to work collaboratively with the person. The notion of being open and collaborating with clients has long been a defining feature of Beck's cognitive therapy. However, until comparatively recently it was discouraged when working with clients with psychotic symptoms as it was thought to be deleterious to discuss, let alone dispute, psychotic ideas. In retrospect this may come to be seen as a policy which further added to the sense of alienation and loneliness experienced by many clients.

Treatment

A last theme of the book, and of cognitive therapy in general, is treatment. A great strength of the cognitive ABC model is that a treatment approach is an integral feature of assessment. No sooner has a therapist identified distress and disturbance and tied it to a belief, than she has a therapeutic strategem for seeking to ease the distress and disturbance. Although there has been much recent criticism of cognitive models on the grounds that they are weak explanations of causation (e.g. Haaga & Davison, 1993) no-one should question the commitment of cognitive therapists to helping clients change or the success with which this has been achieved.

In relation to delusions and voices, it is too early to offer beguiling statistics about the likely outcome for clients receiving cognitive therapy—and to do so might be to resurrect the assumption that outcome is determined only by clients, rather than a gelling of client, therapist and therapy. It is only in the past ten, perhaps even five years, that cognitive therapy for delusions and voices has come to be seen as feasible. Standard texts on cognitive therapy as late as the early 1990s were reporting the impossibility of modifying delusions using cognitive therapy. Moreover, outcome is a very complex matter. In relation to delusions an individual might become less certain a delusion is true, or may modify its content but not conviction in it, or may become less distressed, disturbed, preoccupied, or prone to act on it. With voices, location or frequency or loudness may be affected; or all associated beliefs, emotion and behaviour may reduce, or perhaps only one belief is weakened (e.g. control) while others remain unchanged (e.g. identity and meaning). Any and all these changes might be said to constitute positive change.

The picture is in fact even more complex than this, because change can be difficult to interpret. Preoccupation, for example, is acknowledged to be an important delusional dimension, and generally therapists seek to reduce it on the grounds that it is unhelpful for clients to spend time thinking about the delusional ideas. However, we are not certain that a fall in preoccupation is to be expected during or even soon after therapy; nor that it would be necessarily a good thing. As part of the process of change many individuals will spend time thinking about their beliefs, perhaps even testing them out, and may therefore show as more preoccupied. Indeed, cognitive therapy encourages greater attention to and consideration of distressing thoughts and beliefs (Beck et al., 1979). The concept of preoccupation therefore may need to be broken down into its constituent parts such that it is possible to predict an increase in one type (e.g. critical analysis of delusion) and a decrease in another (e.g. unquestioning acceptance). A similar concern applies to the use of behaviour change as an outcome measure: some individuals show an increase in delusion related behaviour during and following intervention because they are actively seeking to reality test the belief (Chadwick & Lowe, 1994).

Obviously if too few clients responded positively to cognitive therapy for delusions and voices, or if there were no empirical evaluation, this would constitute a considerable problem. However, there is now a substantial and coherent body of evidence to show that cognitive therapy is an effective treatment approach for delusions and voices. It is sure to be the case that successful efforts are more likely to appear in the published literature than unsuccessful ones, but notwithstanding this the published evidence, plus our own clinical endeavour and that of countless other clinicians, leaves us in no doubt that cognitive therapy is an important and beneficial treatment approach for delusions and voices.

SHORTCOMINGS OF THE SYMPTOM MODEL

The symptom model has yielded much in a short space of time; our own work with symptoms has yielded encouraging models of the way delusions are maintained, and in some cases formed, and we have a credible treatment in cognitive therapy. So why do we think that the symptom model is inadequate?

Well, the clue lies in the phrase 'symptom model'—the starting point is a symptom, an abnormal behaviour, a medical concept tied to the idea of illness. Now, while faith in an underlying illness such as schizophrenia may be contested this cannot disguise the fact that conceptually a symptom is a product of something. Thus, if clinicians merely reject an individual syndrome as invalid without offering an alternative conceptual frame, then they may struggle to address certain questions and issues which concern the place of a symptom in a wider context.

Aetiology may be just such an issue. Imagine first a client who hears a voice, which he believes to be malevolent. While our research might help to account for an individual's unpleasant emotional and behavioural reaction to this experience, if one adhered strictly to a symptom model what explanation might be offered for how the voice began in the first place? The danger is that of falling back on the notion of a cognitive deficit or bias as being 'causal'. So for example, in relation to voices, which are defined as one's own thoughts attributed to someone else, it might be argued a misattribution lies at the heart of the emergence of voices. Yet this is circular and incomplete because it fails to explain why it is only a specific and tiny fraction of the individual's thoughts which are so misattributed. It is noticeable that clinical cognitive models frequently are weak on explaining how symptoms emerge and strong on explaining maintenance and treatment effects.

Why this is important becomes clear if one considers the question of what remains once a symptom has disappeared. It seems sensible to assume that once a voice or a delusion goes, the person is still in some way vulnerable. The medical model is clear about this; the individual retains a vulnerability to a particular form of mental illness. But what does the symptom model have to say here? At present the answer must be precious little—the only lead is perhaps that a recovered hallucinator retains a tendency to misattribute internal thoughts to external sources, or that a recovered paranoid retains a tendency towards making an external attribution for failure and an internal one for success (an empirical claim and easily tested) so as to protect shaky self-esteem. These insights are important and have increased understanding on voices and delusions, but they do not constitute compelling theories of psychological vulnerability.

And even if a theory of delusions, or voices, was sufficiently well developed to be able to specify what earlier experience lays down what vulnerability and what threats trigger it, would we seek one such theory for each of the several symptoms an individual typically experiences? This would be an enormously difficult task, and one that was theoretically absurd. And it is noteworthy that the most impressive attempts to date, such as Bentall's theory of paranoia, are grounded in general psychological theory—in Bentall's case, it is Higgins self-discrepancy theory.

So, the symptom model stands accused of lacking an overarching theory with which to make sense of the emergence of symptoms, that it relies upon concepts like self which have complex and hidden meanings, and that it is imprecise about what psychological vulnerability outlives a symptom. In this sense the banner of symptom based work may be seen as signifying more a rejection of syndromes than itself being a viable comprehensive psychological approach to clinical problems.

FROM A SYMPTOM MODEL TO A PERSON MODEL

The root of the problem is if one abandons the syndrome model and replaces it with no other overarching theory then an analysis of symptoms runs the risk of being groundless. It has happened this way historically, and understandably so, but the lack of a general conceptual frame becomes more and more apparent and embarrassing as approaches to symptoms become more mature. What is needed is a new wider context within which to understand symptoms.

We believe that the solution to this problem is to conceptualise a symptom or collection of symptoms that an individual experiences as reflecting an enduring psychological vulnerability.

To achieve this researchers and clinicians seeking psychological under standing of delusions and voices (or other symptoms) need first to state a general theory of ordinary psychological development, and only then to consider how to account for the emergence of symptoms. Because the symptom model has no overarching theory, it reverses this process and begins with a symptom, an extraordinary behaviour, and then tries to generate an account for its emergence—often within a theoretical vacuum.

Now what is striking is that over the last few years this problem has been implicitly recognised by many cognitive therapists and researchers in the sense that so-called symptom work is going well beyond a symptom model. Increasingly, cognitive researchers and therapists who work with delusions and voices borrow concepts from, and assume much implicit knowledge of, other more general theories. In other words while the focus of much current research and thinking in cognitive approaches to psychosis remains the symptom, it does not adhere to a symptom model.

We do not see this as a problem, nor are we seeking to be pedantic—rather the intention is to acknowledge the necessity of a wider psychological theory, and in so doing to hasten and encourage the process of more fully and explicitly stating one.

THE BUILDING BLOCKS OF A PERSON MODEL

We believe the wider psychological theory we are looking for should be rooted in ordinary human psychology—in other words, rather obviously, a psychological theory of the person. But what should be the building blocks of such a person model? A clue lies in the work described in this book, which we believe in fact already goes well beyond a symptom model. Our work on delusions, paranoia and voices does not simply reflect a symptom model, even though it focuses on symptoms. Rather it reflects a cognitive developmental theory of the person.

In the opening chapters on cognitive theory and therapy we saw how an ABC assessment of present functioning rests on a developmental theory concerning the fundamental human need for attachment and autonomy (Beck, 1983; Blatt & Zuroff, 1992), and how cognitive models seek to understand psychological vulnerability in terms of a lack of one or both of these.

In the chapters on delusions and voices we saw how in these symptoms the same themes of interpersonal vulnerability, expressed with greatest clarity through the core evaluations of self and others, were visible. In particular, we speculated that the *content* of voices and delusions reflected strong interpersonal themes, and we gave case examples to back up this speculation. We also saw how the *triggers* that sparked voice activity, or delusional thinking, gained their potency because individuals interpret them as posing a psychological threat. We also saw how in cognitive therapy it may often be possible and helpful to connect symptoms to psychological vulnerability and early experience, particularly loss and trauma. In making these important connections, which help to make the symptoms more understandable to clients and therapists, we go well beyond a symptom approach because we seek to understand the symptom by reference to a wider perspective—an appreciation of a theory of an individual's psychological development and vulnerability.

In the chapter on paranoia we described our unique separation of paranoia into two distinct types—punishment and persecution. We showed how current cognitive theories accounted for the maintenance of persecution paranoia, but not punishment paranoia, and we described our elaboration of a cognitive developmental theory. We offered a theory of self and the process of self-construction, and described two fundamental threats to this process—alienation and insecurity (Trower & Chadwick, 1995). In doing this we hoped to show why attachment and autonomy are so fundamental to a person's psychology—because without both an individual is unable to construct a sense of self. And we went on to argue that the two types of paranoia might be understood as defences against these specific and distinct threats to self. It is in the paranoia work that we most clearly show how an overarching psychological theory may strengthen symptom work.

Thus we believe that the building block, the foundation stone, for a person model from which to approach psychotic phenomena is the central human endeavour of trying to construct a sense of self that is both valued and authentic (i.e. constructed by the person, not imposed by others). Furthermore, although jargon differs, there is widespread agreement that self-construction relies on a balance of attachment and autonomy (Blatt & Zuroff, 1992).

Indeed, this suggestion should be unsurprising. The making of a self is widely acknowledged by a number of eminent authors to be a, perhaps the, fundamental human passion and need (e.g. Rogers, 1961; Maslow, 1954; Kohut, 1977). More specifically, the topic of the self was well recognised by the founding fathers of the classification and development of the concept of the psychoses. Kraepelin, Bleuler, Jaspers, Meyer, Schneider, Sullivan and Freud himself have argued that major disruption in the integrity of self is a core component in these disorders.

Other researchers have similarly placed the concept of self at the heart of understanding psychosis. Bentall (1994) has shown how paranoid people use an extreme form of the cognitive self-serving bias to preserve vulnerable self-esteem. Davidson and Strauss (1992) discovered that a *sense of self* appears to be a major component in the everyday experience of severe mental illness. It is a component that people with these disorders often describe, and which they often see as a core factor in processes of illness and change. Indeed of the 32 out of 66 subjects shown to be improving in their study, practically all described experiences involving the rediscovery and reconstruction of a dynamic sense of self, and placed great importance on this in the process of their recovery. (For a scholarly and helpful critique of the concept of self, and its application to neurosis, see Cheshire & Thomae, 1986).

Moreover, the role of self is a key component in cognitive psychotherapy—self-evaluative beliefs are a cornerstone of the B in the ABC model described in the introductory chapter. Time and again in this book we have shown how threat to self is experienced at point B, in the form of inferences about others' intentions (they want to harm me) and evaluations (they see me as totally bad). And we have seen how the most significant threat to the individual is either negative self-evaluation, with associated despair and guilt, or loss of a sense of self altogether.

As yet we do not know how useful this model will prove to be, and it has clear limits to its explanatory power. For example, the theory does not account for why an individual who is deficient in attachment or autonomy should become deluded rather than depressed or anxious. It is possible that there is a biological vulnerability which partly accounts for this.

Advantages of a Person Model

We have argued that people with delusions and voices, in common with all human beings, have a general need to construct a sense of self and are subject to threat to that construction. In asserting this, and making it the foundation of an approach to psychotic phenomena, we believe that the approach becomes truly person-centred and based on notions of continuity.

In addition to supplying a plausible psychological theory from which to approach individual symptoms, the major advantage of this person perspective is that it informs other psychosocial interventions such as family work, early intervention and relapse prevention, such that the overall service an individual receives is psychologically driven and coherent. In the final section of this book we shall discuss how this might work.

At present it is our experience that services to people with a psychosis reflect a confusing mix of either medical and psychological theory, or different and conflicting psychological theories, or both.

Family (or carer) and client education groups usually are medical in so far as they pass on information about an illness, its likely biological base, the likelihood of the sufferer's offspring having the illness, etc. The psychology is usually restricted to elaborating an adjunct role, such as reducing an individual's stress and the families' possible guilt. They do not typically offer an understanding of psychotic phenomena and interpersonal relationships with families and carers which reflects a psychological model of the person. They do not emphasise how a likely biological vulnerability (as yet undemonstrated) combines with early experience and adolescence to lay down a psychological vulnerability, which may or may not be manifest in psychotic and neurotic symptoms.

And yet the same individuals may also be offered cognitive therapy for voices or delusions, or other forms of psychotherapy, and within this context it is quite common for therapists to seek quite different explanations for the emergence of symptoms.

Also, much family work, such as that looking at expressed emotion (EE), seems to us to reflect a behavioural model—an A–C approach as opposed to an ABC cognitive approach. The essence of the EE argument is that certain families behave in ways which may produce problems (e.g. distress, relapse) in vulnerable individuals. Nowhere is a cognitive analysis offered, which would say that: certain families behave in ways which an individual *may interpret* as controlling, rejecting, critical etc.; this interpretation is made because of an enduring interpersonal vulnerability to rejection, or loss of autonomy; and it is interpretations such as these, not behaviour of others, which increase distress and may trigger relapse.

Again, work on early signs and early intervention has been very empowering for clients in that it offers them the opportunity to monitor their own levels of distress and disturbance and to detect signs of change. Clients are usually told that declines and relapses are biological and triggered by stress—but what stress? What is lacking is an explanation of why particular stressors have such a devastating effect.

Similarly, it is possible to work with a client to understand his or her first episode as having been triggered by an event which posed a significant interpersonal threat. In other words, it is not the event so much as its meaning which sparks off distress and an episode of acute symptomatology.

We have then a potentially mixed picture of models and approaches which is unlikely to add up to a coherent and understandable whole for either the health care deliverers or the clients and their families. We believe there is considerable danger here for clients to feel both misunderstood and confused.

The person model is we believe an alternative concept which unifies the various approaches and components. It is easy to understand and is 'normalising' and empowering for clients, families and workers alike. We are currently exploring the use of this person model in constructing a psychologically coherent input for people with psychoses. The proposal is that the fundamental therapeutic task is to understand an individual's psychological vulnerability, in terms of attachment or autonomy, evaluative beliefs about self and others with associated disturbed affect and dysfunctional behaviour. This is what we routinely seek to do when working with voices and delusions. A person model thus drives not only a therapist's attempts to address the distress occasioned by delusions, voices and paranoia, the major symptoms of psychosis; it also may be used to conceptualise and guide other aspects of psychological case (e.g. education, working with families, relapse prevention) to create a safer, more consistent and therefore containing environment for clients.

GENERAL CONCLUSION

We began this book by discussing a significant paradigm shift in the study of psychosis—the move from the study of syndromes to symptoms. The book embodies a further significant paradigm shift in our own understanding—a move away from a symptom model towards a person model. The work described on cognitive assessment and treatment for delusions, voices and paranoia is first and foremost based on an understanding of ordinary psychological processes and development. This shift has deepened our understanding of these problems and we advocate this person model as a unifying framework for future research and development into psychosis.

REFERENCES

Abramson, L.Y., Seligman, M.E.P. & Teasdale, J.D. (1978). Learned helplessness in humans: Critique and reformulation. *Journal of Abnormal Psychology*, **27**, 49–74.

Alford, B.A. (1986). Behavioural treatment of schizophrenic delusions: A single case experimental analysis. *Behaviour Therapy*, **17**, 637–644.

Alford, B.A. & Beck, A.T. (1994). Cognitive therapy for delusions. *Behaviour Research and Therapy*, **32**, 369–380.

American Psychiatric Association (1987). *Diagnostic and Statistical Manual of Mental Disorders* (3rd edn). Washington, DC: American Psychiatric Association.

American Psychiatric Association (1994). *Diagnostic and Statistical Manual of Mental Disorders* (4th edn). Washington, DC: American Psychiatric Association.

Antaki, C. (ed.) (1981). *The Psychology of Ordinary Explanations of Social Behaviour.* London: Academic Press.

Asaad, G. & Shapiro, M.D. (1986). Hallucinations: Theoretical and Clinical Overview. *American Journal of Psychiatry*, **143**, 1088–1097.

Austin, J.L. (1976). *Words and How to Use Them.* Oxford: Oxford University Press.

Bauer, S. (1979). The function of hallucinations: An inquiry into the relationship of hallucinatory experience to creative thought. In M. Keup (ed.) *Origin and Mechanisms of Hallucinations.* New York: Plenum, 191–205.

Beck, A.T. (1952). Successful outpatient psychotherapy of a chronic schizophrenic with a delusion based on borrowed guilt. *Psychiatry*, **15**, 305–312.

Beck, A.T. (1976). *Cognitive Therapy and the Emotional Disorder.* New York: International Universities Press.

Beck, A.T. & Steer, R. (1987). *Beck Depression Inventory Scoring Manual.* The Psychological Corporation. NY: Harcourt Brace Jovanovich.

Beck, A.T., Rush, A.J., Shaw, B.F. & Emery, G. (1979). *Cognitive Therapy of Depression.* New York: Guilford.

Beck, A.T., Epstein, N. & Harrison, R. (1983). Cognitions, attitudes and personality dimensions in depression. *British Journal of Cognitive Psychotherapy*, **1**, 1–11.

Beck, A.T., Freeman, A. et al. (1990). *Cognitive Therapy of Personality Disorders.* New York: Guilford.

Bellack, A.S. (1986). Schizophrenia: behavior therapy's forgotten child. *Behaviour Therapy*, **17**, 199–214.

Benjamin, L.S. (1989). Is chronicity a function of the relationship between the person and the auditory hallucination? *Schizophrenia Bulletin*, **15**, 291–230.

Bentall, R.P. (1990). *Reconstructing Schizophrenia.* London: Routledge.

Bentall, R.P. (1994). Cognitive biases and abnormal beliefs: Towards a model of persecutory delusions. In: A.S. David & J. Cutting (eds), *The Neuropsychology of Schizophrenia.* London: Lawrence Erlbaum Associates.

Bentall, R.P., Kinderman, P. & Kaney, S. (1994). Cognitive processes and delusional beliefs: Attributions and the self. *Behaviour Research and Therapy*, **32**, 331–341.

Bentall, R.P., Jackson, H.F. & Pilgrim, D. (1988). Abandoning the concept of schizophrenia: Some implications of validity arguments for psychological research into psychotic phenomena. *British Journal of Clinical Psychology*, **27**, 303–324.

Berrios, G. (1991). Delusions as 'wrong' beliefs: A conceptual history. *British Journal of Psychiatry*, **159**, 6–13.

Birchwood, M.J., Hallet, S. & Preston, M. (1988). *Schizophrenia: An Integrated Approach to Research and Treatment*. London, England: Longman.

Birchwood, M.J. & Tarrier, N. (1992). *Innovations in the Psychological Management of Schizophrenia*. Chichester: Wiley.

Blackburn, I. & Davison, K.M. (1990). *Cognitive Therapy for Depression and Anxiety*. Oxford: Blackwell.

Blatt, S. & Zuroff, (1992). Interpersonal relatedness and self-definition: Two prototypes for depression. *Clinical Psychology Review*, **12**, 527–562.

Boyle, M. (1990). *Schizophrenia—A Scientific Delusion?* London: Routledge.

Brehm, J.W. (1962). *A Theory of Psychological Reactance*. New York: Academic Press.

Brett-Jones, J., Garety, P.A., & Hemsley, D.R. (1987). Measuring delusional experiences: A method and its application. *British Journal of Clinical Psychology*, **26**, 257–265.

Brewin, C.R. (1988). *Cognitive Foundations of Clinical Psychology*. Hove: Lawrence Erlbaum Associates.

Brockington, I.F. (1991). Factors involved in delusion formation. *British Journal of Psychiatry*, **159** (suppl.), 42–46.

Bruner, J.S. (1990). *Acts of Meaning*. Cambridge, MA: Harvard University Press.

Buchanan, A., Reed, A., Wessley, S. et al. (1993). Acting on delusions II. The phenomenological correlates of acting on delusions. *British Journal of Psychiatry*, **163**, 77–81.

Burns, D.D. (1992). *Feeling Good: The New Mood Therapy*. New York: Avon Books.

Cavendish, R. (1980). *The Great Religions*. London: W.H. Smith.

Chadwick, P.D.J. & Birchwood, M.J. (1994). The omnipotence of voices: A cognitive approach to auditory hallucinations. *British Journal of Psychiatry*, **165**, 190–201.

Chadwick, P.D.J. & Birchwood, M.J. (1995). The omnipotence of voices II: The beliefs about voices questionnaire. *British Journal of Psychiatry*, **166**, 11–19.

Chadwick, P.D.J. & Birchwood, M.J. (1996). Cognitive therapy for voices. In: G. Haddock & P. Slade (eds). *Cognitive Behavioural Interventions for Psychosis*. Routledge.

Chadwick, P.D.J., & Lowe, C.F. (1990). Measurement and modification of delusional beliefs. *Journal of Consulting and Clinical Psychology*, **58**, 225–232.

Chadwick, P.D.J., & Lowe, C.F. (1994). A cognitive approach to measuring delusions. *Behaviour Research and Therapy*, **32**, 355–367.

Chadwick, P.D.J. & Trower, P. (1993). The evaluative belief scale. Unpublished.

Chadwick, P.D.J., & Trower, P. (in press). Cognitive therapy for 'bad me' paranoia: A single case experiment. *Behaviour Research and Therapy*.

Chadwick, P.D.J. & Trower, P. (in submission). Examining the paranoid defence: A brief report. Manuscript submitted for publication.

Chadwick, P.D.J., Lowe, C.F., Horne, P.J. & Higson, P. (1994). Modifying delusions: The role of empirical testing. *Behaviour Therapy*, **25**, 35–49.

Cheshire, N.M. & Thomae, H. (1986). *Self, Symptoms and Psychotherapy*. Chichester: Wiley.

Claridge, G. (1990). Can a disease model of schizophrenia survive? In R.P. Bentall (ed.), *Reconstructing Schizophrenia*. London: Routledge.

Clarke, D.M. (1986). A cognitive approach to panic. *Behaviour Research and Therapy*, **24**, 461–470.

Clarkson, P. (1989). *Gestalt Counselling in Action*. London: Sage.

Cochrane, R. (1983). *The Social Creation of Mental Illness*. Essex: Longman.

Costello, C.G. (1992). Research on symptoms versus research on syndromes: Arguments in favour of allocating more research time to the study of symptoms. *British Journal of Psychiatry*, **160**, 304–308.

Costello, C.G. (1993). *Symptoms of Schizophrenia*. New York: Wiley.

Davidson, L. & Strauss, J.S. (1992). Sense of self in recovery from severe mental illness. *British Journal of Medical Psychology*, **65**, 131–145.

Dowd, E.T. (1994). Implicit learning, tacit knowledge, and implications for stasis and change in cognitive psychotherapy. Paper presented at the annual meeting of the Association for Advancement of Behavior Therapy, Boston, MA.

Dryden, W. & Rentoul, R. (1991). *Adult Clinical Problems*. London: Routledge.

Egan, G. (1990). *The Skilled Helper: A Systematic Approach to Effective Helping*. Monterey, CA: Brooks/Cole.

Ellis, A. (1962). *Reason and Emotion in Psychotherapy*. New York: Lyle Stuart.

Ellis, A. (1994). *Reason and emotion in psychotherapy: Revised and expanded edition*. New York: Lyle Stuart.

Fennell, M.J. (1989). Depression. In: K. Hawton, P. Salkovskis, J. Kirk & D.M. Clark (eds), *Cognitive Behavioural Therapy for Psychiatric Problems*, 169–234. Oxford: Oxford University Press.

Fowler, D. & Morley, S. (1989). The cognitive behavioural treatment of hallucinations and delusions: A preliminary study. *Behavioural Psychotherapy*, **17**, 267–282.

Garety, P.A. (1985). Delusions: Problems in definition and measurement. *British Journal of Medical Psychology*, **58**, 25–34.

Garety, P.A. (1991). Reasoning and delusions. *British Journal of Psychiatry*, **159** (suppl.), 14–18.

Garety, P.A. (1992). Assessment of symptoms and behaviour. In M. Birchwood & N. Tarrier (eds), *Innovations in the Psychological Management of Schizophrenia*. Chichester: Wiley.

Garety, P.A., Wessely, S. & Hemsley, D.R. (1991). Reasoning in deluded schizophrenic and paranoid patients: Biases in performance on a probabilistic inference task. *Journal of Nervous and Mental Disease*, **179**, 194–201.

Gilbert, P. (1992a). *Depression: The Evolution of Powerlessness*. Hove: Lawrence Erlbaum.

Gilbert, P. (1992b). *Counselling for Depression*. London: Sage.

Goffman, E. (1959). *The Presentation of Self in Everyday Life*. Harmondsworth: Penguin Books.

Goodwin, D.W. (1971). Clinical significance of hallucinations in psychiatric disorders. *Archives of General Psychiatry*, **24**, 76–80.

Haage, D.A.F., Dyck, M.J. & Ernst, D. (1991). Empirical status of cognitive theory of depression. *Psychological Bulletin*, **110**, 215–236.

Haddock, G., Bentall, R.P. & Slade, P. (1993). Psychological treatment of chronic auditory hallucinations: Two case studies. *Behavioural and Cognitive Psychotherapy*, **21**, 335–346.

Harper, D.J. (1992). Defining delusions and the serving of professional interests: The case of 'paranoia'. *British Journal of Medical Psychology*, **65**, 357–369.

Harré, R. (1979). *Social Being: A Theory for Social Psychology*. Oxford: Basil Blackwell.

Harrow, M., Rattenbury, F. & Stoll, F. (1988). Schizophrenic delusions. In: T. Oltmanns and B. Maher (eds), *Delusional Beliefs*. New York: Wiley.

Hartman, L.M. & Cashman, F.E. (1983). Cognitive behavioural and psychopharmacological treatment of delusional symptoms: A preliminary report. *Behavioural Psychotherapy*, **11**, 50–61.

Hawton, K., Salkovskis, P., Kirk, J., & Clark, D.M. (eds), *Cognitive Behavioural Therapy for Psychiatric Problems*. Oxford: Oxford University Press.

Heise, D.R. (1988). Delusions and the construction of reality. In: T. Oltmanns and B. Maher (eds), *Delusional Beliefs*. New York: Wiley.

Higgins, E.T. (1987). Self-discrepancy: A theory relating self and affect. *Psychological Review*, **94**, 319–340.

Hole, R.W., Rush, A.J. & Beck, A.T. (1979). A cognitive investigation of schizophrenic delusions. *Psychiatry*, **42**, 312–319.

Hustig, H.H. & Hafner, R.J. (1990). Persistent auditory hallucinations and their relationship to delusions of mood. *Journal of Nervous and Mental Diseases*, **178**, 264–267.

Jacoby, M. (1994/1991). *Shame and the Origins of Self-Esteem: A Jungian Approach*. London: Routledge.

James, W. (1983/1890). *The Principles of Psychology*. Cambridge, MA: Harvard University Press.

Jaspers, K. (1962). *General Psychopathology*. Chicago: University of Chicago Press. (Originally published 1923).

Johnson, W.G., Ross, J.M. & Mastria, M.A. (1977). Delusional behaviour: An attributional analysis. *Journal of Abnormal Psychology*, **86**, 421–426.

Jones, E.E. (1990). *Interpersonal Perception*. New York: W.H. Freeman.

Juninger, J. & Frame, C.L. (1985). Self report of the frequency and phenomenology of verbal hallucinations. *Journal of Nervous and Mental Disease*, **173** 149–155.

Kant, I. (1787). Critique of Pure Reason, 2nd edn (translated by J. Meiklejohn, 1934). London: Dent.

Kazdin, A.E. (1982). *Single Case Research Designs*. New York: Oxford University Press.

Kelly, G.A. (1955). *The Psychology of Personal Constructs*. New York: Norton.

Kendler, K.S., Glazer, W.M. & Morgenstern, H. (1983). Dimensions of delusional experience. *American Journal of Psychiatry*, **140**, 466–469.

Kingdon, D.G., & Turkington, D. (1994). *Cognitive-Behavioral Therapy of Schizophrenia*. Hove: Lawrence Erlbaum.

Kohut, H. (1972). Thoughts on narcissism and narcissistic rage. *Psychoanalytic Study of the Child*, **27**, 360–400.

Kohut, H. (1977). *The Restoration of the Self*. New York: International Universities Press.

Lazarus, A.A. (1992). Clinical/therapeutic effectiveness. In J. Zeig (ed.) *The Evolution of Psychotherapy*. New York: Brunner/Mazel.

Levin, J.D. (1992). *Theories of the Self*. Washington: Hemisphere Publishing Corporation.

Lowe, C.F. & Chadwick, P.D.J. (1990). Verbal control of delusions. *Behaviour Research and Therapy*, **21**, 461–479.

Magee, B. (1987). *The Great Philosophers*. Oxford: Oxford University Press.

Maher, B.A. (1974). Delusional thinking and perceptual disorder. *Journal of Individual Psychology*, **30**, 98–113.

Maher, B.A. (1988). Anomalous experience and delusional thinking: The logic of explanation. In: T.F. Oltmanns and B.A. Maher (eds). *Delusional Beliefs*. New York: Wiley.

Maher, B. & Ross, J.S. (1984). Delusions. In H.E. Adams & P. Sutker (eds), *Comprehensive Handbook of Psychiatry*, 383–409. New York: Plenum.

Mahoney, M. (1974). *Cognition and Behaviour Modification*. Cambridge, MA: Ballinger.

Malan, D. (1979). *Individual Psychotherapy and the Science of Psychodynamics*. Oxford: Butterworth-Heinemann.

Marmor, J. (1992). The essence of dynamic psychotherapy. In: J. Zeig (ed.). *The Evolution of Psychotherapy*. New York: Brunner/Mazel.

Maslow, A.H. (1954). *Motivation and Personality*. New York: Harper.

McGarry, P., Singh, D.S. & Copolor, D.L. (1990). Royal Park Multi-diagnostic instrument for psychosis. *Schizophrenia Bulletin*, 16, 501–536.

Milgram, S. (1974). *Obedience to Authority*. New York: Harper & Row.

Miller, D.T., & Ross, M. (1975). Self serving biases in the attribution of causality: Fact or fiction? *Psychological Bulletin*, 82, 213–225.

Milton, F., Patwa, K. & Hafner, R.J. (1978). Confrontation vs. belief modification in persistently deluded patients. *British Journal of Medical Psychology*, 51, 127–130.

Montgomery, J. (1993). The ancient origins of cognitive therapy: The re-emergence of stoicism. *Journal of Cognitive Psychotherapy*, 17, 6–20.

Muran, J.C. (1991). A reformulation of the ABC model in psychotherapies. *Clinical Psychology Review*, 11, 399–418.

Neale, J.M. (1988). Defensive functions of manic episodes. In: T. Oltmanns and B. Maher (eds), *Delusional Beliefs*. New York: Wiley.

Oltmanns, T. (1988). Approaches to the definition and study of delusions. In: T. Oltmanns and B. Maher (eds), *Delusional Beliefs*. New York: Wiley.

Perris, C. (1988). *Cognitive Therapy with Schizophrenic Patients*. New York: Cassell.

Phillips, J.P.N. (1977). Generalized personal questionnaire techniques. In P. Slater (ed.), *Dimensions of Intrapersonal Space*, Vol. 2. New York: Wiley.

Piasecki, J., & Hollon, S. (1987). Cognitive therapy for depression: Unexplicated schemata and scripts. In: N.S. Jacobson (ed.), *Psychotherapists in Clinical Practice*. New York: Guilford.

Popper, K.R. (1977). On hypotheses. In: P.N. Johnson-Laird & P.C. Wason (eds), *Thinking: Readings in Cognitive Science*. Cambridge: Cambridge University Press.

Rogers, C.R. (1961). *On Becoming a Person*. London: Constable.

Romme, M.A. & Escher, S. (1989). Hearing voices. *Schizophrenia Bulletin*, 15, 209–216.

Romme, M.A. & Escher, S. (1994). *Accepting Voices*. London: England: Mind.

Romme, M., Honig, A., Noorthoorn, E. & Escher, A. (1992). Coping with hearing voices: An emancipatory approach. *British Journal of Psychiatry*, 161, 99–103.

Ryle, G. (1949). *The Concept of Mind*. Harmondsworth: Penguin.

Salkovskis, P.M. (1989). Obsessions and compulsions. In J. Scott, J.M.G. Williams & A.T. Beck (eds). *Cognitive Therapy: A Clinical Casebook*. London: Routledge, pp. 50–77.

Sampson, E.E. (1993). *Celebrating the Other: A Dialogic Account of Human Nature*. New York: Harvester Wheatsheaf.

Sarbin, T.R. (1990). Towards the obsolescence of the schizophrenia hypothesis. *Journal of Mind and Behaviour*, 11, 259–284.

Sarbin, T.R. & Mancuso, J.C. (1980). *Schizophrenia: Medical Diagnosis or Moral Verdict?* New York: Pergamon.

Schlenker, B.R. (1980). *Impression Management: The Self-concept, Social Identity, and Interpersonal Relations*. Monterey, CA: Brooks/Cole.

Schlenker, B.R., & Leary, M.R. (1982). Social anxiety and self-presentation: A conceptualization and model. *Psychological Bulletin*, 92, 641–669.

Searle, J. (1983). *Intentionality*. Cambridge: Cambridge University Press.

Segal, Z.V. & Blatt, S.J. (1993). *The Self in Emotional Distress*. New York: Guilford.

Shapiro, M.B. & Ravenette, A.T. (1959). A preliminary experiment on paranoid delusions. *Journal of Mental Science*, **105**, 296–312.

Slade, P.D. & Bentall, R.P. (1988). *Sensory Deception: A Scientific Analysis of Hallucination*. Chichester: Wiley.

Storr, A. (1979). *The Art of Psychotherapy*. London: Secker & Warburg.

Strauss, J.S. (1969). Hallucinations and delusions as points on continua functions. *Archives of General Psychiatry*, **21**, 581–586.

Strauss, J.S. (1989). Subjective experience of schizophrenia. *Schizophrenia Bulletin*, **15**, 179–185.

Strauss, J.S. (1991). The person with delusions. *British Journal of Psychiatry*, **159** (suppl.), 57–62.

Tarrier, N. (1992). Management and modification of residual positive psychotic symptoms. In: M. Birchwood & N. Tarrier (eds). *Innovations in the Psychological Management of Schizophrenia*. Chichester: Wiley.

Tarrier, N., Beckett, R., Harwood, S. et al. (1993). A trial of two cognitive-behavioural methods of treating drug-resistant residual psychotic symptoms in schizophrenia patients: I. Outcome. *British Journal of Psychiatry*, **162**, 524–532.

Tarrier, N., Harwood, S., Yussof, L., et al. (1990). Coping strategy enhancement (C.S.E.): A method of treating residual schizophrenic symptoms. *Behavioural Psychotherapy*, **18**, 643–662.

Trower, P., Casey, A. & Dryden, W. (1988). *Cognitive Behavioural Counselling in Action*. London, UK: Sage.

Trower, P. & Chadwick, P.D.J. (1995). Pathways to defence of the self: A theory of two types of paranoia. *Clinical Psychology: Science and Practice*, **2**, 263–278.

Vygotsky, L.S. (1962). *Thought and Language*. Massachusetts: MIT Press.

Watts, F.N., Powell, E.G. & Austin, S.V. (1973). The modification of abnormal beliefs. *British Journal of Medical Psychology*, **46**, 359–363.

Wessler, R.A., & Wessler, R.L. (1980). *The Principles and Practice of Rational Emotive Therapy*. San Francisco: Jossey Bass.

Winnicott, D.W. (1960). Ego distortion in terms of true and false self. In: *The Maturational Processes and the Facilitating Environment*. London: Hogarth.

Williams, J.M.G. (1992). The Psychological Treatment of Depression; A Guide to the Theory and Practice of Cognitive Behaviour Therapy (2nd edn). London: Routledge.

Wing, J.K., Cooper, J.E., & Sartorius, N. (1974). *The Measurement and Classification of Psychiatric Syndromes*. Cambridge, UK: Cambridge University Press.

World Health Organization (1973). *International Pilot Study of Schizophrenia*. Geneva: WHO.

Yalom, Il (1970). *The Theory and Practice of Group Psychotherpay*. New York: Basic Books.

Zajonc, R.B. (1980). Feeling and thinking: Preferences need no inferences. *American Psychologist*, **35**, 151–175.

Zigler, E. & Glick, M. (1988). Is paranoid schizophrenia really camouflaged depression? *American Psychologist*, **43**, 284–290.

APPENDIX 1: EVALUATIVE BELIEFS SCALE

Below is a list of beliefs people sometimes report. Please read each one and tick how much you believe it to be true. Please give your 'gut' response.

	Agree strongly	Agree slightly	Unsure	Disagree slightly	Disagree strongly
Other people are worthless					
I am a total failure					
People think I am a bad person					
Other people are inferior to me					
People see me as worthless					
I am worthless					
Other people are total failures					
Other people are totally weak and helpless					
People see me as a total failure					
Other people are bad					
I am totally weak and helpless					

	Agree strongly	Agree slightly	Unsure	Disagree slightly	Disagree strongly
People see me as unlovable					
I am a bad person					
People see me as totally weak and helpless					
Other people are unlovable					
Other people look down on me					
I am an inferior person					
I am unlovable					

APPENDIX 2: COGNITIVE ASSESSMENT OF VOICES: INTERVIEW SCHEDULE

The following semi-structured schedule is intended to guide the cognitive assessment interview (Chadwick & Birchwood, 1994). The schedule enquires about the voice, the individual's feelings and behaviour in relation to the voice, and his or her beliefs about the voice's identity, power, purpose or meaning and about the likely consequences of obedience and disobedience.

Do try to use it flexibly; the structure is for convenience based on the cognitive ABC model and will not be the order in which all individuals will want to talk.

It is important that you familiarise yourself with the schedule prior to the interview—certain sections contain detailed notes for the interviewer.

VOICE

How many voices do you hear?

Does the voice come through the ears or from inside your head?

Is the voice a man or woman, or are you unsure?

CONTENT

Does the voice talk to you or about you?

Has the voice used your name?

Can you tell me what kinds of things the voice says? (Record 2 or 3 recent examples)

. . . .

. . . .

. . . .

Explore if the voice ever says the following (record examples)

Commands: Does the voice ever tell you to do something

. . . .

. . . .

Advice: Does the voice ever give you advice or suggestions

. . . .

. . . .

Commentary: Does the voice ever comment on what you are doing or thinking?

. . . .

. . . .

Criticism and Abuse: Does the voice say unpleasant things about you or someone else?

Self . . . . .Other . . . .

. . . .

Hostility: Does the voice ever threaten to harm you or someone else?

Self . . . . .Other . . . .

. . . .

ANTECEDENTS (CUES)

We have found that most people's voices are more active at certain times: perhaps last thing at night, or when they are shopping or in pubs, or when they are feeling nervous. Are there certain times or occasions when your voice is more active?

. . . .

. . . .

. . . .

Are there times when you don't hear the voice? Perhaps when you have company and are talking to someone?

. . . .

. . . .

AFFECT

How do you feel when the voice speaks? (scared, tormented, reassured, amused, indifferent, etc.). . . . .

. . . .

Are there times when you hear the voice and do not feel this way? (record feelings)

. . . .

BEHAVIOUR

When the voice talks what do you usually do?

. . . .

. . . .

. . . .

Do you:

	Usually	Sometimes	Never
Listen because you feel you have to			
Listen because you want to			

Shout and swear at the voices

Talk to the voice

Do what the voice says willingly

Comply unwillingly

Ignore the voice

Try and stop it talking

Is there anything you have found to do that makes the voice go away or seem less intense (e.g. TV, talking, reading, drugs . . .)

. . . .

. . . .

IDENTITY

[Often individuals will initially not reveal the identity. Encouragement at this point can be helpful: something like 'Have you ever had any vague ideas, however strange they might have seemed' or 'Many people I've spoken to have thought their voices might be some kind of god or devil, others have thought their voices might be a friend or member of their family. Have you ever wondered something similar?' If unsuccessful simply move on and be prepared to return.]

Do you have an idea whose voice you hear?

How sure are you that the voice is (give name)?

What makes you think the voice is (give name)?

> 0. Voice identifies itself
>
> 1. Inferred from voice ('sounds like her', 'it talks about the Bible', 'only he could know that')
>
> 2. Belief is based on guilt, visual hallucinations etc.
>
> 3. Other (please specify) . . . .

MEANING

We say something like 'Most people I've spoken to have found that they really needed to try and make sense of hearing voices, some thought the voice might be punishing them or getting at them in some way, others that it might be trying to help them'.

Have you any idea why it is that *you* hear this particular voice?

. . . .

. . . .

Do you think the voice is trying to harm you in some way (e.g. punishment for bad deed, undeserved persecution . . . .

. . . . .How sure are you that this is true? . . . .

Is the voice trying to help you (e.g. protecting you, developing special power . . .)

. . . .

. . . . .How sure are you that this is true? . . . .

Has the voice said this is its purpose?   Yes/No

If no, explore evidence: say something like 'So you have worked this out for yourself. What makes you think the voice is (give meaning)?'

. . . .

. . . .

POWER

Do you think that the voice might be very powerful?

What makes you think this? (e.g. Voice makes me do things, reads my mind . . .)

. . . .

. . . .

Can you control the voice?   Yes/No   How sure are you of this . . . .

Can you 'call up' the voice?

Can you stop it talking?

Can you have a conversation with it (e.g. ask questions and get answers)?

COMPLIANCE

The following section is intended for those individuals whose voices give commands.

[We have found it helpful to explore the feelings and thoughts that influence if someone obeys or disobeys a command. However, the act of compliance can be very significant and often produces a secondary 'chain' of thoughts and feelings. For this reason we also explore people's reactions to having complied with a command.]

Usually people comply either because they think it in their best interest, or because the voice leaves them alone once they have complied, or because they are frightened of what will happen to them if they don't. This meaning then determines how they subsequently view their compliance. For example, if they comply unwillingly through fear, they may subsequently feel very guilty and down, have thoughts of self-harm and view themselves as weak and bad people.

Ask about how individual feels when he or she complies/resists, and probe for associated thoughts and beliefs.

. . . .

. . . .

. . . .

. . . .

Explore secondary feelings, behaviour and thoughts about the preced ing act of compliance/resistance.

. . . .

. . . .

. . . .

. . . .

APPENDIX 3: BAVQ (CHADWICK & BIRCHWOOD, 1995)

There are many people who hear voices. It would help us to find out how you are feeling about your voices by completing the enclose questionnaire which simply asks you to circle 'Yes' or 'No' to the following questions.

If you hear more than one voice, please fill in the questionnaire for the dominant voice.

Thank you for your help.

Name:. . . . .

1.	My voice is punishing me for something I have done.	YES	NO
2.	My voice wants to help me.	YES	NO
3.	My voice is persecuting me for no good reason.	YES	NO
4.	My voice wants to protect me.	YES	NO
5.	My voice is evil.	YES	NO
6.	My voice is helping to keep me sane.	YES	NO
7.	My voice wants to harm me.	YES	NO
8.	My voice is helping me to develop my special powers or abilities.	YES	NO
9.	My voice wants me to do bad things.	YES	NO
10.	My voice is helping me to achieve my goal in life.	YES	NO
11.	My voice is trying to corrupt or destroy me.	YES	NO
12.	I am grateful for my voice.	YES	NO
13.	My voice is very powerful.	YES	NO
14.	My voice reassures me.	YES	NO
15.	My voice frightens me.	YES	NO
16.	My voice makes me happy.	YES	NO
17.	My voice makes me feel down.	YES	NO
18.	My voice makes me feel angry.	YES	NO
19.	My voice makes me feel calm.	YES	NO
20.	My voice makes me feel anxious.	YES	NO
21.	My voice makes me feel confident	YES	NO

WHEN I HEAR MY VOICE, *USUALLY* . . .

22.	I tell it to leave me alone.	YES	NO
23.	I try and take my mind off it.	YES	NO
24.	I try and stop it.	YES	NO
25.	I do things to prevent it talking.	YES	NO
26.	I am reluctant to obey it.	YES	NO
27.	I listen to it because I want to.	YES	NO
28.	I willingly follow what my voice tells me to do.	YES	NO
29.	I have done things to start to get in contact with my voice.	YES	NO
30.	I seek the advice of my voice.	YES	NO

APPENDIX 4: TOPOGRAPHY OF VOICES RATING SCALE (from Hustig & Hafner, 1990)

Over the last few days my voices have been

1	2	3	4	5
VERY FREQUENT (every hour)	FAIRLY FREQUENT (several times a day but not every hour)	AVERAGE (once a day)	FAIRLY INFREQUENT (several times this week but not every day)	ABSENT (not at all lately)

1	2	3	4	5
VERY LOUD	FAIRLY LOUD	AVERAGE	FAIRLY QUIET	VERY QUIET

1	2	3	4	5
VERY CLEAR	FAIRLY CLEAR	AVERAGE	FAIRLY MUMBLED	VERY MUMBLED

1	2	3	4	5
VERY DISTRES-SING	FAIRLY DISTRES-SING	NEUTRAL	FAIRLY COMFORT-ING	VER COMFORT-ING

1	2	3	4	5
VERY EASY TO IGNORE	SLIGHTLY DISTRACT-ING	FAIRLY DISTRACT-ING	VERY DISTRACT-ING	COMPELLING ME TO OBEY THEM

INDEX

A (activating event), *see* Activating
    events
ABC model 1–10
  B notation
    as key 176–7, 183
    meaning 2–4
  clinical psychological problems are
    Cs 4–5
  core Bs from early experience 8–10
  delusions 13–17, 19
    as symptoms 175–6
  dysfunctional assumptions 2, 4
  evaluations 2, 3–4, 8, 10
  images 2
  inferences 2–3, 4, 8, 10
  person evaluations 3–4, 8
  philosophical origins 6–7
  predictable B–C connections 8
  problems arise from Bs not As 5–6
  therapeutic principles 26–43
    assessing C 27–30
    assessing A 30
    assessing B 31–2
    challenging beliefs 34–7, 41–2
    confirming A–C is the problem
      30–1
    connecting Bs and Cs 32–3
    developmental assessments 33
    engagement problem 37–43
    goal setting and options 33–4
    homework 36–7
    prerequisites 25–6
    problem focus 27
  therapist/client collaboration 177
  treatment/assessment integral
    177–8
  voices 17–23
  weakening beliefs 10
  see also Delusions; Paranoia; Voices
Accommodation measure, assessing
  delusions 57

Activating events (As) 1
  assessment of voices 101–4
  delusion assessment 50–1
  problems arise from Bs not As 5–6,
    10, 14, 19, 20
  therapy principles 30–1
Affect
  coping behaviour and belief 21,
    22–3
  delusion assessment 51–2
  delusion challenges 76–7
  voices 22–3, 98–9, 105–6
Aggression, B–C connections 8
Alienated self, theory of paranoia 157,
  159–61, 182
Anger, B–C connections 8
Anxiety, B–C connections 8
'A's, *see* Activating events (As)
Attachment-autonomy balance 9–10
  paranoia and 161
  person model 181–3
  therapy principles 33
Auditory hallucinations 18, 103
  see also Voices
Automatic thoughts, *see* Inferences
Autonomy, *see* Attachment-autonomy
  balance
Avoidance behaviour
  bad me paranoia 160–1
  delusion assessment 53

B, *see* Beliefs (Bs) about activating
  events
Bad me paranoia, *see* Punishment-
  persecution paranoia
BAVQ 22, 109, 201–2
Behavioural consequences (C), *see*
  Consequences
Behavioural measures, delusion
  assessment 52–3, 55

Beliefs About Voices Questionnaire (BAVQ) 22, 109, 201–2
Beliefs (Bs) about activating events 1
    delusion assessment 53–64
        conviction 53–5, 85–6
        core evaluative beliefs 61–4
        evidence 56–8
        formation 55–6
        preoccupation 53–4, 55, 178
        reaction to hypothetical contradiction 58–60, 86
    delusion challenges 73–7, 86
    key to cognitive approach 176–7, 183
    meaning of B notation 2–4
        dysfunctional assumptions 2, 4
        evaluations 2, 3–4
        images 2
        inferences 2–3, 4
    model principles
        early experience 8–10
        predictable B–C connections 8
        problems arise from Bs not As 5–6, 14, 19, 20
        weakening distress 10
    therapy principles
        assessment 31–2
        challenges 34–7, 41–2
    voices
        assessment 22–3, 106–14, 169–70
        challenges 115–34, 169–70
Benevolent voices, see Malevolent/ benevolent voices
Blocking beliefs, engagement 38, 40–1
    clients who hear voices 92, 94–8, 131–2
Bs, see Beliefs (Bs) about activating events

C, see Consequences (Cs)
Capgras, cognitive ABC 15
Childhood development, see Personality development
Cognitive ABC model, see ABC model
Cognitive therapy principles 25–44
    assessing C 27–30
    assessing A 30
    assessing B 31–2
    challenging beliefs 34–7, 41–2
    confirming A–C is the problem 30–1
    connecting Bs and Cs 32–3
    developmental assessments 33

engagement problem 37–43
goal setting and options 33–4
homework 36–7
prerequisites 25–6
problem focus 27
Consequences (Cs) 1
    model principles 4–5, 8
    therapy principles
        assessing C 27–30
        confirming A–C is the problem 30–1
        connecting Bs and Cs 32–3
        voices, assessment 105–6, 197–8
Control, cognitive ABC 15
Conviction about beliefs, ABC assessment 53–5, 85–6
Coping behaviour, voices assessment 105–6
    coping strategy enhancement 98–9
empirical support for ABC model 22–3
Cotard, cognitive ABC 15
Cs, see Consequences (Cs)

Delusions 13–17, 19
    alternative therapies 172
    assessment 45–64
        purpose 45–6
        first steps 46–7
        clarifying the problem 47–50
        assessing activating events 50–1
        assessing affect and behaviour 51–3, 55
        assessing beliefs 53–64
    challenges to 69–90
        assessing alternatives to delusion 79–81, 87–8
        case examples 79–81, 84–9
        challenge process 71–3
        desirability 70–1
        evaluative thinking 72–3, 79, 80, 84, 88
        evidence for beliefs 73–7, 86
        inconsistency and irrationality 77–8, 79–80, 87
        inferential thinking 72, 79
        modifiability of delusions 69–70
        psychological functions 78–9, 80, 87
        reality testing 72, 81–4, 88–9
        shame-attacking 84

verbal challenges 72–3, 77–81, 83,
84, 86, 87–8
weakening processes 72–89
definitions 11–13
formulation 64–7
symptom model
or person model 180–5
shortcomings 179–80
therapeutic challenges
clients get worse 167–9
no change 163–4
symptom substitution 165–7
therapists 172–3
therapeutic outcomes 177–8
voices and 19
see also Paranoia; Voices
Depression
B–C connections 8
challenging delusions 76
omnipotent voices 21, 22–3
theories of paranoia and 135–7, 139,
161
therapeutic challenges 163–4
client selection 171, 172
when symptoms are not a
problem 169–70
worsening of symptoms 167, 168
Development, *see* Personality
development
Diaries
accommodation measure and 57
voices 101
Discontinuity gap, therapist
empathy 39
DSM IV, delusions 13
DSM IIIR, delusions 11–13
Dysfunctional assumptions 2, 4, 36

EE (expressed emotions), person
model and 184, 185
Emotion, cognitive ABC therapy 51–2
Emotional consequences, ABC
model 1, 28–9
clinical psychological problems are
Cs 4–5
predictable B–C connections 8
see also Affect; Consequences
Empathy, engagement in therapy 38–9
Empirical testing
beliefs about voices 122–3
delusions 72, 81–4, 88–9
Engagement 37–43

therapist empathy 38–9
therapist beliefs 38, 39–40
client's blocking beliefs 38, 40–1
relationship threat 38, 41
viewing delusions as beliefs 38, 41–2
rationale for questioning
delusions 38, 42–3
voice hearers 91–100, 126, 130–1
blocking beliefs 92, 94–8
case examples 126, 130–1
coping strategy enhancement 98–9
malevolent–benevolent
connections 94
process 91–2
universality 100, 131
worries about therapist 92–3, 94–5
Evaluative beliefs 2, 3–4, 10
connection with inferences 8, 61–4
delusions 14
assessment 61–4
challenging process 72–3, 79, 80,
84, 88
formulation 64–7
shame-attacking 84
paranoia 137–8
persecution type 114, 141–4,
146–9, 158–9
punishment type 73, 114, 144–5,
150–2, 153, 154, 159–61
therapy principles 31–2, 35–6
voices, assessment 109, 113–14,
125–6, 130–1, 169–70
Evaluative Beliefs Scale (EBScale) 4,
193–4
Exploratory psychotherapy 172
Expressed emotion (EE), person model
and 184, 185

Family therapy 171–2
person model and 184, 185
Formation of beliefs, ABC
assessment 55–6

Grandiose delusions 15, 17
benevolent voices 109, 113
core evaluative beliefs 63, 73
theory of poor me paranoia 158–9

Hallucinations, auditory 18, 103
see also Voices
Homework, therapy 36–7
Hypothetical contradiction, *see*
Reaction to hypothetical
contradiction

Identity and meaning beliefs,
   voices 108, 116, 117, 133, 198–9
Images, in ABC model 2
Inconsistency, challenging
   delusions 77–8, 79–80, 87–8, 148
Inferences 2–3, 4, 10
   connection with evaluations 8, 61–3
   delusions 14
      assessment 48–9, 61–4
      challenge process 71–2, 79
   disputing beliefs about voices 120
   paranoia 137–8
   therapy principles 31–2, 34–5
Infestation, cognitive ABC 15
Insecure self, theory of paranoia 157,
   158–9, 161, 182
Interview schedule, assessment of
   voices 20, 22, 102, 195–200
Irrationality, challenging
   delusions 77–8, 79–80, 87–8, 148

Kantian philosophy, ABC model
   origins 6–7

Malevolent/benevolent voices 21–2
   assessment 109–14
   engagement in therapy 94
   punishment–persecution
      distinction 21–2, 109, 114, 139
   thought chaining 113
Meaning and identity beliefs,
   voices 108, 116, 117, 133, 198–9
Mind reading 15
   delusion challenging case
      examples 147–9, 151–2
   reality testing 82
   symptom substitution 165

Objective self, paranoia 155, 156, 157
Omnipotent voices
   beliefs about 107, 127–9
   coping strategy enhancement 99
   empirical support for ABC
      model 20–1, 22–3
   engagement in therapy 93, 95–8
Omniscient voices
   beliefs about 108, 120–2
   engagement in therapy 93–4
Other, paranoia 155, 156, 157, 160
Outcomes of therapy 177–8
   client selection 170–1
   clients getting worse 164, 167–9

no change 163–4
symptom substitution 164, 165–7
when symptoms not
   problematic 169–70

Paranoia 15, 17
   assessment 62
   concepts 135–8, 182–3
   a definition of paranoid
      delusions 140
   person model 182–3
   punishment–persecution types 138–
      45
      cognitive therapy case
         examples 146–53
      as defence of self 155–61, 179–80,
         182
      origins 161
      therapeutic relationship 153–4
      symptom model shortcomings 179
Persecution paranoia, see Punishment–
   persecution paranoia
Person evaluations 3–4
   connection with inferences 8
   delusions
      assessment 61–4
      case example 64–7
      challenge process 73
   measurement tools 4
   paranoia 137–8
      persecution type 114, 141–4,
         146–9, 158–9
      punishment type 73, 114, 144–5,
         150–2, 153, 154, 159–61
   therapy principles 32, 35–6
   towards a person model 183
Person model
   building blocks 181–5
   from symptom model 180–1
Personality development 8–10
   ABC formulation 64–7
   attachment–autonomy balance 9–10,
      33, 161, 181–3
   paranoia 137, 161
   therapy principles 33
Poor me paranoia, see Punishment–
   persecution paranoia
Preoccupation with beliefs, ABC
   assessment 53–4, 55, 178
Psychodynamic psychotherapy,
   dealing with symptoms 166–7
Punishment–persecution
   paranoia 138–45

malevolent voices 21–2, 109, 114,
    139
persecution (poor me) type 114, 138,
    139–40, 141–4, 146–50, 153–4
punishment (bad me) type 73, 114,
    138, 139–40, 145–6, 150–4
theory of 154–61, 182
    major differences between
        types 158–62
    origins 161
    threats to self 158–62

Reactance, belief reinforcement
    and 73–4
Reaction to hypothetical contradiction
    (RTHC)
    delusion assessment 57, 58–60, 86
    voices 119
Reality testing
    challenging beliefs about
        voices 122–3
    challenging delusions 72, 81–4, 88–9
    delusion assessment 53, 55
Reasoning bias, delusions 15–17
Reference 15, 17
    assessment 56
    delusion challenging 84–9, 147–9
Risk taking, challenging beliefs 34–5
RTHC
    delusion assessment 57, 58–60, 86
    voices 119

Schizophrenia
    auditory hallucinations 18
    symptom model xv–xx, 175
Self
    as building block for person
        model 182–3
    paranoia as defence of 155–61, 182
        construction conditions 155
        making of self 155–6
        poor me/bad me differences
            157–61
        poor me/bad me origins 161
        symptom model
            shortcomings 179–80
    see also Evaluative beliefs
Self-evaluative beliefs, see Evaluative
    beliefs
Self-presentations, constructing
    self 156, 157
Self-report measures, voices 20, 22,
    104, 109, 201–2, 203

Self-serving bias
    paranoia 135–7, 154, 159–60, 182–3
    of therapists 163
Shame-attacking 36
    challenging delusions 84
    paranoia 153
Socratic method, challenging
    beliefs 34, 42
Somatic delusions 15
    core evaluative beliefs 63–4
    problem clarification 48–50
Subjective self, paranoia 155, 156, 157,
    160
Supervision, of therapists 173
Symptom model xv–xx, 175–85
    delusions/voices/paranoia as
        symptoms 175–6
    or person model 180–5
    personal meaning 176–7
    shortcomings 178–80
    therapist/client collaboration 177
    treatment integral to
        assessment 177–8
Symptom substitution 164, 165–7
    psychodynamic psychotherapy
        and 166–7

Therapeutic principles 25–44
Therapists
    collaboration with client 177
    engagement problems 38, 39–40,
        92–3, 94–5
    overwhelming challenges 164, 172–3
    self-serving bias 163
    supervision 173
    therapeutic relationship in
        paranoia 153–4
    when clients do not change 163–4
Thought broadcast 15, 17
    assessment 56
    delusion challenging 84–9
Thought chaining
    assessment of voices 113–14
    delusions
        assessment 61–4
        challenges 80, 88
        persecution paranoia 142–4
        punishment paranoia 144–5
Thought insertion 15, 17
Transference, paranoid ideation 153–4

Verbal challenges, delusions 72–3,
    77–81, 83, 84, 86, 87–8

Voices
  ABC model 17–23
  alternative therapies 171–2
  assessment 100–14
  self-report measures 20, 22, 104, 109,
      201–2, 203
    activating events 101–4
    behaviour and affect 105–6
    beliefs 106–14
    case examples 125–6, 130–2
    interview schedule 20, 22, 102,
        195–200
  challenges to beliefs about 20, 95–8,
      115–34
    case examples 124–33
    disputing beliefs 119–22
    empirical testing 122–3
    motivation to change 118–19
    rationale for collaborative
        empiricism 116–18
    reaction to hypothetical
        contradiction 119
    tackling delusions in order 116
    targeting multiple delusions 116
    testing control of voices 123–4,
        127–8, 132–3
  compliance with 94, 106–7
    challenging beliefs 116, 120, 133
    interview schedule 200
  concurrent symptoms 103
  content 23, 101–2, 195–6
  coping behaviours 22–3, 98–9, 105–6
  cues and contexts 103–4, 123–4,
      128–9, 197
  delusions and 19
  engagement 91–100
    blocking beliefs 92, 94–8
    case examples 126, 130–1
    coping strategy enhancement 98–9

  malevolent–benevolent
      connections 94
  process 91–2
  universality 100, 131
  worries about therapist 92–3, 94–5
  evaluative beliefs 109, 113–14,
      125–6, 130–1, 169–70
  identity and meaning beliefs 108,
      116, 117, 133, 198–9
  locus 103
  loss of confidence through 94
  malevolence/benevolence 109–14
    engagement in therapy 94
    punishment–persecution
        distinction 21–2, 109, 114, 139
    thought chaining 113
  power of 106–8, 109
    challenging beliefs 116, 120–2,
        127–9, 132–3
    interview schedule 199
    omnipotent type 93, 95–8, 107,
        127–9
    omniscient type 93–4, 108,
        120–2
  symptom model
    or person model 180–5
    shortcomings 179–80
  therapeutic challenges
    client selection 171–2
    clients get worse 167–9
    symptom substitution 165–7
    therapist's own feelings 173
    when symptoms are not a
        problem 169–70
  therapeutic outcomes 178
  topography 104, 203

Index compiled by Liz Granger

The Wiley Series in

CLINICAL PSYCHOLOGY

Graham C.L. Davey and Frank Tallis (Editors)	Worrying: Perspectives on Theory, Assessment and Treatment
Paul Dickens	Quality and Excellence in Human Services
Edgar Miller and Robin Morris	The Psychology of Dementia
Ronald Blackburn	The Psychology of Criminal Conduct: Theory, Research and Practice
Ian H. Gotlib and Constance L. Hammen	Psychological Aspects of Depression: Toward a Cognitive-Interpersonal Integration
Max Birchwood and Nicholas Tarrier (Editors)	Innovations in the Psychological Management of Schizophrenia: Assessment, Treatment and Services
Robert J. Edelmann	Anxiety: Theory, Research and Intervention in Clinical and Health Psychology
Alastair Agar (Editor)	Microcomputers and Clinical Psychology: Issues, Applications and Future Developments
Bob Remington (Editor)	The Challenge of Severe Mental Handicap: A Behaviour Analytic Approach
Colin A. Espie	The Psychological Treatment of Insomnia

Martin Herbert   Clinical Child Psychology: Social Learning, Development and Behaviour

David Peck and   Measuring Human Problems: A Practical
C.M. Shapiro (Editors)   Guide

Roger Baker (Editor)   Panic Disorder: Theory, Research and Therapy

Friedrich Fösterling   Attribution Theory in Clinical Psychology

Anthony Lavender and   Community Care in Practice: Services for
Frank Holloway (Editors)   the Continuing Care Client

J. Mark G. Williams,   Cognitive Psychology and Emotional
Fraser N. Watts   Disorders
Colin MacLeod and
Andrew Mathews

John Clements   Severe Learning Disability and Psychological Handicap

Related titles of interest from Wiley...

Multiple Selves, Multiple Voices
Working with Trauma, Violation and Dissociation
Phil Mollon

Shows how new understanding of trauma and dissociation can transform our view of many severe personality disturbances, including the extreme condition of Multiple Personality/Dissociative Identity Disorder (MPD/DID).

0471 95292 3   232pp   1996   Hardback
0471 96330 5   232pp   1996   Paperback

Obsessive Compulsive Disorder
A Cognitive and Neuropsychological Perspective
Frank Tallis

Reviews the nature and incidence of OCD in light of the related research on cognitive processes and cognitive neuropsychology, with special reference to treatment using behavioural and cognitive therapies.

0471 95775 5   222pp   1995   Hardback
0471 95772 0   222pp   1995   Paperback

Cognitive Behaviour Therapy for Psychosis
Theory and Practice
David Fowler, Philippa Garety and Elizabeth Kuipers

Focuses on the four main problems presented by people with psychosis: emotional disturbance; psychotic symptoms like delusions and bizarre beliefs; social disabilities; and relapse risk.

0471 93980 3   212pp   1995   Hardback
0471 95618 X   212pp   1995   Paperback

Psychological Management of Schizophrenia
Edited by Max Birchwood and Nicholas Tarrier

Offers a practical guide for mental health professionals wanting to develop and enhance their skills in new treatment approaches.

0471 95056 4   176pp   1994   Paperback